The Esdaile notebook; a volume of early poems

Percy Bysshe Shelley 1792-1822,
Kenneth Neill Cameron ed

Nabu Public Domain Reprints:

You are holding a reproduction of an original work published before 1923 that is in the public domain in the United States of America, and possibly other countries. You may freely copy and distribute this work as no entity (individual or corporate) has a copyright on the body of the work. This book may contain prior copyright references, and library stamps (as most of these works were scanned from library copies). These have been scanned and retained as part of the historical artifact.

This book may have occasional imperfections such as missing or blurred pages, poor pictures, errant marks, etc. that were either part of the original artifact, or were introduced by the scanning process. We believe this work is culturally important, and despite the imperfections, have elected to bring it back into print as part of our continuing commitment to the preservation of printed works worldwide. We appreciate your understanding of the imperfections in the preservation process, and hope you enjoy this valuable book.

THE ESDAILE NOTEBOOK

WATER-COLOR SKETCH OF SHELLEY,
probably by Edward Ellerker Williams, 1821-1822

THE
Esdaile Notebook

A Volume of Early Poems

by PERCY BYSSHE SHELLEY

Edited by Kenneth Neill Cameron
*from the Original Manuscript in
The Carl H. Pforzheimer Library*

NEW YORK

Alfred · A · Knopf

1964

L. C. catalog card number: 64-13444

THIS IS A BORZOI BOOK,
PUBLISHED BY ALFRED A. KNOPF, INC.

Copyright © 1964 by THE CARL AND LILY PFORZHEIMER FOUNDATION, INC. All rights reserved. No part of this book may be reproduced in any form without permission in writing from the publisher, except by a reviewer, who may quote brief passages and reproduce not more than three illustrations in a review to be printed in a magazine or newspaper. Manufactured in the United States of America, and distributed by Random House, Inc. Published simultaneously in Toronto, Canada, by Random House of Canada, Limited.

FIRST EDITION

Foreword

PUBLICATION of the Esdaile Notebook, separately and at this time, in the midst of continuing progress in editing material for *Shelley and his Circle,* represents both a tribute to the strength in spirit and in resources with which my late father, Carl H. Pforzheimer (1879-1957), endowed his Library and a desire to make available at the earliest possible moment the only major body, so far as is known, of hitherto unpublished poetry by Percy Bysshe Shelley.

Quite aside from the number of scholars using it—through study there, constant flow of correspondence, and a steady provision of microfilm or photostats and other modern scholarly apparatus—the Library maintains its vitality by a selective but vigorous acquisition policy. From April 1957 to date, The Carl H. Pforzheimer Library has acquired over 500 manuscripts and books, chiefly relating to the *Shelley and his Circle* project. More than half are manuscripts. These include over a dozen items in the poet's own hand, five in Mary W. Shelley's, three letters from Charles Bysshe Shelley (who died at the age of twelve) to his sister Eliza Ianthe (who married an Esdaile), and of course the Esdaile Notebook, the most important Library acquisition since my father's death.

The Esdaile Notebook is appealingly simple in appearance. A book 7.3 by 4.8 inches, 0.8 inch thick, in marbled boards, it resembles a medium-sized diary. Of its total of 276 pages, the first 189 contain the poems (and a few blank leaves at the beginning), 57 poems by Percy Bysshe Shelley, one probably by his first wife, Harriet Westbrook Shelley. The final 87 pages are blank. Of the 57 poems by Shelley, only eight have been published in full from the Esdaile Notebook text, and six from other manuscript sources. The total number of lines in the poems is 2925. Of these, 511 have been published from the Esdaile Notebook text, 553 from other manuscripts, and, of these latter, 225 "differ in wording, in one degree or another, from the corresponding lines in the Esdaile Notebook," as detailed in the Publication History below.

The Esdaile Notebook, as I have indicated, contains the only major body of unpublished poetry by Shelley. The reason for this is that it has a different provenance from most of Shelley's other literary manuscripts. These were inherited by Shelley's second wife, Mary Shelley, and passed from her to their son, Sir Percy Florence Shelley. Sir Percy Florence Shelley died without issue in 1889; Shelley's literary manuscripts subsequently went to the Bodleian Library in Oxford. Most of them were included by Mary Shelley in her editions of Shelley's poetry and prose and others have been published in later editions.

The Esdaile Notebook, however, was written before Shelley married Mary. It was in the possession of his first wife, Harriet Westbrook, and apparently was presented to her by Shelley.

It is not known exactly when Shelley gave the Esdaile Notebook to Harriet. As noted in the Introduction, the Notebook is really two entities in one. The first section ends with "The wandering Jew's soliloquy." This section, some 2774 lines, Shelley intended for publication, and he had finished compiling it probably by the spring of 1813.

FOREWORD

It was turned down for publication by Shelley's friend, the publisher Thomas Hookham, a few weeks later. But Shelley kept the Notebook, and, presumably in the fall of 1813, copied into it two sonnets, one on Harriet and one on Ianthe, his infant daughter. After these sonnets come five poems in Harriet's hand, four of them by Shelley, one probably by Harriet. This latter section containing the two sonnets and the poems in Harriet's hand is designated the keepsake section, for the poems in it were not part of the original group put together for publication by Hookham. It seems likely that Shelley gave the Notebook to Harriet shortly after Hookham turned it down and that it was hers when he copied the sonnets into it for her. We know that she had it by 1815 because she dates one of the poems in her hand "1815." Whether it was with her in her lodgings when she committed suicide in November 1816 we do not know. But if it was not with her it was presumably in her father's house. All we actually know is that Ianthe, whose name appears on the inside cover, later inherited it, and we can presume that it was given to her by the Westbrooks, most probably by her aunt Eliza Westbrook.

In 1837 Ianthe married Edward Jeffries Esdaile, of a well-known banking family, by whom she had three children who survived to adulthood. On Ianthe's death in 1876 the Notebook went to her daughter, Eliza Margaret Esdaile, who often moved from one house to another and therefore placed the Notebook for safekeeping with her brother, Charles Edward Jeffries Esdaile, who resided at the family seat, Cothelstone House, near Taunton in Somerset. On Eliza Margaret's death in 1930 the Notebook was willed to her niece, Mrs. Lettice A. Worrall (nee Esdaile), Shelley's great-granddaughter. Mrs. Worrall sold the Notebook on July 2, 1962.

FOREWORD

The Notebook has been in the hands of Shelley's descendants from 1816 until 1962. Throughout these years the Esdaile family refused permission for its publication as a whole, but Charles Edward Jeffries Esdaile, during the time he held custody for his sister, allowed Edward Dowden to publish some of the poems of biographical import in his life of Shelley in 1886. Dowden at this time copied the poems into two copybooks and made some notes on them. In 1961 The Carl H. Pforzheimer Library purchased the first of these copybooks from Mrs. Lennox Robinson, Dowden's granddaughter.

All my contacts with the Worrall family have been most stimulating and friendly, one particularly happy result being the acquisition by The Carl H. Pforzheimer Library, from these direct descendants of the poet, of the three letters written by the nine-year-old son of the poet in 1823-4 to his older sister Ianthe. There also has been acquired directly from the family such memorabilia as Shelley's baby shirt, christening robe, silver whistle and rattle with a ring handle (clearly indicating that even the infancy of one Percy Bysshe Shelley was not immune to the excruciating need for solace while teething). All of these items were presumably given by Shelley's mother to Harriet on the birth of Ianthe. More intimately related to the background of this volume was the acquisition—also from the Worrall family—of the beautiful, gem-studded ring which Harriet received from the youthful poet.

All these contacts and purchases are consistent with, and in furtherance of, the policies of the Foundation in administering and maintaining the Library to concentrate mainly on material relating to *Shelley and his Circle* and the Romantic period in general. It should be further noted here that the manuscripts in The Carl H. Pforzheimer Library collection of Shelley and those associated with him will eventually appear in their entirety in *Shelley and his Circle*. The first two volumes of this work appeared in 1961, published by the Harvard University Press in this country and the Oxford University Press in Great Britain, and the total work may well run to some eight volumes. The Esdaile Notebook will, in accordance with policy, also be included in a later volume of *Shelley and his Circle,* and will be presented therein according to the editorial procedures established for that work. Its text will represent a duplication of Shelley's manuscript as closely as type will allow, retaining the original wording and punctuation, and including bibliographical notes and collations as well as textual notes.

The obvious measure of intellectual generosity, mutual respect, and understanding between the two primary publishers and the editor involved, should not be overlooked. It is perhaps not unjustified to express a feeling that this has come about because of admiration for the collection and its founder. With great satisfaction in this spirit of scholarly collaboration The Carl H. Pforzheimer Library presents *The Esdaile Notebook,* dedicating this volume to those who pause in these parlous times to read and enjoy it.

CARL H. PFORZHEIMER, JR.

Vigil Hill
Purchase, New York
October 1963

Acknowledgments

PERHAPS the most satisfying, and certainly the easiest, task assigned to me as president of The Carl and Lily Pforzheimer Foundation, Inc., which maintains and administers The Carl H. Pforzheimer Library, is the privilege of thanking the many persons whose combined efforts have materially aided the editing and publication of this volume.

The Foreword makes brief allusion to two publishers and an editor, which requires further elaboration here. The Foundation had reached an agreement early in 1960 with the Harvard University Press to publish *Shelley and his Circle;* Volumes I and II appeared in 1961; and the Library staff was heavily engaged in putting copy for Volumes III and IV into final form when the Esdaile Notebook was acquired. Much hitherto unpublished Shelley material became suddenly available. This certainly demanded both an early publication and a format designed for a wider audience than could be reached by the specialized editorial presentation developed for other Shelleyana in The Carl H. Pforzheimer Library, as represented in *Shelley and his Circle.*

One of the first to recognize this was the director of the Harvard University Press, Mr. Thomas J. Wilson. With characteristic understanding and insight, he agreed not only that the Library staff should concentrate its efforts on the Esdaile Notebook but also that this present volume

ACKNOWLEDGMENTS

would not detract from later inclusion of the Notebook in *Shelley and his Circle*. Gratitude to this distinguished leader in the field of scholarly publishing is deep and very personal.

We are all very proud that this volume bears the imprint of Alfred A. Knopf, whom Mr. Wilson in a recent article described as "the most exciting personality in American book publishing, the individual who has done most in the last forty years to make taste in content and design of books a matter of economic as well as cultural importance." Yet even more important to the undersigned is the pleasure of working with a warm friend and good neighbor, both happy circumstances which my parents thoroughly enjoyed for many years.

This is a welcome opportunity to express agreement with Tom Wilson and to say "thank you" to Blanche and Alfred Knopf.

The editor, Professor Kenneth Neill Cameron, whom my father considered the outstanding Shelley scholar in the United States, has been associated with The Carl H. Pforzheimer Library since 1952. His scholarship is coupled with a versatility and capacity for accomplishment which has made this volume possible without adversely affecting the total effort on *Shelley and his Circle*. We are all grateful for his having assumed a double burden.

It should be emphasized here that preparing the Notebook for publication represents a collective effort by the staff of The Carl H. Pforzheimer Library. Miss Winifred M. Davis, Library Editorial Assistant, worked out some of the more difficult sections of the original transcript and checked it all. She assisted in the preparation of the text and Textual Notes, a task beset with complex punctuation and other problems. She read all editorial writing, including the Commentaries and Introduction, hunted out

ACKNOWLEDGMENTS

errors, and made critical suggestions. Mrs. Edith S. Degani, Library Cataloguer, compiled the Index of Titles and the Index of First Lines and researched some of the basic material for the Publication History. Mrs. Margot M. Smith, Library Secretary, transcribed most of the original manuscript, taking in her stride many readings of extremely difficult words, compiled the tables included in the Publication History, and also did research on specific points as required. Mrs. Smith did most of the typing of several drafts of the whole book. All three have continued their work on *Shelley and his Circle*.

Invaluable liaison has been continuously provided between the Library and the office of the Foundation by its Assistant Secretary, Mr. Joseph F. Quigley, who maintained a focal point for clearing the multitude of detail necessary to prepare this volume.

Thanks are also extended to Messrs. Lewis A. Spence and Martin F. Richman of Root, Barrett, Cohen, Knapp & Smith, New York, for their painstaking counsel to the Foundation whenever legal problems arose.

Thanks go to Mr. Sidney R. Jacobs, production manager, and to Mr. Patrick Gregory, editor, and the many at Alfred A. Knopf, Inc., who have helped on this volume. Thanks also to Miss Doris Charrington, the present owner of Field Place, Horsham, for permission to photograph the house; and to the Director and Trustees of The Pierpont Morgan Library for permission to reproduce the portrait of P. B. Shelley by Edward Ellerker Williams.

Finally, the undersigned is very indebted to the officers and directors of the Carl and Lily Pforzheimer Foundation, Inc., for their co-operation and support.

C.H.P., Jr.

October 1963

Contents

Introduction	*3*
Poems	*35*
Commentaries	*175*
Publication History	*313*
Bibliographical Description	*329*
Textual Notes	*331*
Reference Sources, Abridged Title List	*371*
Index of Titles	*375*
Index of First Lines	*377*

Poems

To Harriet ("Whose is the love")	37
A sabbath Walk	38
The Crisis	40
Passion	41
To Harriet ("Never, O never")	43
Falshood and Vice	44
To the Emperors of Russia and Austria	48
To November	50
Written on a beautiful day in Spring	52
On leaving London for Wales	53
A winter's day	56
To Liberty	58
On Robert Emmet's tomb	60
a Tale of Society as it is	62
The solitary	67
The Monarch's funeral	68
To the Republicans of North America	71
Written at Cwm Ellan	73
To Death	74
Dark Spirit of the desart rude	77

POEMS

The pale, the cold and the moony smile	79
Death-spurning rocks!	81
The Tombs	83
To Harriet ("It is not blasphemy")	85
Sonnet. To Harriet on her birth day	88
Sonnet. To a balloon, laden with Knowledge	89
Sonnet. On launching some bottles	90
Sonnet. On waiting for a wind	91
To Harriet ("Harriet! thy kiss to my soul is dear")	92
Mary to the Sea-Wind	94
A retrospect of Times of Old	95
The Voyage	98
A Dialogue	108
How eloquent are eyes!	110
Hopes that bud in youthful breasts	112
To the Moonbeam	113
Poems to Mary	115
To Mary I	116
To Mary II	118
To Mary III	119
To the Lover of Mary	121
Dares the Lama	123
I will kneel at thine altar	125
Fragment . . . bombardment of Copenhagen	127
On an Icicle	128
Cold are the blasts	129
Henry and Louisa	131
A Translation of The Marsellois Hymn	144
Written in very early youth	147
Zeinab and Kathema	148

(xviii)

POEMS

The Retrospect	155
The wandering Jew's soliloquy	161
To Ianthe	163
Evening—to Harriet	164
To Harriett ("Thy look of love")	165
Full many a mind	167
To Harriet ("Oh Harriet, love like mine")	168
Late was the night	170
To St Irvyne	171

Illustrations

FRONTISPIECE

Water-color sketch of Shelley, probably by
Edward Ellerker Williams, 1821-1822
[By permission of the Director and Trustees of
The Pierpont Morgan Library]

MAP

Shelley's travels and places of residence, 1809-1813 *page* 2

FOLLOWING PAGE 200

I The Esdaile Notebook
   [Photo by Urs Zangger]

II "Field Place," a recent photograph
    [By permission of the present owner, Miss Doris Charrington; photo by John Jackson, Horsham]

III The dedicatory poem, with the title in Harriet's hand

IV The last line of "A retrospect of Times of Old," with Shelley's line count following it; the opening of "The Voyage"; the conclusion of the final footnote of "A retrospect of Times of Old"

V The first page of "Henry and Louisa"

VI The final page of "Zeinab and Kathema," showing Shelley's corrections

VII The first page of "To Harriett ('Thy look of love')," in Harriet Shelley's hand

VIII Shelley's "St. Irvyne"
      [By permission of the Trustees of the British Museum]

THE ESDAILE NOTEBOOK

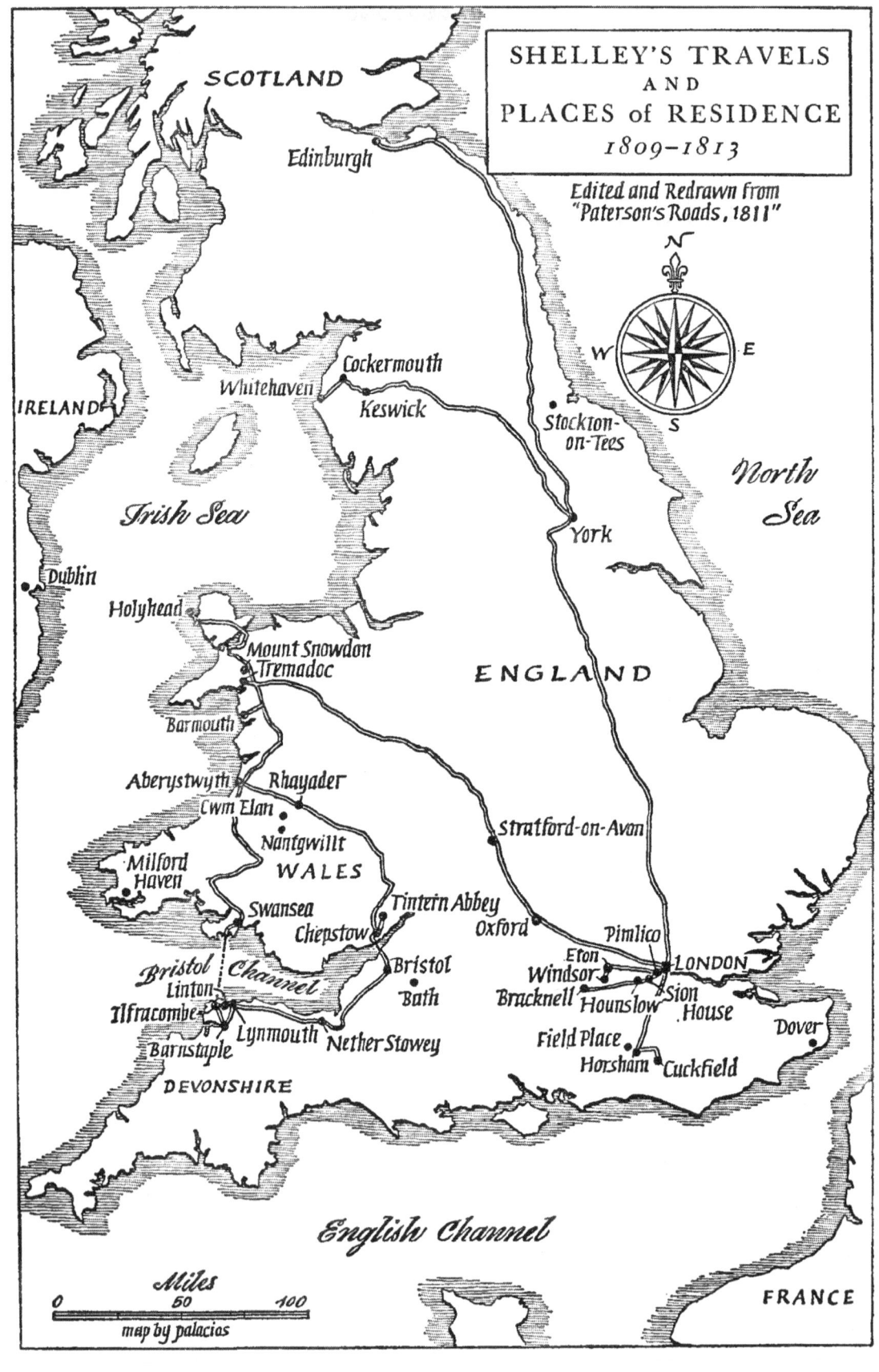

Introduction

THE POEMS in the Esdaile Notebook are, it must be understood at the outset, early poems, poems not of fulfillment but of promise. Shelley was probably only sixteen when he wrote the earliest of them and just turned twenty when he wrote the latest. They are not the product of the rich years with Mary in Italy, the years of *Adonais* and *Prometheus Unbound,* but of Eton and Oxford, the two Harriets, and the breaking of family ties. To those acquainted only with the later works, some of these poems— with their frequent crudities and stumblings, eighteenth-century touches, sentimental echoes from Scott and Campbell, and imitations of Southey's irregular blank verse— will seem strange, sometimes even harsh, but those who have read *Queen Mab* and the other early poems will recognize both the manner and the matter. To this we must add that the Esdaile Notebook is being published 150 years after it was planned for publication. A work intended for the world of 1813, in an England at war with Napoleon, is coming out in the world of the 1960's; a volume by a talented beginner is appearing after he has become one of England's classic poets.

Shelley himself had mixed feelings about the volume.

"My poems, will, I fear," he wrote to his publisher friend Thomas Hookham, "little stand the criticism even of friendship. Some of the later ones have the merit of conveying a meaning in every word, and these all are faithful pictures of my feelings at the time of writing them. But they are, in a great measure, abrupt and obscure—all breathing hatred to government and religion, but I think not too openly for publication. One fault they are indisputably exempt from, that of being a volume of *fashionable literature*." Shelley was aware also of another element in the poems. As he wrote in a footnote to one of the earliest of them: "These defects I do not alter now, being unwilling to offer any outrage to the living portraiture of my own mind; bad as it may be pronounced." It would be difficult to put the essence of the book more concisely. It is a "living portraiture" of Shelley's mind and life during his formative period.

In this Introduction, I shall discuss, first, the poems themselves, giving some of the facts about them which I have been able to uncover, second, the Notebook as a manuscript, and, third, editorial method.

THE POEMS

The poems in the Esdaile Notebook fall into two main categories—personal and political. The political poems are angry poems, the poems of a young aristocrat hurled out of the orbit of his class and seeing English society for the first time from the viewpoint of such men as Paine and Blake—with the eyes of the dispossessed: a society of wealth and power concentrated at the apex, and mass poverty, churned up by the Industrial Revolution, at the base, a society of 11,000,000 of whom 11,000 had the franchise, a society torn by conflicting aristocratic and commercial interests. The poems attack social injustice, political tyranny, and organized religion. They advocate — sometimes directly, sometimes by implication — a democratic republic and a social order based on economic equality, peace, religious tolerance, and civil liberties. The personal poems reflect Shelley's boyhood romance with his cousin Harriet Grove and his marriage to Harriet Westbrook.

Few poets have had a more stormy formative period than Shelley. In the fall of 1810 his engagement to Harriet Grove was broken. The following spring he was expelled from Oxford for writing *The Necessity of Atheism.* In the summer of 1811 he eloped with Harriet Westbrook, then went to Dublin and spoke at a mass meeting with Daniel O'Connell (the great "Liberator" himself). Later he was spied upon in Devon by government agents and tracked to Wales. He wrote an impassioned defense of an imprisoned radical publisher, Daniel Isaac Eaton, and a revolutionary poem, *Queen Mab,* which later became the Bible of Owenites and Chartists. "Tameless and swift and proud" he seemed as he looked back at himself some seven years later.

It is easy to misread this period. The "Ariel" caricature of the aimless, delicate romantic dies hard. The young Shelley was, in fact, neither aimless nor delicate. True, he was often unhappy, hurt, and bewildered, but he knew where he was going and moved with courage, determination, and vigor. When attacked he struck back, often savagely. "I go on until I am stopped," he once told Trelawny, "and I never am stopped." Certainly, in this early period nothing stopped him. Anything that stood in his way was swept aside, including both family ties and the marriage for which he had broken those ties.

It is wrong too to regard this early period as one of

ideological radicalism from which he later recovered. The views on society, politics, religion, and sex that he developed during these years really changed very little. It was primarily the manner that changed, as he found that his early directness had cut him off from his audience. The social message of *Prometheus Unbound* — although not the style or metaphysics — is essentially the same as that of *Queen Mab*. The spirit of the Preface to *Hellas* is as revolutionary as the *Letter to Lord Ellenborough*. The poems in the Esdaile Notebook represent, not a radical rash soon to disappear, but the beginnings of a social philosophy which animated all the major works in one way or another. It is present in the pounding rhythms of indignation in *The Masque of Anarchy*, in the attacks on the Tory reviewers in *Adonais*, in the hatred of tyranny and parental domination in *The Cenci*, in the political science of *A Philosophical View of Reform*.

In the personal poems we find not only the later lyrical powers in embryo but also the penchant for psychological probing (in *Alastor, Julian and Maddalo, Epipsychidion*, and *Adonais*).

Shelley himself regarded his early poems as being divided chronologically into "younger poems" and "the later ones." As it was in December 1811 that he referred to his "younger poems," he must have been speaking of those written before, say, the middle of 1811; the comment on "later ones" was made on January 2, 1813, indicating that these were written from about mid-1811 to the end of 1812. Thus his marriage to Harriet Westbrook in August 1811 can be taken as a convenient dividing line. On this basis the last of the "younger poems" would be those written at Cwm Elan in Wales just before eloping with Harriet; the "later ones" begin in the late fall of 1811 at Keswick. (His wanderings may be traced on the map on page 2.)

INTRODUCTION

When he compiled the Esdaile Notebook, however, Shelley did not adopt a chronological sequence. "Later" poems, with a few "younger" ones mixed in, come first, ending with "The Voyage"; then some "younger" ones, beginning with "A Dialogue"; then "The Retrospect," which was written in the summer of 1812, and "The wandering Jew's soliloquy," which, though it cannot be dated exactly, may be an 1812 poem.

There would, of course, be obvious advantages in rearranging the poems into chronological sequence, and doubtless some future editors will do so, but it has seemed best on this first publication to present the book as Shelley himself compiled it. It might be helpful, for this and other reasons, to present a chronological outline.

1808-1809 (Eton). Shelley entered Eton in 1804 and left in 1810 at the age of seventeen (he was born on August 4, 1792) to go to Oxford. While still at Eton he wrote two novels, *Zastrozzi: A Romance* and *St. Irvyne: or The Rosicrucian.* In the fall of 1810 he published a volume of poems in collaboration with his sister Elizabeth, *Original Poetry* by "Victor" (Shelley) and "Cazire" (Elizabeth); some of these verses date from the Eton period. In the winter of 1809 Shelley and his cousin Thomas Medwin began an anti-religious poem, *The Wandering Jew,* which seems to have been finished in the spring. The novels are a sort of juvenile Gothic with anti-clerical overtones, the "Original" poems, with the exception of "The Irishman's Song," which laments the wrongs inflicted on Ireland, are romantic trivia. Such, in essence, is the Eton record as we have it without considering the contents of the Esdaile Notebook. What do these poems add?

First and foremost they add "Henry and Louisa." "Henry and Louisa" is a narrative poem of 315 lines, and is apparently Shelley's first attempt at a major work. The opening stanza runs:

> Where are the Heroes? sunk in death they lie.
> > What toiled they for? titles and wealth and fame.
> > But the wide Heaven is now their canopy,
> > And legal murderers their loftiest name.
> > Enshrined on brass their glory and their shame
> > What tho' torn Peace and martyred Freedom see?
> > What tho' to most remote posterity
> > Their names, their selfishness for ay enscrolled,
> > A shuddering world's blood-boltered eyes behold,
> > Mocking mankind's unbettered misery?
> > Can this perfection give, can valour prove
> > One wish for others' bliss, one throb of love . . .

Certainly no one can claim that this is great poetry, but to find it in Shelley's Eton period is something of a revelation. Both in technical skill and in sustained effort, it is far above any other poetry he was then writing. Mostly in Spenserian stanza (showing an influence from Spenser much earlier than had been suspected), the verse is quite skillfully handled for a boy of seventeen. And we have to remember that this is the poet of *Adonais*—also in Spenserian stanza—serving his apprenticeship.

The content is no less surprising, for, as even this first stanza shows, Shelley is voicing anti-war and republican sentiments as an Eton schoolboy in 1809.

In another 1809 poem, "I will kneel at thine altar" (which is almost the "Hymn to Intellectual Beauty" in embryo), we find the beginnings of that philosophy of love—anticipating, in some respects, Eric Fromm and other modern thinkers—which was to become central to Shelley's work. It was, in fact, the counterpart of his social views: in the existing inegalitarian society, humanity's instinct for love—which is the essence of life—has been thwarted and distorted, but it still exists, and in a future society will come to fruition (the theme of *Prometheus*

Unbound). Then, and then only, will one be able "to live as if to love and live were one."

We also learn from these two poems that Shelley had, by late 1809, been influenced by William Godwin's *Political Justice*. Up to now it had been thought that Godwinian radicalism made its first appearance in Shelley's poetry in *Queen Mab* (1812-1813). But the influence of *Political Justice* upon these 1809 poems is unmistakable.

These poems, moreover, give us new insights into Shelley's life. We had known, for instance, that his boyhood romance with Harriet Grove began in his Eton years, but we had not known how deeply he was attached to her. "Henry and Louisa," "To St Irvyne," "To the Moonbeam," and other early poems now enable us to trace more exactly the course of this romance and its psychological impact on the young Shelley. They indicate that, as Newman White surmised, the parents attempted to break up the affair in the fall of 1809, a year before it was actually dissolved.

1810 (Eton — Oxford). The year 1810 was, for Shelley, a comparatively calm year. He left Eton in the summer and was taken to Oxford in the fall by his father, Timothy Shelley (later Sir Timothy), who saw him safely settled in his old college, University. There Shelley acquired a reputation as something of a literary phenomenon: *Zastrozzi* had already been published; *St. Irvyne* and two books of poems, the *Original Poetry* and *The Posthumous Fragments of Margaret Nicholson*, appeared in the fall. At University College he met a kindred spirit in Thomas Jefferson Hogg, later to be his biographer. The engagement with Harriet Grove had been broken, but Shelley had not given up hope.

To this record the Esdaile Notebook poems add two radical poems, "The Monarch's funeral" (in which Shelley not unhappily anticipates the demise of George III) and "To the Emperors of Russia and Austria" (an anti-war poem which possibly dates from early 1811), and an agitated series of poems on the suicide of a girl named Mary, of whom we know little more than the poems themselves reveal. We find, too, that some of the poems which Shelley represented in letters to Hogg in 1811 as having just flowed from his pen ("by the midnight moon last night") had really been written a year or more earlier. And he similarly pulled Hogg's leg in regard to his poem on the bombardment of Copenhagen, telling him that it was by his sister Elizabeth in order to stimulate Hogg's romantic instincts.

1811 (Cwm Elan—Keswick). The decisive year in Shelley's life was 1811, the year in which he was expelled from Oxford (in March) and in which he eloped with Harriet Westbrook (in August) and was driven from the ranks of upper-class society to be turned into a confirmed and persecuted rebel. Before the elopement he had spent a month at the estate of his cousin John Grove at Cwm Elan, near Rhayader in Wales. After the elopement he and Harriet (aged sixteen) were joined in Edinburgh by Hogg and then by Harriet's older sister, Eliza (aged twenty-nine or thirty), at York. After Hogg attempted to seduce Harriet, Shelley whisked her off to Keswick in November and remained there for the rest of the year.

Shelley wrote a great many letters during 1811, some of them revealing much about his life and ideas, but his only published work was the pamphlet that led to his expulsion from Oxford, *The Necessity of Atheism*. He also worked on a novel, *Hubert Cauvin*, which apparently is now lost, and on essays, some of which may have found their way into the Notes to *Queen Mab*. The only poems of 1811 which have survived are those in the Esdaile Notebook.

These poems fall into three categories: those written at

Cwm Elan before the elopement, those written at Keswick after the quarrel with Hogg, and "Zeinab and Kathema."

When "Zeinab and Kathema" was written we do not exactly know, but various indications point to the summer of 1811. It is, like "Henry and Louisa," a narrative poem outlining the adventures of two lovers but really concerned with social issues (on both counts also anticipating *The Revolt of Islam*). It is, however, bolder than "Henry and Louisa" both in its narrative and in its message. Here we have no gentle Louisa but a woman driven into prostitution and brutally executed; her lover commits suicide on the gibbet chains from which she is hanging. In place of the "republican" attacks on war and tyrants, we find an explosive condemnation of society as a cesspool of vice, crime, and corruption:

> A universe of horror and decay,
> Gibbets, disease, and wars, and hearts as hard as they.

We had known from Shelley's letters that he had periods of depression at Cwm Elan, but the poems written there—"Written at Cwm Ellan," "Dark Spirit of the desart rude," and "Death-spurning rocks!"—reveal a severe spiritual crisis of which we had not known. As the full impact of the events of the past months—his rejection by Harriet Grove, his expulsion, his alienation from his family—struck him he was reduced to suicidal despair. Adding to the turmoil was his newly unfolding passion for Harriet Westbrook, with whom he had spent some time in London before leaving for Cwm Elan. As the weeks passed, the whirl of emotions began to center on this new passion and the depression receded—indeed, in the final days was supplanted by an almost manic exaltation (as a letter of August 3 to Hogg on the projected elopement shows). One poem, "Oh Harriet, love like mine," copied into the Notebook in Harriet's hand, seems to be a (rather tangled) verse letter sent to her in this period by Shelley, promising to "save" her and love her forever.

Much of the Cwm Elan verse is technically poor, a fact which strikes a warning note against attempting to date Shelley's earlier poetry on stylistic grounds alone. Some of the 1811 poetry is worse than some of the 1810; and the Mary poems of late 1810 are worse than some written in 1809. Shelley is developing, but by no means in a simple upward curve. We find considerable variation, depending on how greatly he was inspired by a particular subject and how much time he spent on the composition. The first of the Mary poems, for instance, gives the impression of having been dashed off abruptly and never revised (at least, one hopes that it was not).

Three of the Keswick poems, "A sabbath Walk," "Passion," and "The Crisis," were doubtless among those described by Shelley to Hookham as "abrupt and obscure" but "conveying a meaning in every word." The change in style is startling:

> When we see Despots prosper in their weakness,
> When we see Falshood triumph in its folly,
> When we see Evil, Tyranny, Corruption,
>   Grin, grow and fatten;
> When Virtue toileth thro' a world of sorrow,
> When Freedom dwelleth in the deepest dungeon,
> When Truth, in chains and infamy, bewaileth
>   O'er a world's ruin.

Gone now are all attempts at a luxurious unfolding of the Spenserian stanza or at lyrical beauty (even though derivative). The style is deliberately harsh, as though the young poet wished it to reflect the despotic, war-torn world around him. This style was not to last, but it did serve to produce in *Queen Mab* the most revolutionary

INTRODUCTION

poem of the age. For the initial turn toward it, Shelley, as we shall see, was indebted to Southey, whom he met at Keswick.

Of other poems probably written at Keswick, two are addressed to Harriet, "To Harriet ('Never, O never')" and "To November." They are, so far as we know, the first Shelley wrote to her after their marriage. Both show rather more technical dexterity and grace than his earlier lyrics. "To November" is a decorative compliment in traditional style:

> Whilst thou obscurest the face of day
> Her radiant eyes can gild the gloom,

but "To Harriet" conveys beneath the conventional prettiness of the verse a sense of deeper feeling — strangely mingled, however, with Shelley's own death-wish fantasies.

1812 (Dublin — Wales — Devon — London). In February, Shelley, Harriet, and Eliza left Keswick for Dublin by way of Whitehaven (passing through, as the road guides show us, Wordsworth's birthplace, Cockermouth). At Dublin, in addition to appearing at the mass meeting with O'Connell, Shelley published *An Address to the Irish People* and other pamphlets, and became acquainted with some of the Irish nationalist leaders. In April he left for Wales, where he settled near his beloved Cwm Elan and began work upon *A Letter to Lord Ellenborough,* making his most powerful plea for religious and political toleration:

> The time is rapidly approaching, I hope that you, my Lord, may live to behold its arrival, when the Mahometan, the Jew, the Christian, the Deist, and the Atheist, will live together in one community, equally sharing the benefits which arise from its association, and united in the bonds of charity and brotherly love. My Lord, you have condemned an innocent man: no crime was imputed

to him — and you sentenced him to torture and imprisonment. I have not addressed this letter to you with the hope of convincing you that you have acted wrong. The most unprincipled and barbarous of men are not unprepared with sophisms to prove that they would have acted in no other manner, and to show that vice is virtue. But I raise my solitary voice to express my disapprobation, so far as it goes, of the cruel and unjust sentence you passed upon Mr. Eaton — to assert, so far as I am capable of influencing, those rights of humanity which you have wantonly and unlawfully infringed.

From Wales, Shelley and Harriet, accompanied as usual by Eliza (plus one or two maidservants and one manservant), moved south to Devon, renting a cottage near the village of Lynmouth on the west coast. There *A Letter to Lord Ellenborough* was printed and *Queen Mab* begun, and there Shelley's Irish servant, Daniel Healey, was arrested for distributing the broadside *Declaration of Rights*, which Shelley had written in Dublin. There, too, the household acquired for some four months a new inhabitant in the person of Shelley's schoolteacher friend Elizabeth Hitchener (later to become "the Brown Demon").

As a result of Shelley's political activities, the town clerk of nearby Barnstable wrote to Lord Sidmouth, the Secretary of State, and to the Earl of Chichester, the Postmaster General. Sidmouth (later to be pilloried in *The Masque of Anarchy*) suggested that Shelley be watched and a list of his correspondents compiled.

Shelley, becoming aware of this surveillance, left Devon at the end of August, after a two months' stay, and headed back to Wales. In September he became interested in a scheme to reclaim land from the sea at Tremadoc by building an embankment, and made a trip to London to try to raise money for it. There he — at last — met William Godwin, his future father-in-law, and Thomas Love Peacock, whose poems he had read in Devon. The last in date of the poems in the Esdaile Notebook as prepared for publication was written as Shelley returned once more to work on the embankment project: "On leaving London for Wales."

It may seem surprising that with all this rushing about Shelley was able to write anything, but he produced not only the prose works mentioned, but a number of poems as well, all of them in the Esdaile Notebook.

The poems, as usual, complement the prose works. Shelley's indignation at the wrongs suffered by the Irish is reflected both in *An Address to the Irish People* and in "On Robert Emmet's tomb" and "The Tombs," the latter a somewhat metaphysical tribute to the fallen Irish patriots of the rebellion of 1798:

> All that could sanctify the meanest deeds,
> All that might give a manner and a form
>   To matter's speechless elements,
>   To every brute and morbid shape
>   Of this phantasmal world ...

Once more we have the unrhymed Southeyan form of the Keswick poems, but Shelley is now learning to infuse into it a richer meaning.

In Dublin, Shelley also wrote a poem hailing the Mexican revolution of 1812-1813, and very probably also "To Liberty," another anti-monarchical poem but one exhibiting a developing ability to add dignity and beauty to directness:

>   The pyramids shall fall ...
>   And Monarchs! so shall ye!
>   Thrones shall rust in the hall
>   Of forgotten royalty.

The only poem we know to have been written in Wales during this year is "The Retrospect," which reflects the psychological crisis of the previous year. The charming (and rather Wordsworthian) "Written on a beautiful day in Spring" may also have been written on this 1812 visit. (At least there does not seem to be any other "Spring" that fits it.)

Of the two best and longest of the Devon poems, "The Voyage" and "A retrospect of Times of Old," only scattered lines have so far been published.

"The Voyage" is, next to "Henry and Louisa," the longest poem in the book. It is not an easy poem to read—and in the Commentary I have attempted an outline—but it is one of the most interesting and suggestive. The first part appears to be autobiographical, reflecting Shelley's own voyagings, both physical and psychological. The second part switches over to a *Queen Mab* type of attack on the press gang and allied social evils.

"A retrospect of Times of Old" also deals with a *Queen Mab* theme, one which Shelley touched upon in the earlier "To Liberty," namely, the passing of former aristocratic glories (with the strong hint that a similar fate awaits present ones also):

> The mansions of the Kings are tenantless...
> Low lie in dust their glory and their shame.
> No tongue survives their victorious Deeds to bless,
> No tongue with execration blasts their fame.

The "Ozymandias" theme has begun.

1813-1815. From Wales, Shelley, Harriet, and Eliza (the "Brown Demon" having been shed in London) went once more to Ireland, but this time on a brief visit, and by early April they were back in London. By late May, *Queen Mab* was in the press and the Esdaile Notebook project had been abandoned. In June, Shelley and Harriet's first child, Eliza Ianthe, was born. The following spring

INTRODUCTION

(1814) the marriage began to break up; in August, Shelley eloped with Mary Godwin; in the fall Shelley and Harriet's second child, Charles Bysshe, was born; and Shelley continued occasionally to visit Harriet during this year and the next. In November 1816, Harriet committed suicide (apparently after an unfortunate love affair), throwing herself into the Serpentine in Hyde Park.

After Shelley had given up hope of publishing, the Notebook passed to Harriet, and in its final pages we find two sonnets copied in by Shelley, one to Harriet and one to the baby, Ianthe, and a number of poems in Harriet's hand. One of these, "To Harriett ('Thy look of love')," was written at the time of the break-up of the marriage, and in the Commentary to the poem I discuss its significance in relation to that event. Another, dated 1815, "Full many a mind," is apparently a poem by Harriet herself.

THE MANUSCRIPTS

The story of the various manuscripts of these poems and their relation to the Esdaile Notebook is a story in itself. It begins with a letter to Elizabeth Hitchener in December 1811: "I think I shall also make a selection of my younger poems for publication." A few weeks later, while Shelley was preparing to leave for Dublin, she was informed that "My Poems will be printed there," that is, in Dublin. There is no reference to the "Poems" in letters from Dublin, but that Shelley did take them with him and give them to a printer we learn from a letter of Harriet Shelley's in June 1812 to her Irish friend Catherine Nugent: "As to the poems I have no idea how and when they will come out. The printers are very slow in their operations." The reason for the slowness appears in August: "His printer refuses to go on with his poems until he is paid. Now such a demand is seldom made, as printers are never paid till the profits arising from the sale of the work come in, and Percy agreed with him to this effect, and as long as we staid in Dublin he wore the mask which is now taken off." The manuscripts of the "younger poems," then, were in a print shop in Dublin and the printer refused to give them up until Shelley paid him. And if he was demanding payment he must have done some work. Some of the poems, then, must have been set up in type and the printer would neither "go on" with the rest nor give them up until he was paid for what he had done.

By fall the situation had become desperate: "Percy says he wishes you to go to Stockdale's, and get all his manuscript poems and other pieces. I am afraid you will be obliged to use a little manoeuvre to get them. In the first place, you can say you wish to look at them, and then you may be able to steal them away from him. I leave it all to you." Behind this desperation must lurk the fact that Shelley did not have copies of the poems with him and that his only manuscripts, either for most or for all of them, were those in Dublin.

Next comes a letter to Thomas Hookham on December 17: "I write hastily again today because I hear from Ireland of my MSS." What Shelley had heard we do not know, but that his informant was Catherine Nugent appears from a letter to her from Harriet on January 16, 1813: "Eliza and Percy desire their kind regards to you, with many thanks for your embassy to Stockdale, who will hear from Mr. S. soon."

It is not clear from these letters whether Shelley had received his poems or not. My impression is that he had not. The securing of the poems had been such an important matter in the correspondence that one would expect some definite and enthusiastic announcement of their receipt rather than the noncommittal (via Harriet) "many thanks for your embassy to Stockdale." Nor do letters to Hookham on January 2, January 26, January 31 (from Harriet), or February 19 state that Shelley has the manuscripts although they refer to the project. The first time that Shelley definitely indicates possession of the poems is in a letter to Hookham in March (the letter is undated but obviously follows closely after one by Harriet on March 12): "I have many other Poems which shall also be sent." This letter was written from Dublin, the previous ones from Wales, and this fact may be significant. Shelley left Tremadoc early in March for a return trip to Ireland. This trip has usually been attributed to wanderlust, but perhaps he took it in order to retrieve his manuscripts. He borrowed £120 before leaving Wales, which may explain how he overcame Stockdale's resistance.

So much for the "younger poems" and their manuscripts.

After writing these "younger poems" Shelley composed others (for instance "The Voyage" in the present volume, which is dated "Devonshire—August 1812") and began work on *Queen Mab*. On December 17, 1812, he told Hookham that he was "preparing a Volume of Minor Poems," and this volume, as the correspondence indicates, was to contain both the "younger" and the later poems, the "younger" ones from the Dublin manuscripts (when he got them), the later ones from manuscripts he had with him. Hookham apparently evinced interest in this project, for Shelley next (January 2, 1813) described the "later" poems, commenting, as we have seen, that the volume was not one of *"fashionable literature."*

From this point on, the fortunes of the projected volume of "Minor Poems" become entangled with those of *Queen*

Mab. On January 26 he informed Hookham: "I expect to have Queen Mab, and the other Poems finished by March. Queen Mab will be in ten cantos and contain about 2800 lines. The other poems probably contain as much more." In February *Queen Mab* was "finished and transcribed" and he was "preparing the notes"; and he added: "You will receive it with the other poems. I think that the whole should form one volume; but of that we can speak hereafter." Shelley, then, intended to produce one book containing *Queen Mab,* its Notes, and the "other Poems." In March, 1813, when he sent the completed manuscript of *Queen Mab* to Hookham, he still adhered to this scheme: "The notes are preparing and shall be forwarded before the completion of the printing of the Poem. I have many other Poems which shall also be sent. The notes will be long, philosophical, and Anti Christian. This will be unnoticed in a Note. Do not let the title page be printed before the body of the Poems. I have a motto to introduce from Shakespeare, and a Preface." The word "Poems" here cannot refer to *Queen Mab* alone, yet its juxtaposition with his comments on *Queen Mab* indicates that Shelley is not thinking only of the "other Poems." Presumably the title page he speaks of would have read "Queen Mab and other Poems" or something similar.

The next we hear of *Queen Mab* is in a letter from Harriet to Catherine Nugent on May 21: "Mr. Shelley continues perfectly well, and his Poem of 'Queen Mab' is begun [apparently, to be printed], tho' it must not be published under pain of death, because it is too much against every existing establishment. It is to be privately distributed to his friends, and some copies sent over to America." And that the book was actually out in the summer of 1813 we learn from Hogg.

Exactly what happened between the middle of March

and May 21 we are not sure. We know that Hookham did not publish *Queen Mab,* for it was privately printed by Shelley himself; and there was a tradition in the Hookham family that he and Shelley had quarreled over the poem. What of the "other Poems"?

In his letter of February 19 Shelley had stated that Hookham would receive *Queen Mab,* its Notes, and the "other Poems" all together. In this mid-March letter, however, he sends him *Queen Mab* only and promises the Notes and "other Poems." As the Notes appeared in the *Queen Mab* volume, and that volume was in the press by May 21, they must have been sent to Hookham not very long after the poem itself, say by late March or mid-April; and the "other Poems" were most probably sent at about the same time, for all three items—*Queen Mab,* the Notes, and the "other Poems"—were to appear in one volume. Presumably, then, what Hookham turned down was not only *Queen Mab* but the whole project. As *Queen Mab* was in the press by May 21, being privately printed by Shelley, and the "other Poems" were never published, Hookham must have rejected the "other Poems" by May 21 at the latest. Shelley had himself apparently given up on them.

What is the connection between these various manuscripts and the Esdaile Notebook? Let us turn to the Notebook itself. When we examine it, we see that up through "The wandering Jew's soliloquy" cumulative line counts are appended to the poems, showing a grand total of 2822 lines at the end. As the usual reason for making such a line count is to give an estimate to a printer, we can assume that this section of the Notebook (running from page 37 to page 162 in the present volume) was compiled for publication. Following this section, as we have seen, there come two poems (sonnets) in Shelley's hand, and five poems in Harriet's hand, one of which is not by Shelley and probably by Harriet. For these poems there are no line counts. The first two were apparently added to the Notebook in the fall of 1813; two, at least, of the later ones, sometime in 1815. These poems, then, were placed in the Notebook — for sentimental and other reasons — after Shelley had given up hope of publication.

Let us pause here to look at some vital statistics:

Total number of lines of poetry	2925
Total number of lines in numbered section	2774
Total number of lines in unnumbered section	151
Unnumbered section, lines in Shelley's hand	28
Unnumbered section, lines in Harriet's hand	123

Shelley's own total for the line-numbered section, we might note, included lines on four pages now torn out, did not include a few other lines apparently added later, and, as we shall see, contains at least one mistake in addition.

It is clear, from this evidence, that the Notebook is really two entities. The first section, with its roughly 2800 lines, was prepared with the problems of publication in mind; the second, of 151 lines, is simply a keepsake section in which poems were copied in later without any connection with plans for publication.

Both the late dates at which the keepsake poems were entered and their placement in the volume show that they can have had no connection with the manuscripts Shelley was preparing for Hookham.

There is, however, obviously a connection, and a very close one, between these manuscripts and the line-numbered section of the Notebook, the first section. (1) Shelley informed Hookham on January 26, 1813, that the "other poems" would "probably" contain about 2800 lines. According to Shelley's calculations, the line-numbered section of the Notebook contained 2822 lines. (2) As we have seen, Shelley spoke of the proposed volume as containing "younger poems" and "later" ones. This is the division of the Esdaile Notebook. (3) In April 1812 Shelley wrote to Elizabeth Hitchener: "I have written some verses on Robert Emmett, which you shall see, and which I will insert in my book of Poems." The Poem on Robert Emmet is in the Notebook. (4) Shelley included "Falshood and Vice" in the *Queen Mab* volume with the comment that "This opportunity is perhaps the only one that will ever occur of rescuing it from oblivion." "Falshood and Vice" is in the Esdaile Notebook. (5) Shelley's description of some of the "later" poems as "abrupt and harsh — all breathing hatred to government and religion," fits, both in style and content. "The Voyage," which he dated August 1812, and other "later" poems in the Esdaile Notebook. (6) Shelley has a reference on the verso of the final leaf of the Notebook (see below, pages 329, 309) to Gibbon's *History of the Decline and Fall of the Roman Empire* that is apparently connected with a Note to *Queen Mab* (which quotes Gibbon). Shelley informed Hookham in February and March 1813 that he was working on both the Notes to *Queen Mab* and the "other poems."

This evidence is, it seems to me, sufficient to establish that the poems in the line-numbered section of the Esdaile Notebook contain either all or most of the "younger" and "later" poems which Shelley writes of in 1811 and 1812 and which he put together for publication.

If we regard this connection as established, certain further deductions can be made. For instance, it is probable that the "juvenilia" part of the Notebook — beginning with "A Dialogue"—roughly corresponds to the "younger poems" and to the manuscripts held by the printer in Dublin. The fact that Shelley was able to come so close in his estimate of the total number of lines on January 26, 1813, may indicate that he had the "younger poems" back by that time. Or it could be that he had totaled the poems he had with him, which probably came to more than half, and estimated the rest. In view of the fact that he does not mention actual possession of the manuscripts until March, when he was in Ireland, the second hypothesis seems to me more likely. And finally, the comment on "Falshood and Vice" in the *Queen Mab* volume substantiates the view that the poems sent to Hookham had been turned down by the time of the printing of *Queen Mab*.

Was the Esdaile Notebook the actual manuscript Shelley sent to Hookham for publication? This is most unlikely, for, in the first place, one would normally send loose sheets rather than a notebook to a printer. Secondly, this particular notebook would have been most unsuitable for a printer. It is comparatively small and nearly every page of writing is crowded, leaving almost no margins, so that a printer would have had little space in which to mark up the copy. We might note, too, that as Stockdale had apparently set up some of the early poems in Dublin, Shelley might have had proof sheets of them. If so, he would be likely to send these to Hookham rather than manuscript.

The Notebook, then, was apparently a copy taken from the manuscripts sent to Hookham. Why did Shelley make such a copy? There seem to be two possible answers: it was compiled as a gift for Harriet; or it was compiled because Shelley's experience with the Dublin printer had convinced him that he should have a copy, and this copy was later given to Harriet. Of these, the second seems the more likely. That the poems were not originally copied as a gift for Harriet is indicated by their casual punctuation, lack of apostrophes, and so on, which stand in sharp contrast to the two poems which apparently were copied into the book for her — in the second section — namely, a sonnet to Ianthe and one to Harriet, both of which are fully punctuated. The probability is that the book was originally compiled as a guarantee against loss of manuscripts. If this was indeed Shelley's motive, the poems must have been copied before the manuscripts were sent to Hookham — that is, by about the middle of April 1813 or earlier. The line count that Shelley made would seem to support this supposition, for such a count, as we have noted, would normally be made to provide an estimate for a printer.

Against this hypothesis several specific objections can be raised; none of them, however, seems insuperable. In the first place, Shelley leaves two stanzas and part of another blank in one poem, "Henry and Louisa." As I suggest in the Commentary, this may mean that he had mislaid a page or so of the manuscript from which he was copying. Secondly, the final stanza of another poem, "To the Lover of Mary," has been added later. It is written with a thinner pen and a different shade of ink and is not included in the line count either for this poem or in the final total. The line count following the preceding stanza, however, has been crossed out as though Shelley intended to make a new count but failed to do so. Perhaps, then, he wrote the stanza in shortly after the copying and simply forgot to add it to the later line counts. Or perhaps he wrote it in considerably later; if so, he may have kept the Notebook with him and made changes after he had sent the manuscripts off to Hookham.

Thirdly, there is some indication that Shelley actually composed a footnote to "To Mary I" as he was copying the poem. If so, presumably he added or intended to add this footnote to a manuscript to be sent for publication.

Finally, Shelley made occasional stylistic and creative changes in the poems. Some of these are in ink of about the same shade as the poems as a whole, but most of them are in a different, usually darker shade. It may be assumed that the alterations in the same shade of ink were made when Shelley was copying the poems into the Notebook; the others were made later. The latter changes, the ones usually in darker ink, may again indicate that Shelley worked on the Notebook after he had sent his manuscripts to Hookham. In fact, a number of them, in widely scattered places, are in a particularly black shade of ink and perhaps indicate a general revision of the Notebook at one time. The changes made in ink of about the same shade apparently represent ideas that occurred to Shelley as he was copying. These, too, he presumably added or intended to add to a manuscript to be sent for publication.

All these objections, then, can be answered on the basis of the hypothesis that the Esdaile Notebook represents a copy originally made as insurance against loss of the original manuscripts (perhaps Shelley mailed them from Ireland) if we assume that Shelley (a) mislaid one or two of his original sheets, (b) made some changes as he went along, (c) perhaps made a few further changes after the original manuscripts had been mailed.

The evidence, as we have seen, indicates that Shelley had completed the line-numbered section of the Esdaile Notebook by the middle of April 1813 and probably before. When did he begin it? It is possible that he had begun when he informed Hookham in December 1812 that "he was preparing a Volume of Minor poems." (The word "Volume" here may mean that he had a manuscript volume in mind as well as a future published volume.)

This hypothesis receives some support from the arrangement of the poems in the line-numbered section, which is that of a group of mainly "later" poems occupying the first half and a group of mainly "younger" poems occupying the second half. The break comes after a run of poems written in the summer of 1812 in Devon, the last of which is "The Voyage." This is followed by "A Dialogue," which Shelley has dated in the title "1809"; then comes a series of similarly dated early poems. Shelley obviously added the dates so that this group would stand out as a kind of juvenilia section. But he did not have these "younger" poems with him in December 1812, for they were still in Dublin. It may be, then, that Shelley started copying with what he did have with him — that is, the "later" poems. On the other hand, of course, he may have intended to place the "later" poems first; in this case he may not have started the actual compilation of the Notebook until shortly before he sent the poems to Hookham. It is not possible, then, to say exactly when Shelley began the Notebook, except that it was probably not much earlier than his announcement to Hookham on December 17, 1812, that he was "preparing" the volume of "Minor Poems" and probably not much later than his statement in mid-March 1813 that the "Poems" would be "sent" to Hookham in the near future.

The poems in the keepsake section, beyond the numbered section, were probably added, as we have noted, between the fall of 1813 and sometime in 1815. The first two, the sonnets, are in Shelley's hand; the last five in Harriet's.

The dedicatory poem, "To Harriet ('Whose is the love')" is a special problem in itself. Let us look first at the placement of this poem in the Notebook. The first three leaves of the Notebook are blank. Then comes the dedication, on the recto of leaf four. The verso of leaf four is blank. On the recto of leaf five is the title, *Poems*, followed by the first of the "Poems" ("A sabbath Walk"). Leaf five is the leaf following the binding string, which makes a natural break and opening point for the volume. It looks as though Shelley started to compile the volume on this leaf.

Next we might note that the lines of the dedicatory poem are not included in Shelley's running line counts, which follow each poem and were totaled as they went along. The final total, however (following "The wandering Jew's soliloquy"), appears as follows:

$$\begin{array}{r} 2796 \\ 16 \\ \hline 2822 \end{array}$$

As the dedicatory poem has sixteen lines and no other sixteen lines are omitted, the "16" here must refer to this poem (regardless of the mistake in addition). We must note also that the whole of the sum appears to have been written at the same time. It is all in ink of the same shade and thickness, and the numbers are of the same size. The "16," then, was almost certainly not added later, but at the same time as the "2796."

To this let us add one other fact. At the top of the leaf 56, verso, Shelley has put the page number 104. For this page to be 104 he must have begun his count with the first poem following the dedication. If he had begun with the dedication the page number would be 106 (assuming that he counted correctly).

From these facts we can deduce that Shelley began his copying not with the dedication but with the body of the poems; that the dedication was probably not in the Notebook when he got to his page 104; and, furthermore, that it either was in the book by the time he got to "The wandering Jew's soliloquy" or was written in immediately after that poem and before he made the final line count. It seems probable that both poems, the dedication at the beginning and "The wandering Jew's soliloquy" at the end of the line-numbered section, were added at about the same time, that is, at the time of the final compilation of that section.

In regard to this dedication, however, one other fact must be noted, namely, that it appears also—though in a somewhat different version—as the dedicatory poem of *Queen Mab*. As *Queen Mab* was in the press by May 21 and out a month or so later, the *Queen Mab* version must have been completed by June 1812 at the latest (allowing for the addition of prefatory matter after the body of the book had been set up).

Which dedication was written first, that for the Esdaile volume or that for *Queen Mab*? The indication is that the Esdaile version came first. The last two lines of the third stanza in both versions have the same wording:

> Thine are these early wilding flowers,
> Tho' garlanded by me.

The phrase "early wilding flowers" is appropriate for the Notebook poems, some of which were written some years previously, but it is not appropriate for *Queen Mab*, which is one long poem and had been composed in the months immediately preceding its publication. It looks as though these lines had been carelessly left over from the Esdaile version. We might note also that the *Queen Mab* version is somewhat better verse. The probability is that the Esdaile dedication was written for the originally planned volume which was to contain both the Esdaile poems and *Queen Mab*.

When did Shelley give the volume to Harriet? We cannot give an exact date, but the implication of the sonnets to her and Ianthe, apparently copied into the book in September 1813, is that the book was then considered to be Harriet's. Possibly Shelley gave it to her shortly after he heard that the poems had been turned down by Hookham and, as he indicates in the comment on "Falshood and Vice" in *Queen Mab*, had despaired of their being published.

Whenever Harriet received the volume, it is apparent from its subsequent history that she kept it with her after Shelley's elopement with Mary Godwin in July 1814. That she had it in October 1814 seems to be indicated in a request that Shelley made to her in a letter of that month: "If you could copy for me & send me one poem called an Indian Tale I wish to have it." Although there is no poem in the manuscript book with the title "An Indian Tale," the reference, as Roger Ingpen argued when editing this letter, is probably to "Zeinab and Kathema," the hero and heroine of which come from Cashmire. Certainly Harriet had the book the next year, for, as we have noted, the final pages contain two poems in her hand dated 1815.

EDITORIAL METHOD

Few who read the poets of the past in modern editions realize how much work — often by generations of scholars — has gone into their production. But when one is faced with a manuscript which has not previously been edited, he is only too aware of it. All the elementary facts of text, dating, and so on which one tends to take for granted become all-important. Without these, the critic and biographer cannot proceed.

In editing the Esdaile Notebook I have placed the emphasis upon these fundamentals. The only way to establish them is by patient sifting of evidence. For some of these poems, for instance, no clue whatsoever to a date appeared at a first, dismayed reading, but, usually, when letters and other pieces of evidence were brought to bear, patterns began to emerge. In such matters the adage about one fool with a fact being able to defeat an army of wise men has particular pertinence. One can spin elaborate (and often convincing) theories about the life, views, and skill of an author in one period only to have someone discover that the works on which the theory is based were written in another.

In editing Shelley's manuscripts for *Shelley and his Circle* I chose to adopt a virtually literal text, one which presented the manuscript, with all its misspellings, slips of the pen, unique punctuation (or lack of it), crossed-out words, inserted words, and so on, preserved intact. For the Esdaile Notebook I have chosen differently. The text is what one might call a minimum clean-up type. What this is I have described in the introduction to the Textual Notes, but I might hasten to allay rising fears by stating that Shelley's wording has not been changed and that what changes have been made — for instance, in correcting spelling and adding capitals — are recorded in the Textual Notes.

Different kinds of texts serve different purposes. *Shelley and his Circle* contains a recording, for scholarly purposes, of manuscripts in The Carl H. Pforzheimer Library — from which other editors can depart as they see fit. The Esdaile Notebook, on the other hand, is a first edition. As such, the text should approximate what Shelley himself would have presented had he published the work (as he did *Queen Mab*). The text is, in places, difficult enough even after a minimum of punctuation has been added, for Shelley tended to delight in complexities of syntax.

As has already been noted, Shelley had other manuscripts of these poems; in fact, all the poems in the Notebook originated in such manuscripts. Shelley, however, did not merely copy; he could not resist making changes and additions as he went along. These, too, are recorded in the Textual Notes.

The final piece of critical apparatus is the Commentaries. Here an editor must choose between a series of footnotes with reference to particular points in each poem or a general commentary on the poem with particular references included in it. There are obvious advantages and disadvantages in both methods. Footnotes make it easier to pinpoint particular problems but more difficult to establish basic general matters: date, over-all meaning, relation to other works, place in biographical or literary development. For first publication it has seemed that these are the most important things to try to establish.

The editorial matter, then, consists of a Biblographical Description, Textual Notes, and Commentaries. We have also added a number of tables — with comments — showing what has and has not been previously published from the volume. These units have been placed at the back so that the poems may be read without the intrusion of editorial matter.

I should like in conclusion to mention the copybook made by Shelley's biographer Edward Dowden, which is referred to in the Foreword and elsewhere. Dowden obtained access to the Esdaile Notebook in 1884 and copied it in two notebooks, word for word, in a remarkably exact and literal text. The second of these notebooks appears to have been lost. The first, which is in The Carl H. Pforzheimer Library, ends, about halfway through, with "The Voyage." This text has been of considerable help in making our transcript. Dowden transcribed on right-hand pages only; on the left-hand pages he sometimes made comments on dating and sources. Wherever these have proved useful — even if only as starting points — they have been noted in the Commentaries.

INTRODUCTION

The portrait of Shelley which forms the frontispiece to the present volume was convincingly argued by Newman I. White in an appendix to his *Shelley* (1940) to be the long-lost water-color sketch of Shelley by Edward Ellerker Williams. After presenting his evidence White added: "More objective proof might have been forthcoming through an expert comparison of the water-colour with Williams's authenticated self-portrait in the British Museum. This examination had already been arranged when the outbreak of the present war forced its indefinite postponement." In October 1963 we wrote to the British Museum to ask whether they could compare the portrait as reproduced in White's *Shelley* with the self-portrait by Williams. We received a reply from Mr. Edward Croft-Murray, Keeper of Prints and Drawings at the Museum, stating that certain techniques employed are "very similar in both cases" and that there is "a very good case for the two drawings being by the same man." This opinion, added to White's evidence, seems to me to put the matter beyond reasonable doubt. The portrait is not so polished (or idealized) as that by Amelia Curran but it probably conveys a better concept of what Shelley actually looked like.

K. N. C.

THE ESDAILE NOTEBOOK

POEMS

To Harriet

Whose is the love that gleaming thro' the world
Wards off the poisonous arrow of its scorn?
   Whose is the warm and partial praise,
     Virtue's most sweet reward?

Whose looks gave grace to the majestic theme,   5
The sacred, free and fearless theme of truth?
   Whose form did I gaze fondly on
     And love mankind the more?

Harriet! on thine:—thou wert my purer soul,
Thou wert the inspiration to my song;   10
   Thine are these early wilding flowers,
     Tho' garlanded by me.

Then twine the withering wreath-buds round thy brow;
Its bloom may deck their pale and faded prime.
   Can they survive without thy love   15
     Their wild and moody birth?

Poems.

A sabbath Walk

    Sweet are the stilly forest glades:
    Imbued with holiest feelings there
    I love to linger pensively
        And court seclusion's smile.
This mountain labyrinth of loveliness   5
Is sweet to me even when the frost has torn
All save the ivy clinging to the rocks
Like friendship to a friend's adversity!
    Yes, in my soul's devotedness,
    I love to linger in the wilds.   10
    I have my God, and worship him,
    O vulgar souls, more ardently
    Than ye the Almighty fiend
        Before whose throne ye kneel.

    'Tis not the soul pervading all,   15
    'Tis not the fabled cause that framed
    The everlasting orbs of Heaven
        And this eternal earth,
Nor the cold Christians' blood-stain'd King of Kings,
Whose shrine is in the temple of my heart;   20
'Tis that divinity whose work and self
Is harmony and wisdom, truth and love,
    Who in the forests' rayless depth
    And in the cities' wearying glare,
    In sorrow, solitude and death   25

A SABBATH WALK

Accompanies the soul
   Of him who dares be free.

It is a lovely winter's day.
Its brightness speaks of Deity
Such as the good man venerates   30
   Such as the Poet loves.
Ah! softly o'er the quiet of the scene
A pealing harmony is felt to rise.
The village bells are sweet but they denote
That spirits love by the clock, and are devout   35
   All at a stated hour. The sound
   Is sweet to sense but to the heart
   It tells of worship insincere,
   Creeds half believed, the ear that bends
   To custom, prejudice and fear,   40
   The tongue that's bought to speak,
      The heart that's hired to feel.

   But to the man sincerely good
   Each day will be a sabbath day
   Consigned to thoughts of holiness   45
      And deeds of living love.
The God he serves requires no cringing creed,
No idle prayers, no senseless mummeries,
No gold, no temples and no hireling priests.
'The winds, the pineboughs and the waters make   50
  Its melody. The hearts of all
  The beings it pervadeth form
  A temple for its purity;
  The wills of those that love the right
    Are offerings beyond   55
      Thanksgivings, prayers and gold.

The Crisis

When we see Despots prosper in their weakness,
When we see Falshood triumph in its folly,
When we see Evil, Tyranny, Corruption,
        Grin, grow and fatten;
When Virtue toileth thro' a world of sorrow,   5
When Freedom dwelleth in the deepest dungeon,
When Truth, in chains and infamy, bewaileth
        O'er a world's ruin;
When Monarchs laugh upon their thrones securely,
Mocking the woes which are to them a treasure,   10
Hear the deep curse, and quench the Mother's hunger
        In her child's murder;
Then may we hope the consummating hour
Dreadfully, sweetly, swiftly is arriving,
When light from Darkness, peace from desolation,   15
        Bursts unresisted;
Then mid the gloom of doubt and fear and anguish
The votaries of virtue may raise their eyes to Heaven
And confident watch till the renovating day-star
        Gild the horizon.   20

Passion

(to the   .

Fair are thy berries to the dazzled sight,
Fair is thy chequered stalk of mingling hues,
   And yet thou dost conceal
   A deadly poison there
     Uniting good and ill.   5

Art thou not like a lawyer whose smooth face
Dost promise good, while hiding so much ill?
   Ah! no. The semblance even
   Of goodness lingereth not
     Within that hollow eye.   10

Art thou the tyrant whose unlovely brow
With rare and glittering gems is contrasted?
   No — thou mayst kill the body,
   He withers up the soul;
     Sweet thou when he is nigh.   15

Art thou the wretch whose cold and sensual soul
His hard-earned mite tears from the famished hind
   Then says that God hath willed
   Many to toil and groan
     That few may boast at ease?   20

Art thou the slave whose mercenary sword
Stained with an unoffending brother's blood
   Deeper yet shews the spot

PASSION

 Of cowardice, whilst the
  Who wears it talks of courage?   25

Ah no! else while I gaze upon thy bane
I should not feel unmingled with contempt
 This awful feeling rise:
 As if I stood at night
  In some weird ruin's shade.   30

Thou art like youthful passion's quenchless fire
Which in some unsuspecting bosom glows
 So wild, so beautiful,
 Possessing wondrous power
  To wither or to warm.   35

Essence of Virtue, blushing virtues' prime,
Bright bud of Truth, producing Falshood's fruit,
 Freedom's own soul that binds
 The human will in chains
  Indissolubly fast;   40

Prime source of all that's lovely, good, and great,
Debasing man below the meanest brute,
 Spring of all healing streams,
 Yet deadlier than the gall
  Blackening a monarch's heart.   45

Why art thou thus, O Passion? Custom's chains
Have bound thee from thine Heaven-directed flight
 Or thou wouldst never thus
 Bring misery to man,
  Uniting good and ill.   50

To Harriet

Never, O never, shall yonder Sun
   Thro' my frame its warmth diffuse
When the heart that beats in its faithful breast
   Is untrue, fair girl, to thee;
     Nor the beaming moon   5
     On its nightly voyage
Shall visit this spirit with softness again,
     When its soaring hopes
     And its fluttering fears
Are untrue — fair girl to thee!   10

O Ever while this frail brain has life
   Will it thrill to thy love-beaming gaze,
And whilst thine eyes with affection gleam
   It will worship the spirit within.
     And when death comes   15
     To quench their fire,
A sorrowful rapture their dimness will shed
     As I bind me tight
     With thine auburn hair
And die, as I lived, with thee.   20

Falshood and Vice

a Dialogue

Whilst Monarchs laughed upon their thrones
To hear a famished nation's groans,
And hugged the wealth, wrung from the woe
That makes their eyes and veins o'erflow,
Those thrones high built upon the heaps 5
Of bones where frenzied Famine sleeps,
Where slavery with her scourge of iron
   Stained in mankind's unheeded gore,
And war's mad fiends the scene environ
   Mingling with shrieks a drunken roar, 10
There Vice and Falshood took their stand
High raised above the unhappy land.

FALSHOOD

Brother, arise from the dainty fare
   Which thousands have toil'd and bled to bestow,
A finer feast for thy hungry ear 15
   Is the news that I bring of human woe.

VICE

And secret one, what hast thou done
   To compare in thy tumid pride with me,
I, whose career thro' the blasted year
   Has been marked by ruin and misery? 20

FALSHOOD

What have I done! I've torn the robe
   From baby Truth's unsheltered form

FALSHOOD AND VICE

And round the desolated globe 25
   Worn safely the bewildering charm.
My tyrant-slaves to a dungeon floor
   Have bound the dauntless innocent,
And streams of fertilizing gore
   Flow from her bosom's hideous rent
   Which this unfailing dagger gave . . .
I dread that blood. No more. This day 30
Is ours tho' her eternal ray
   Must shine upon our grave . . .
Yet know, proud Vice, had I not given
To thee the mask I stole from Heaven,
Thy shape of ugliness and fear 35
Had never gained admission here.

VICE

And know that had I disdained to toil
But sate in my noisome cave the while
And ne'er to these hateful sons of Heaven,
   GOLD, MONARCHY or MURDER given, 40
Hadst thou with all thine art essayed
One of thy games then to have played,
With all thine overweening boast
Falshood, I tell thee thou had lost!—
But wherefore this dispute . . . we tend 45
Fraternal to one common end.
In this cold grave beneath my feet
Will our hopes, our fears and our labours meet.

FALSHOOD

I brought my daughter RELIGION on Earth.
She smothered its sweetest buds in their birth 50
But dreaded Reason's eye severe
So the crocodile slunk off slily in fear

FALSHOOD AND VICE

And loosed her bloodhounds from the den.
They started from dreams of slaughtered men
And by the light of her poison eye 55
Did her work o'er the wide Earth frightfully.
The deathy stench of her torches' flare,
Fed with human fat, polluted the air.
The curses, the shrieks, the ceaseless cries
Of the many mingling miseries, 60
As on she trod, ascended high
And trumpeted my Victory!
Brother, tell what thou hast done.

VICE

I have extinguished the noonday sun
In the carnage smoke of battles won. 65
Famine, Murder, Hell, and Power
Were sated in that joyous hour
Which searchless fate had stampt for me
With the seal of his security,
For the bloated Wretch on yonder throne 70
    Commanded the bloody fray to rise.
Like me he joyed at the stifled moan
    Wrung from a Nation's miseries
Whilst the snakes, whose slime *even him* defiled,
In extacies of malice smiled. . . . 75
They thought 'twas theirs!! — but mine the deed.
Theirs is the toil, but mine the meed.
Ten thousand victims madly bleed.
They think that tyrants goad them there
With poisonous war to taint the air, 80
[But hired assassins! 'tis not vice,
'Tis her sweet sister Cowardice . . . .]
    These tyrants on their beds of thorn
Swell in their dreams of murderous fame

And with their gains to lift my name 85
   Restless they plan from night to morn.
I — I do all. Without my aid,
Thy daughter, that relentless maid,
Could never o'er a deathbed urge
The fury of her venomed scourge. 90

FALSHOOD

Brother, well. — The world is ours.
   And whether thou or I have won,
The pestilence expectant lowers
   On all beneath yon blasted Sun.
Our joys, our toils, our honors meet 95
In the milkwhite and wormy winding sheet.
A short-lived joy, unceasing care,
Some heartless scraps of godly prayer,
A moody curse and a frenzied sleep
Ere gapes the grave's unclosing deep, 100
A tyrant's dream, a coward's start,
The ice that clings to a priestly heart,
A judge's frown, a courtier's smile,
Make the great whole for which we toil.
And Brother! Whether thou or I 105
Have done the work of misery,
It little boots. — Thy toil and pain
Without my aid were more than vain,
And but for thee I ne'er had sate
The guardian of Heaven's palace gate. 110

To the Emperors of Russia and Austria who eyed the battle of Austerlitz from the heights whilst Buonaparte was active in the thickest of the fight

Coward Chiefs! who, while the fight
 Rages in the plain below,
Hide the shame of your affright
 On yon distant mountain's brow,
Does one human feeling creep   5
Thro' your hearts' remorseless sleep
On that silence cold and deep?
 Does one impulse flow
Such as fires the Patriot's breast,
Such as breaks the Hero's rest?   10

No, cowards! ye are calm and still,
 Keen frosts that blight the human bud,
Each opening petal blight and kill
 And bathe its tenderness in blood.
Ye hear the groans of those who die,   15
Ye hear the whistling death-shots fly,
And when the yells of Victory
 Float o'er the murdered good
Ye smile secure.— On yonder plain
The game, if lost, begins again.   20

Think ye the restless fiend who haunts
 The tumult of yon gory field,

TO THE EMPERORS OF RUSSIA AND AUSTRIA

Whom neither shame nor danger daunts,
   Who dares not fear, who cannot yield,
Will not with Equalizing blow 25
Exalt the high, abase the low,
And in one mighty shock o'erthrow
   The slaves that sceptres wield
Till from the ruin of the storm
Ariseth Freedom's awful form? 30

Hushed below the battle's jar
   Night rests silent on the Heath,
Silent save where vultures soar
   Above the wounded warrior's death.
How sleep ye now, unfeeling Kings! 35
Peace seldom folds her snowy wings
On poisoned memory's conscience-stings
   Which lurk bad hearts beneath,
Nor downy beds procure repose
Where crime and terror mingle throes. 40

Yet may your terrors rest secure.
   Thou, Northern chief, why startest thou?
Pale Austria, calm those fears. Be sure
   The tyrant needs such slaves as you.
Think ye the world would bear his sway 45
Were dastards such as you away?
No! they would pluck his plumage gay
   Torn from a nation's woe
And lay him in the oblivious gloom
Where Freedom now prepares your tomb. 50

To November

O month of gloom, whose sullen brow
   Bears stamp of storms that lurk beneath,
No care or horror bringest thou
   To one who draws his breath
Where Zephyrs play and sunbeams shine   5
Unstained by any fog of thine.

Whilst thou obscurest the face of day
   Her radiant eyes can gild the gloom,
Darting a soft and vernal ray
   On Nature's leafless tomb.   10
Yes! tho' the landscape's beauties flee
My Harriet makes it spring to me.

Then raise thy fogs, invoke thy storms,
   Thy malice still my soul shall mar,
And whilst thy rage the Heaven deforms   15
   Shall laugh at every care,
And each pure feeling shall combine
To tell its Harriet "I am thine!"

It once was May; the Month of Love
   Did all it could to yield me pleasure,   20
Waking each green and vocal grove
   To a many-mingling measure,
But warmth and peace could not impart
To such a cold and shuddering heart.

TO NOVEMBER

Now thou art here — come! do thy worst 25
    To chill the breast that Harriet warms.
I fear me sullen Month thou'lt burst
    With envy of her charms
And finding nothing's to be done
Turn to December ere thou'st won! 30

Written on a beautiful day in Spring

In that strange mental wandering when to live
To breathe, to be, is undivided joy,
When the most woe-worn wretch would cease to grieve,
When satiation's self would fail to cloy;
When unpercipient of all other things   5
Than those that press around, the breathing Earth
The gleaming sky and the fresh season's birth,
Sensation all its wondrous rapture brings
And to itself not once the mind recurs—
   Is it foretaste of Heaven?   10
So sweet as this the nerves it stirs,
And mingling in the vital tide
   With gentle motion driven,
Cheers the sunk spirits, lifts the languid eye,
And scattering thro' the frame its influence wide   15
Revives the spirits when they droop and die.
The frozen blood with genial beaming warms
And to a gorgeous fly the sluggish worm transforms.

On leaving London for Wales.

Thou miserable city! where the gloom
   Of penury mingles with the tyrant's pride,
And virtue bends in sorrow o'er the tomb
   Where Freedom's hope and Truth's high Courage died.
May floods and vales and mountains me divide
   From all the taints thy wretched walls contain,
That life's extremes in desolation wide
   No more heap horrors on my beating brain
Nor sting my shuddering heart to sympathy with pain.

With joy I breathe the last and full farewell
   That long has quivered on my burdened heart,
My natural sympathies to rapture swell
   As from its day thy cheerless glooms depart,
Nor all the glare thy gayest scenes impart
   Could lure one sigh, could steal one tear from me,
Or lull to languishment the wakeful smart
   Which virtue feels for all 'tis forced to see,
Or quench the eternal flame of generous Liberty.

Hail to thee, Cambria, for the unfettered wind
   Which from thy wilds even now methinks I feel
Chasing the clouds that roll in wrath behind
   And tightening the soul's laxest nerves to steel!
True! Mountain Liberty alone may heal
   The pain which Custom's obduracies bring,
And he who dares in fancy even to steal
   One draught from Snowdon's ever-sacred spring
Blots out the unholiest rede of worldly witnessing.

And shall that soul to selfish peace resigned
   So soon forget the woe its fellows share?
Can Snowdon's Lethe from the freeborn mind
   So soon the page of injured penury tear?
Does this fine mass of human passion dare
   To sleep, unhonouring the patriot's fall,
Or life's sweet load in quietude to bear
   While millions famish even in Luxury's hall
And Tyranny high-raised stern lowers over all?

No, Cambria! never may thy matchless vales
   A heart so false to hope and virtue shield,
Nor ever may thy spirit-breathing gales
   Waft freshness to the slaves who dare to yield.
For me! . . . the weapon that I burn to wield
   I seek amid thy rocks to ruin hurled
That Reason's flag may over Freedom's field,
   Symbol of bloodless victory, wave unfurled—
A meteor-sign of love effulgent o'er the world.

Hark to that shriek! my hand had almost clasped
   The dagger that my heart had cast away
When the pert slaves, whose wanton power had grasped
   All hope that springs beneath the eye of day,
Pass before memory's gaze in long array.
   The storm fleets by and calmer thoughts succeed,
Feelings once more mild reason's voice obey.
   Woe be the tyrants' and murderers' meed,
But Nature's wound alone should make their
     Conscience bleed.

Do thou, wild Cambria, calm each struggling thought;
   Cast thy sweet veil of rocks and woods between,
That by the soul to indignation wrought
   Mountains and dells be mingled with the scene.

Let me forever be what I have been,
    But not forever at my needy door 60
Let Misery linger, speechless, pale and lean.
    I am the friend of the unfriended poor;
Let me not madly stain their righteous cause in gore.

No more! the visions fade before my sight
    Which Fancy pictures in the waste of air 65
Like lovely dreams ere morning's chilling light,
    And sad realities alone are there.
Ah! neither woe nor fear nor pain can tear
    Their image from the tablet of my soul,
Nor the mad floods of Despotism where 70
    Lashed into desperate furiousness they roll,
Nor passion's soothing voice, nor interest's cold control.

A winter's day

O! wintry day! that mockest spring
   With hopes of the reviving year!
That sheddest softness from thy wing
And near the cascade's murmuring
   Awakenest sounds so clear 5
That peals of vernal music swing
   Thro' the balm atmosphere.

Why hast thou given, O year! to May
   A birth so premature,
To live one incompleted day 10
That the mad whirlwind's sullen sway
   May sweep it from the moor
And winter reassume the sway
   That shall so long endure?

Art thou like Genius's matin bloom 15
   Unwelcome promise of its prime
That scattereth its rich perfume
   Around the portals of the tomb
   Decking the scar of time
In mockery of the early doom? 20

Art thou like Passion's rapturous dream
   That o'er life's stormy dawn
Doth dart its wild and flamy beam
Yet like a fleeting flash doth seem
   When many chequered years are gone 25
And tell the illusion of its gleam
   Life's blasted springs alone?

A WINTER'S DAY

Whate'er thou emblemest, I'll breathe
   Thy transitory sweetness now,
And whether Health with roseate wreathe   30
May bind mine head, or creeping Death
   Steal o'er my pulse's flow,
Struggling the wintry winds beneath
   I'll love thy vernal glow.

To Liberty

O let not Liberty
   Silently perish;
May the groan and the sigh
   Yet the flame cherish
Till the voice to Nature's bursting heart given,   5
   Ascending loud and high
   A world's indignant cry,
   And, startling on his throne
   The tyrant grim and lone,
Shall beat the deaf vault of Heaven.   10

Say, can the Tyrant's frown
   Daunt those who fear not
Or break the spirits down
   His badge that wear not?
Can chains or death or infamy subdue   15
   The free and fearless soul
   That dreads not their control,
   Sees Paradise and Hell,
   Sees the Palace and the cell,
Yet bravely dares prefer the good and true?   20

Regal pomp and pride
   The Patriot falls in scorning,
The spot whereon he died
   Should be the despot's warning.
The voice of blood shall on his crimes
      call down Revenge!   25
   And the spirits of the brave

TO LIBERTY

    Shall start from every grave
    Whilst from her Atlantic throne
    Freedom sanctifies the groan
That fans the glorious fires of its change.   30

Monarch! sure employer
    Of vice and want and woe,
Thou conscienceless destroyer,
    Who and what art thou! —
The dark prison house that in the dust shall lie,   35
    The pyramid which guilt
    First planned, which man has built;
    At whose footstone want and woe
    With a ceaseless murmur flow
And whose peak attracts the tempests of the sky.   40

The pyramids shall fall . . . . . .
    And Monarchs! so shall ye!
Thrones shall rust in the hall
    Of forgotten royalty
Whilst Virtue, Truth and Peace shall arise   45
    And a Paradise on Earth
    From your fall shall date its birth,
    And human life shall seem
    Like a short and happy dream
Ere we wake in the daybeam of the skies.   50

On Robert Emmet's tomb

May the tempests of Winter that sweep o'er thy tomb
Disturb not a slumber so sacred as thine;
May the breezes of summer that breathe of perfume
Waft their balmiest dews to so hallowed a shrine.

May the foot of the tyrant, the coward, the slave, 5
Be palsied with dread where thine ashes repose,
Where that undying shamrock still blooms on thy grave
Which sprung when the dawnlight of Erin arose.

There oft have I marked the grey gravestones among,
Where thy relics distinguished in lowliness lay, 10
The peasant boy pensively lingering long
And silently weep as he passed away.

And how could he not pause if the blood of his sires
Ever wakened one generous throb in his heart?
How could he inherit a spark of their fires 15
If tearless and frigid he dared to depart?

Not the scrolls of a court could emblazon thy fame
Like the silence that reigns in the palace of thee,
Like the whispers that pass of thy dearly loved name,
Like the tears of the good, like the groans of the free. 20

No trump tells thy virtues — the grave where they rest
With thy dust shall remain unpolluted by fame,
Till thy foes, by the world and by fortune caresst
Shall pass like a mist from the light of thy name.

When the storm cloud that lowers o'er the daybeam
    is gone,
Unchanged, unextinguished its lifespring will shine,
When Erin has ceased with their memory to groan
She will smile thro' the tears of revival on thine.

a Tale of Society as it is
from facts

1811

She was an Aged Woman, and the years
Which she had numbered on her toilsome way
Had bowed her natural powers to decay.
She was an Aged Woman, yet the ray
Which faintly glimmered thro' the starting tears 5
Pressed from their beds by silent misery
Hath soul's imperishable energy.
She was a cripple, and incapable
To add one mite to golden luxury,
And therefore did her spirit clearly feel 10
That Poverty — the crime of tainting stain —
Would merge her in its depths never to rise again.

One only son's love had supported her.
She long had struggled with infirmity
Lingering from human lifescenes, for to die 15
When fate has spared to send some mental tie
Not many wish, and surely fewer dare.
But when the tyrant's bloodhounds forced her Child
For tyrant's power unhallowed arms to wield,
Bend to another's will, become a thing 20
More senseless than the sword of battle field,
Then did she feel keen sorrow's keenest sting
And many years had past ere comfort they would bring.

For seven years did this poor woman live
In unparticipated solitude.   25
Thou might'st have seen her in the desert rude
Picking the scattered remnants of its wood.
If human, thou might'st there have learned to grieve.
The gleanings of precarious charity
Her scantiness of food did scarce supply;   30
The proofs of an unspeaking sorrow dwelt
Within her ghastly hollowness of eye;
Each arrow of the Season's change she felt,
Yet still she yearned ere her sad course were run —
One only hope it was — once more to see her son.   35

It was an eve of June, when every star
Spoke peace from Heaven to those on Earth that live.
She rested on the moor . . . 'twas such an eve
When first her soul began indeed to grieve —
Then he was here . . . now he is very far.   40
The freshness of the balmy evening
A sorrow o'er her weary soul did fling,
Yet not devoid of rapture's mingled tear;
A balm was in the poison of the sting.
This aged sufferer for many a year,   45
Had never felt such comfort . . . . she supprest
A sigh, and turning round — clasp'd William to her breast.

And tho' his form was wasted by the woe
Which despots on their victims love to wreak,
Tho' his sunk eyeball, and his faded cheek,   50
Of slavery, violence, and scorn did speak,
Yet did the aged Woman's bosom glow;
The vital fire seemed reillumed within
By this sweet unexpected welcoming.
O! consummation of the fondest hope   55

That ever soared on Fancy's dauntless wing!
O! tenderness that foundst so sweet a scope!
Prince! who dost swell upon thy mighty sway
When thou canst feel such love thou shalt be great as they!

Her son, compelled, the tyrant's foes had fought, 60
Had bled in battle, and the stern control
That ruled his sinews and coerced his soul
Utterly poisoned life's unmingled bowl
And unsubduable evils on him wrought.
He was the shadow of the lusty child 65
Who, when the time of summer season smiled,
For her did earn a meal of honesty
And with affectionate discourse beguiled
The keen attacks of pain and poverty
Till power as envying this, her only joy, 70
From her maternal bosom tore the unhappy boy.

And now cold charity's unwelcome dole
Was insufficient to support the pair,
And they would perish rather than would bear
The law's stern slavery and the insolent stare 75
With which law loves to rend the poor man's soul,
The bitter scorn, the spirit-sinking noise
Of heartless mirth which women, men and boys
Wake in this scene of legal misery . . .
Oh! William's spirit rather would rejoice 80
On some wild heath with his dear charge to die.
The death that keenest penury might give
Were sweeter far than cramped by slavery to live.

And they have borne thus long the winter's cold,
The driving sleet, the penetrating rain; 85

It seemeth that their element is pain
And that they never will feel life again,
For is it life to be so deathlike old? —
The same kind light feeds every living thing
That spreads its blossoms to the breath of spring, 90
But who feeds thee, unhappy wanderer?
With the fat slaves, who from the rich man's board
Lick the fallen crumbs thou scantily dost share
And mutterest for the gift a heartless prayer,
The flowers fade not thus. Thou must poorly die. 95
The changeful year feeds them. The tyrant, man, feeds thee.

And is it life that in youth's blasted morn
Not one of youth's dear raptures are enjoyed,
All natural bliss with servitude alloyed,
The beating heart, the sparkling eye, destroy'd, 100
And manhood of its brightest glories shorn
Debased by rapine, drunkenness and woe,
The foeman's sword, the vulgar tyrant's blow,
Ruined in body and soul till Heaven arrive,
His health and peace insultingly laid low, 105
Without a fear to die or wish to live,
Withered and sapless, miserably poor,
Relinquished for his wounds to beg from door to door?

Seest thou yon humble sod where oziers bind
The pillow of the monumentless dead? 110
There since her thorny pilgrimage is sped
The aged sufferer rests on the cold bed
Which all who seek or who avoid must find.
O let her sleep! and there at close of eve
'Twere holiness in solitude to grieve 115
And ponder on the wretchedness of Earth.

With joy of melancholy I would leave
A spot that to such deep-felt thoughts gives birth,
And tho' I could not pour the useless prayer
Would weep upon the grave and leave a blessing there. 120

The solitary

1810

Darest thou amid this varied multitude
To live alone, an isolated thing,
To see the busy beings round thee spring
And care for none? — in thy calm solitude,
A flower that scarce breathes in the desert rude   5
    To Zephyr's passing wing?

Not the swarth Pariah in some Indian Grove
Lone, lean and hunted by his brothers' hate,
Hath drunk so deep the cup of bitter fate
As that poor wretch who cannot, cannot love.   10
He bears a load which nothing can remove —
    A killing, withering weight.

He smiles ... 'tis sorrow's deadliest mockery;
He speaks ... the cold words flow not from his soul;
He acts like others; drains the genial bowl;   15
Yet, yet he longs, altho he fears, to die.
He pants to reach what yet he seems to fly,
    Dull Life's extremest goal.

The Monarch's funeral

An Anticipation

1810

The glowing gloom of eventide
   Has quenched the sunbeam's latest glow
And lowers upon the woe and pride
   That blasts the city's peace below.

At such an hour how sad the sight,
   To mark a Monarch's funeral
When the dim shades of awful night
   Rest on the coffin's velvet pall;

To see the Gothic Arches shew
   A varied mass of light and shade,
While to the torches' crimson glow
   A vast cathedral is displayed;

To see with what a silence deep
   The thousands o'er this death scene brood
As tho' some wizard's charm did creep
   Upon the countless multitude;

To see this awful pomp of death
   For one frail mass of mouldering clay
When nobler men the tomb beneath
   Have sunk unwept, unseen away.

THE MONARCH'S FUNERAL

For who was he, the uncoffined slain,
   That fell in Erin's injured isle
Because his spirit dared disdain
   To light his country's funeral pile?

Shall he not ever live in lays 25
   The warmest that a Muse may sing
Whilst monumental marbles raise
   The fame of a departed King?

May not the Muse's darling theme
   Gather its glorious garland thence 30
Whilst some frail tombstone's Dotard dream
   Fades with a monarch's impotence!

—Yes, 'tis a scene of wondrous awe
   To see a coffined Monarch lay
That the wide grave's insatiate maw 35
   Be glutted with a regal prey!

Who *now* shall public councils guide?
   Who rack the poor on gold to dine?
Who waste the means of regal pride
   For which a million wretches pine? 40

It is a child of earthly breath,
   A being perishing as he,
Who throned in yonder pomp of death
   Hath now fulfilled his destiny.

Now dust to dust restore! ... O Pride, 45
   Unmindful of thy fleeting power,
Whose empty confidence has vied
   With human life's most treacherous hour,

THE MONARCH'S FUNERAL

One moment feel that in the breast
    With regal crimes and troubles vext 50
The pampered Earthworms soon will rest,
    One moment feel . . . and die the next.

Yet deem not in the tomb's control
    The vital lamp of life can fail,
Deem not that e'er the Patriot's soul 55
    Is wasted by the withering gale.

The dross, which forms the *King*, is gone,
    And reproductive Earth supplies,
As senseless as the clay and stone
    In which the kindred body lies. 60

The soul which makes the *Man* doth soar
    And love alone survives to shed
All that its tide of bliss can pour
    Of Heaven upon the blessed dead.

So shall the Sun forever burn, 65
    So shall the midnight lightnings die,
And joy that glows at Nature's bourn
    Outlive terrestrial misery.

And will the crowd who silent stoop
    Around the lifeless Monarch's bier, 70
A mournful and dejected group,
    Breathe not one sigh, or shed one tear?

Ah! no. 'Tis wonder, 'tis not woe.
    Even royalists might groan to see
The *Father of the People* so 75
    Lost in the Sacred Majesty.

To the Republicans of North America

    Brothers! between you and me
       Whirlwinds sweep and billows roar,
    Yet in spirit oft I see
       On the wild and winding shore
    Freedom's bloodless banner wave,   5
    Feel the pulses of the brave,
    Unextinguished by the grave,
       See them drenched in sacred gore,
    Catch the patriot's gasping breath
    Murmuring Liberty in death.   10

    Shout aloud! let every slave
       Crouching at corruption's throne
    Start into a man, and brave
       Racks and chains without a groan!
    Let the castle's heartless glow   15
    And the hovel's vice and woe
    Fade like gaudy flowers that blow,
       Weeds that peep and then are gone,
    Whilst from misery's ashes risen
    Love shall burst the Captive's prison.   20

    Cotopaxi! bid the sound
       Thro' thy sister mountains ring
    Till each valley smile around
       At the blissful welcoming.
    And O! thou stern Ocean-deep,   25
    Whose eternal billows sweep
    Shores where thousands wake to weep
       Whilst they curse some villain King,

TO THE REPUBLICANS OF NORTH AMERICA

On the winds that fan thy breast
Bear thou news of freedom's rest.   30

Earth's remotest bounds shall start,
　　Every despot's bloated cheek,
Pallid as his bloodless heart,
　　Frenzy, woe and dread shall speak . . .
Blood may fertilize the tree   35
Of new bursting Liberty.
Let the guiltiness then be
　　On the slaves that ruin wreak,
On the unnatural tyrant-brood
Slow to Peace and swift to blood.   40

Can the daystar dawn of love
　　Where the flag of war unfurled
Floats with crimson stain above
　　Such a desolated world . . .
Never! but to vengeance driven   45
When the patriot's spirit shriven
Seeks in death its native Heaven,
　　Then to speechless horror hurled.
Widowed Earth may balm the bier
Of its memory with a tear.   50

Written at Cwm Ellan

1811

When the peasant hies him home, and the day planet reposes
Pillowed on the azure peaks that bound the western sight,
When each mountain flower its modest petal tremulously closes
And sombre shrouded twilight comes to lead her sister Night,
Vestal dark! how dear to me are then thy dews of lightness
That bathe my brow so withering scorched beneath the daybeam's brightness.
More dear to me, tho' day be robed in vest of dazzling whiteness,
Is one folding of the garment dusk that wraps thy form, O Night!

With thee I still delight to sit where dizzy Danger slumbers,
Where 'mid the rocks the fitful blast hath wak'd its wildest lay 10
Till beneath the yellow moonbeam decay the dying numbers
And silence, even in fancy's throne, hath seized again the sway.
Again she must resign it, hark! for wildest cadence pouring
Far, far amid the viewless glen beneath the Ellan roaring
Mid tongued woods, and shapeless rocks with moonlight summits soaring 15
It mingles its magic murmuring with the blast that floats away.

To Death

    Death, where is thy victory!
    To triumph whilst I die,
    To triumph whilst thine ebon wing
    Infolds my shuddering soul,
    O Death, where is thy sting? 5
    Not when the tides of murder roll,
When Nations groan that Kings may bask in bliss,
Death, couldst thou boast a victory such as this?
        When in his hour
        Of pomp and power 10
Thy slave, the mightiest murderer, gave
        Mid nature's cries
        The sacrifice
    Of myriads to glut the grave,
    When sunk the tyrant, sensualism's slave, 15
    Or Freedom's life-blood streamed upon thy shrine,
    Stern despot, couldst thou boast a Victory such
      as mine?

    To know, in dissolution's void,
    That Earthly hopes and fears decay,
    That every sense, but Love, destroyed, 20
    Must perish with its kindred clay.
    Perish ambition's crown!
    Perish its sceptered sway!
From Death's pale front fade Pride's fastidious frown.
In death's damp vault the lurid fires decay 25
Which Envy lights at heaven-born virtue's beam
    That all the cares subside

TO DEATH

    Which lurk beneath the tide
    Of life's unquiet stream ....
    Yes! this were Victory!   30
And on some rock whose dark form glooms the sky
To stretch these pale limbs when the soul is fled,
To baffle the lean passions of their prey,
To sleep within the chambers of the dead! —
Oh! not the Wretch around whose dazzling throne   35
His countless courtiers mock the words they say,
Triumphs, amid the bud of glory blown,
As I on Death's last pang and faint expiring groan.

Tremble, ye Kings whose luxury mocks the woe
That props thy column of unnatural state,   40
    Ye, the curses deep, tho' low,
      From misery's tortured breast that flow,
    Shall usher to your fate. —
Tremble, ye conquerors, at whose fell command
The War-fiend Riots o'er an happy land —   45
    Ye, desolation's gory throng
    Shall bear from victory along
    To Death's mysterious strand.
'Twere well that Vice no pain should know
    But every scene that memory gives   50
Tho' from the selfsame fount might flow
    The joy which Virtue aye receives ...
It is the grave—no conqueror triumphs now;
    The wreathes of bay that bound his head
    Wither around his fleshless brow.   55
    Where is the mockery fled
    That fired the tyrant's gaze?
'Tis like the fitful glare that plays
On some dark-rolling thunder cloud,
    Plays whilst the thunders roar,   60

TO DEATH

    But when the storm is past
    Fades like the warrior's name.
Death! in thy vault when Kings and peasants lie
Not power's stern rod or fame's most thrilling blasts
Can liberate thy captives from decay.   65
My triumph, their defeat; my joy, their shame!
Welcome then, peaceful Death, I'll sleep with thee—
Mine be thy quiet home, and thine my Victory.

Dark Spirit of the desart rude

Dark Spirit of the desart rude
That o'er this awful solitude,
Each tangled and untrodden wood,
Each dark and silent glen below,
Where sunlight's gleamings never glow, 5
Whilst jetty, musical and still,
In darkness speeds the mountain rill;
That o'er yon broken peaks sublime,
Wild shapes that mock the scythe of time,
And the pure Ellan's foamy course, 10
Wavest thy wand of magic force;
Art thou yon sooty and fearful fowl
   That flaps its wing o'er the leafless oak
That o'er the dismal scene doth scowl
   And mocketh music with its croak? 15

I've sought thee where day's beams decay
   On the peak of the lonely hill,
I've sought thee where they melt away
   By the wave of the pebbly rill;
I've strained to catch thy murky form 20
Bestride the rapid and gloomy storm;
Thy red and sullen eyeball's glare
Has shot, in a dream, thro' the midnight air
   But never did thy shape express
   Such an emphatic gloominess. 25

And where art thou, O thing of gloom? ...
On Nature's unreviving tomb

Where sapless, blasted and alone
She mourns her blooming centuries gone! —
From the fresh sod the Violets peep, 30
The buds have burst their frozen sleep,
Whilst every green and peopled tree
Is alive with Earth's sweet melody.
   But thou alone art here,
Thou desolate Oak, whose scathed head 35
For ages has never trembled,
Whose giant trunk dead lichens bind
Moaningly sighing in the wind,
With huge loose rocks beneath thee spread,
   Thou, Thou alone art here! 40
Remote from every living thing,
   Tree, shrub or grass or flower,
Thou seemest of this spot the King
   And with a regal power
Suck like that race all sap away 45
And yet upon the spoil decay.

The pale, the cold and the moony smile

The pale, the cold and the moony smile,
   Which the meteor beam of a stormy night
Sheds on a lonely and seagirt isle
   Till the dawning of morn's undoubted light,
Is the taper of life so fickle and wan   5
That flits round our steps till their strength is gone.

Oh! Man, hold thee on with courage of soul
   Thro' the long, long night of thy doubtful way,
And the billows of cloud that around thee roll
   Shall subside in the calm of eternal day,   10
For all in this world we can surely know
Is a little delight and a little woe.

All we behold, we feel that we know;
   All we perceive, we know that we feel;
And the coming of death is a fearful blow   15
   To a brain unencompassed by nervestrings of steel —
When all that we know, we feel and we see
Shall fleet by like an unreal mystery.

The secret things of the grave are there
   Where all but this body must surely be,   20
Tho' the fine-wrought eye and the wondrous ear
   No longer will live to hear or to see
All that is bright and all that is strange
In the gradual path of unending change.

Who telleth the tales of unspeaking Death?   25
   Who lifteth the veil of what is to come?

THE PALE, THE COLD AND THE MOONY SMILE

Who painteth the beings that are beneath
    The wide-stretching realms of the peopled tomb
And uniteth the hopes of what shall be
With the fears and the love for that which we see?   30

Death-spurning rocks!

Death-spurning rocks! here have ye towered since Time
    Sprung from Tradition's mist-encircled height
Which Memory's palsied pinion dreads to climb,
    Awed by the phantoms of its beamless night.
        Death-spurning rocks! Each jagged form   5
        Shall still arrest the passing storm
        Whilst rooted there the aged Oak
        Is shivered by the lightning's stroke.
Years shall fade fast, and centuries roll away —
Ye shall spurn death no more but like your Oak decay.   10

A maniac-sufferer soared with wild intent
    Where Nature formed these wonders. On the way
There is a little spot. Fiends would relent
    Knew they the snares that there for memory lay —
        How many a hope and many a fear   15
        And many a vain and bitter tear —
        Whilst each prophetic feeling wakes
        A brood of mad and venomed snakes
To make the lifesprings of his soul their food,
To twine around his veins and fatten on his blood.   20

To quench his pangs he fled to the wild moor.
    One fleeting beam flashed but its gloom to shew,
Turned was the way-worn wanderer from the door
    Where Pity's self promised to soothe his woe.
        Shall he turn back? The tempest there   25
        Sweeps fiercely thro' the turbid air

DEATH-SPURNING ROCKS!

  Beyond a gulph before that yawns.
  The daystar shines, the daybeam dawns.
God! Nature! Chance! remit this misery—
It burns!—why need he live to weep who does not fear
 to die?   30

The Tombs

These are the tombs. O cold and silent Death,
Thy Kingdom and thy subjects here I see.
    The record of thy victories
      Is graven on every speaking stone
        That marks what once was man.   5

These are the tombs. Am I, who sadly gaze
On the corruption and the skulls around,
    To sum the mass of loathsomeness,
      And to a mound of mouldering flesh
        Say——"thou wert human life!"   10

In thee once throbbed the Patriot's beating heart,
In thee once lived the Poet's soaring soul,
    The pulse of love, the calm of thought,
      Courage and charity and truth
        And high devotedness;   15

All that could sanctify the meanest deeds,
All that might give a manner and a form
    To matter's speechless elements,
      To every brute and morbid shape
        Of this phantasmal world: 20

That the high sense which from the stern rebuke
Of Erin's victim-patriot's death-soul shone,
    When blood and chains defiled the land,
      Lives in the torn uprooted heart
        His savage murderers burn.   25

THE TOMBS

   Ah, no! else while these tombs before me stand
My soul would hate the coming of its hour,
      Nor would the hopes of life and love
      Be mingled with those fears of death
         That chill the warmest heart.   30

To Harriet

It is not blasphemy to hope that Heaven
More perfectly will give those nameless joys
Which throb within the pulses of the blood
And sweeten all that bitterness which Earth
Infuses in the heaven-born soul — O Thou,   5
Whose dear love gleamed upon the gloomy path
Which this lone spirit travelled, drear and cold,
Yet swiftly leading to those awful limits
Which mark the bounds of Time and of the space
When Time shall be no more: wilt thou not turn   10
Those spirit-beaming eyes and look on me,
Until I be assured that Earth is Heaven
And Heaven is Earth? — will not thy glowing cheek,
Glowing with soft suffusion, rest on mine
And breathe magnetic sweetness thro' the frame   15
Of my corporeal nature, thro' the soul
Now knit with these fine fibres? I would give
The longest and the happiest day that fate
Has marked on my existence but to feel
One soul-reviving kiss . . . oh, thou most dear,   20
'Tis an assurance that this Earth is Heaven
And Heaven the flower of that untainted seed
Which springeth here beneath such love as ours.
Harriet! let death all mortal ties dissolve
But ours shall not be mortal — the cold hand   25
Of Time may chill the love of Earthly minds,
Half frozen now, the frigid intercourse
Of common souls lives but a summer's day,
It dies, where it arose, upon this Earth,

TO HARRIET

But ours! oh 'tis the stretch of fancy's hope 30
To portray its continuance as now,
Warm, tranquil, spirit-healing. Nor when age
Has tempered these wild extacies, and given
A soberer tinge to the luxurious glow
Which blazing on devotion's pinnacle 35
Makes virtuous passion supersede the power
Of reason, nor when life's aestival sun
To deeper manhood shall have ripened me,
Nor when some years have added judgment's store
To all thy woman sweetness, all the fire 40
Which throbs in thine enthusiast heart, not then
Shall holy friendship (for what other name
May love like ours assume?) not even then
Shall custom so corrupt, or the cold forms
Of this desolate world so harden us 45
As when we think of the dear love that binds
Our souls in soft communion, while we know
Each other's thoughts and feelings, can we say
Unblushingly a heartless compliment,
Praise, hate or love with the unthinking world 50
Or dare to cut the unrelaxing nerve
That knits our love to Virtue — can those eyes
Beaming with mildest radiance on my heart
To purify its purity e'er bend
To soothe its vice or consecrate its fears? 55
Never, thou second self! is confidence
So vain in virtue that I learn to doubt
The mirror even of Truth? — Dark Flood of Time,
Roll as it listeth thee. I measure not
By months or moments thy ambiguous course; 60
Another may stand by me on thy brink
And watch the bubble whirled beyond his ken
Which pauses at my feet — the sense of love,

TO HARRIET

The thirst for action, and the impassioned thought
Prolong my being. If I wake no more   65
My life more actual living will contain
Than some grey veteran's of the world's cold school
Whose listless hours unprofitably roll
By one enthusiast feeling unredeemed.
Virtue and Love! unbending Fortitude,   70
Freedom, Devotedness and Purity—
That life my Spirit consecrates to you.

Sonnet

To Harriet on her birth day

August 1, 1812

O thou, whose radiant eyes and beamy smile —
Yet even a sweeter somewhat indexing —
Have known full many an hour of mine to guile
Which else would only bitter memories bring,
O ever thus, thus! as on this natal day,   5
Tho' age's frost may blight those tender eyes,
Destroy that kindling cheek's transparent dyes
And those luxuriant tresses change to grey,
Ever as now with Love and Virtue's glow
May thy unwithering soul not cease to burn.   10
Still may thine heart with those pure thoughts o'erflow
Which force from mine such quick and warm return,
And I must love thee even more than this
Nor doubt that Thou and I part but to meet in bliss.

Sonnet

To a balloon, laden with Knowledge

Bright ball of flame that thro' the gloom of even
Silently takest thine etherial way
And with surpassing glory dimmst each ray
Twinkling amid the dark blue Depths of Heaven;
Unlike the Fire thou bearest, soon shalt thou   5
Fade like a meteor in surrounding gloom,
Whilst that, unquencheable, is doomed to glow
A watch light by the patriot's lonely tomb,
A ray of courage to the opprest and poor,
A spark, tho' gleaming on the hovel's hearth,   10
Which thro' the tyrants' gilded domes shall roar,
A beacon in the darkness of the Earth,
A Sun which o'er the renovated scene
Shall dart like Truth where Falshood yet has been.

Sonnet

*On launching some bottles filled with
Knowledge into the Bristol Channel.*

Vessels of Heavenly medicine! may the breeze,
Auspicious, waft your dark green forms to shore;
Safe may ye stern the wide surrounding roar
Of the wild whirlwinds and the raging seas;
And oh! if Liberty e'er deigned to stoop 5
From yonder lowly throne her crownless brow,
Sure she will breathe around your emerald group
The fairest breezes of her west that blow.
Yes! she will waft ye to some freeborn soul
Whose eyebeam, kindling as it meets your freight, 10
Her heaven-born flame on suffering Earth will light
Until Its radiance gleams from pole to pole
And tyrant-hearts with powerless envy burst
To see their night of ignorance dispersed.

Sonnet

*On waiting for a wind to cross the
Bristol Channel from Devonshire to Wales.*

Oh! for the South's benign and balmy breeze!
Come, gentle Spirit! thro' the wide Heaven sweep;
Chase inauspicious Boreas from the seas,
That gloomy tyrant of the unwilling deep.
These wilds where Man's profane and tainting hand 5
Nature's primaeval loveliness has marred,
And some few souls of the high bliss debarred
Which else obey her powerful command,
I leave without a sigh. Ye mountain piles
That load in grandeur Cambria's emerald vales, 10
Whose sides are fair in cultivation's smiles,
Around whose jagged heads the storm cloud sails—
A heart that's all thine own receive in me,
With Nature's fervour fraught and calm in purity.

To Harriet

Harriet! thy kiss to my soul is dear;
   At evil or pain I would never repine
If to every sigh and to every tear
   Were added a look and a kiss of thine.
Nor is it the look when it glances fire,   5
   Nor the kiss when bathed in the dew of delight,
Nor the throb of the heart when it pants desire
   From the shadows of eve to the morning light,

But the look when a lustre of joy-mingled woe
   Has faintly obscured all its bliss-beaming Heaven,   10
Such a lovely, benign and enrapturing glow
   As sunset can paint on the clouds of even,
And a kiss, which the languish of silent love,
   Tho' eloquent, faints with the toil of expressing,
Yet so light, that thou canst not refuse, my dove!   15
   To add this one to the debt of caressing.

Harriet! adieu to all vice and care.
   Thy love is my Heaven, thy arms are my world;
While thy kiss and thy look to my soul remain dear
   I should smile tho' Earth from its base be hurled.   20
For a heart as pure and a mind as free
   As ever gave lover, to thee I give,
And all that I ask in return from thee
   Is to love like me and with me to live.

This heart that beats for thy love and bliss,   25
   Harriet! beats for its country too;

TO HARRIET

And it never would thrill with thy look or kiss
   If it dared to that country's cause be untrue.
Honor, and wealth and life it spurns,
   But thy love is a prize it is sure to gain,   30
And the heart that with love and virtue burns
   Will never repine at evil or pain.

Mary to the Sea-Wind

I implore thee, I implore thee, softly swelling Breeze,
Waft swift the sail of my lover to the shore
That under the shadow of yon darkly-woven trees
I may meet him, I may meet him to part with him no more.
For this boon, for this boon, sweet Sea-Wind, will I weave
A garland wild of heath flowers to breathe to thee perfume.
Thou wilt kiss them, yet like Henry's thy kisses will but leave
A more heaven-breathing fragrance and sense-enchanting bloom.

And then on Summer evens I will hasten to inhale —
Remembering that thou wert so kind — thy balmy, balmy breath; 10
And when thy tender pinions in the gloom begin to fail
I will catch thee to my bosom ere thou diest on the heath.

I will catch thee to my bosom — and if Henry's oaths are true,
A softer, sweeter grave thou wilt never find than there.
Nor is it, lovely Sea-Wind, nor is it to undo 15
That my arms are so inviting, that my bosom is so fair.

A retrospect of Times of Old

The mansions of the Kings are tenantless . . . .
Low lie in dust their glory and their shame.
No tongue survives their virtuous Deeds to bless,
No tongue with execration blasts their fame,
But in some ruined pile, where yet the gold*   5
Casts purple brilliance o'er colossal snow,
Where sapphire eyes in breathing statues glow
And the tainted blast sighs mid the reeds below,
Where grim effigies of the Gods of old
In mockery stand of ever-changing men,   10
Their ever-changing worship. Oh how vain!
(Yet baubles aye must please the multitude.)
There Desolation dwells! — Where are the Kings?
Why sleep they now if sleep be not eternal?
Cannot Oblivion's silent tauntings call   15
The kings and heroes from their quietude
Of Death to snatch the Scrolls from her palsying hand,
To tell the world how mighty once they were ——
They dare not wake . . . thy Victory is here
O Death! — . Yet I hear unearthly voices cry,   20
"Death, thou'lt be swallowed up in Victory!"

Yes, Dream of fame! the halls are desolate
Where whitened skeletons of thine heroes lie . . .
Stillness keeps watch before each grass-grown gate
Save where amid thy towers the Simoon's sigh   25
Wakes the lone lyre whose mistress sleeps below
And bids it thrill to notes of awfulness and woe.

---
* Gilding yet remains on the cornices of the ruined palace of Persepolis—

There, ages since, some Royal Bloodhound crept
When on these pillared piles a midnight lay —
Which, but from visioned memories, long has fled —   30
To work ambition whilst his brother slept,
And reckless of the peaceful smile that played
Around his dream-fraught features — when betrayed
They told each innocent secret of the day —
Wakened the thoughtless victim, bade him stare   35
Upon the murderous steel . . . The chaste pale glare
Of the midnight moonbeam kissed its glittering blade —
A moment! and its brightness, quenched in blood,
Distained with murder the moon's silver flood.
The blushing moon, wide-gathering vapours shrouded.   40
One moment did he triumph; — but remorse,
Suspicion, anguish, fear, all triumph clouded.
Destruction . . Suicide . . his last resource . . .
Wider yawned the torrent. The moon's stormy flash
Disclosed its black tumultuousness . . . the crash   45
Of rocks and boughs mixed with its roarings hoarse.
A moment! And he dies! Hark to the awful dash! *

Such were thy works, Ambition, even amid
The darksome times of generations gone,
Which the dark veil of viewless hours has hid, —   50
The veil of hours forever onward flown.
Swift roll the waves of Time's eternal tide:
The peasant's grave, marked by no tribute stone,
No less remembered than the gilded bed
On which the hero slept! now ever gone, —   55
Passion and will and power, flesh, heart and brain and bone!

---

* I believe it was only in those early times when Monarchy was in its apprenticeship that its compunction for evil deeds was unendurable . . There is no instance upon record parallel to that related above, but I know that neither men, nor sets of men become vicious but slowly and step by step, each less difficult than the former.

Each trophied bust where gore-emblazoned Victory
In breathing marble shook the ensanguined spear,
Flinging its heavy purple canopy
In cold expanse o'er martyred Freedom's bier, 60
Each gorgeous altar where the victims bled
And grim Gods frowned above their human prey,
Where the high temple echoing to the yells
Of death-pangs, to the long and shuddering groan,
Whilst sacred hymns along the aisles did swell 65
And pitiless priests drowned each discordant moan —
All, all have faded in past time away!
New Gods, like men, changing in ceaseless flow,
Ever at hand as antient ones decay,
Heroes and Kings and laws have plunged this world in
   woe. 70

Sesostris, Caesar, and Pizarro come!
Thou Moses! and Mahommed,* leave that gloom!
Destroyers! never shall your memory die!
Approach, pale Phantom, to yon mould'ring tomb
Where all thy bones, hopes, crimes and passions lie. 75
And thou, poor peasant, when thou pass't the grave
Where deep enthroned in monumental pride
Sleep low in dust the mighty and the brave,
Where the mad conqueror whose gigantic stride
The Earth was too confined for, doth abide, 80
Housing his bones amid a little clay,
In gratitude to Nature's Spirit bend
And wait in still hope for thy better end.

---

* To this innumerable list of legal murderers our own age affords numerous addenda. Frederic of Prussia, Buonaparte, Suwarroff, Wellington and Nelson are the most skilful and notorious scourges of their species of the present day.—

The Voyage

A Fragment

Devonshire—August 1812

    Quenched is old Ocean's rage;
    Each puissant wave that flung
Its neck, that writhed beneath the tempest's scourge
    Indignant up to Heaven,
Now breathes in its sweet slumber   5
    To mingle with the day
    A spirit of tranquillity.
    Beneath the cloudless sun
    The gently swelling main
    Scatters a thousand colourings   10
And the wind that wanders vaguely thro' the void
With the flapping of the Sail, and the dashing at the prow,
And the whistle of the sailor in that shadow of a calm,
    A ravishing harmony makes.
O! why is a rapt soul e'er recalled   15
    From the palaces of visioned bliss
        To the cells of real sorrow?

That little vessel's company
Beheld the sight of loveliness—
The dark grey rocks that towered   20
    Above the slumbering sea,
    And their reflected forms
Deep in its faintly-waving mirror given.
    They heard the low breeze sighing
    The listless sails and ropes among,   25

THE VOYAGE

    They heard the music at the prow,
    And the hoarse, distant clash
      Sent from yon gloomy caves
Where Earth and Ocean strive for mastery.

    A mingled mass of feeling   30
    Those human spirits prest
      As they heard, and saw, and felt
Some fancied fear, and some real woe
Mixed with those glimpses of heavenly joy
      That dawned on each passive soul.   35
Where is the woe that never sees
One joybeam illumine the night of the mind?
      Where is the bliss that never feels
One dart from the quiver of earthly pain?

Tho' young and happy spirits now   40
Along the world are voyaging,
Love, friendship, virtue, truth,
Simplicity of sentiment and speech,
    And other sensibilities
Known by no outward name.   45
Some faults that Love forgives,
Some flaws that Friendship shares,
    Hearts passionate and benevolent,
    Alive, and urgent to repair
The errors of their brother heads —   50
    All voyage with them too.

They look to land . . . . they look to Sea;
Bounded one is, and palpable
Even as a noonday scene . .
The other indistinct and dim,   55
Spangled with dizzying sunbeams,

THE VOYAGE

Boundless, untrod by human step,
Like the vague blisses of a midnight dream
   Or Death's immeasurable main,
Whose lovely islands gleam at intervals   60
Upon the Spirit's visioned solitude
Thro' Earth's wide woven and many-colour'd veil.

   It is a moveless calm.
   The sailor's whistle shrill
Speeds clearly thro' the sleeping atmosphere—   65
   As country curates pray for rain
   When drought has frustrated full long—
   He whistles for a wind
   With just the same success.
Two honest souls were they   70
And oft had braved in fellowship the storm,
   Till from that fellowship had sprung
   A sense of right and liberty.
Unbending, undismayed, aye they had seen
Where danger, death and terror played   75
   With human lives in the boiling deep,
   And they had seen the scattered spray
Of the green and jagged mountain-wave
Hid in the lurid tempest-cloud,
With lightnings tinging all its fleeting form,   80
   Rolled o'er their fragile bark.
   A dread and hopeless month
   Had they participated once
   In that diminutive bark:—
Their tearless eyes uplifted unto Heaven   85
   So fruitlessly for aid!
Their parched mouths oped eager to the shower,
So thin and sleety in that arctic clime.
   Their last hard crust was shared

THE VOYAGE

  Impartial in equality   90
And in the dreadful night
Where all had failed ... even hope,
Together they had shared the gleam
Shot from yon lighthouse tower
  Across the waste of waves;   95
And therefore are they brave, free, generous.
For who that had so long fought hand to hand
With famine, toil and hazard, smil'd at Death
When leaning from the bursting billow's height
He stares so ghastly terrible, would waste   100
One needless word for life's contested toys?
Who that had shared his last and nauseous crust
With Famine and a friend, would not divide
A landsman's meal with one who needed it?
Who that could rule the elements and spurn   105
Their fiercest rage, would bow before a slave
Decked in the fleetingness of Earthly power?
Who that had seen the soul of Nature work—
Blind, changeless and eternal in her paths—*
Would shut his eyes and ears, quaking before   110
The bubble of a Bigot's blasphemy?

  The faintly moving prow
Divided Ocean's smoothness languidly.
  A landsman there reclined,

---

* It is remarkable that few are more experimentally convinced of the doctrine of necessity than old sailors, who have seen much and various service. The peculiarly engaging and frank generosity of seafaring men probably is an effect of this cause. Those employed in small and ill-equipped trading vessels seem to possess this generosity in a purer degree than those of a King's ship. The habits of subjection and coercion imbued into the latter may suffice to explain the cause of the difference.

    With lowering close-contracted brow 115
        And mouth updrawn at intervals
As fearful of his fluctuating bent,
        His eyes wide-wandering round
        In insecure malignity,
Rapacious, mean, cruel and cowardly, 120
        Casting upon the loveliness of day
        The murkiness of villainy ...
By other nurses than the battling storm,
        Friendship, Equality and Sufferance,
        His manhood had been cradled,— 125
Inheritor to all the vice and fear
Which Kings and laws and priests and conquerors spread
        On the woe-fertilized world.
        Yes! in the dawn of life,
When guileless confidence and unthinking love 130
        Dilate all hearts but those
Which servitude or power has cased in steel,
He bound himself to an unhappy woman;
Not of those pure and heavenly links that Love
        Twines round a feeling to Freedom dear, 135
But of vile gold, cank'ring the breast it binds,
Corroding and inflaming every thought
        Till vain desire, remorse and fear
            Envenom all the being.
Yet did this chain, tho' rankling in the soul 140
Not bind the grosser body; he was wont
        All means to try of striving.
To those above him, the most servile cringe
That ignorance e'er gave to titled Vice
        Was simperingly yielded; 145
To those beneath, the frown which Commerce darts
On cast-off friends, unprofitably poor,
        Was less severe than his.

THE VOYAGE

There was another too ...
    One of another mould.   150
He had been cradled in the wildest storm
    Of Passion, and tho' now
The feebler light of worn-out energies
    Shone on his soul, yet ever and anon
        A flash of tempests long past by   155
            Would wake to pristine visions.
Now he was wrapt in a wild, woeful dream.
    Deeply his soul could love,
And as he gazed on the boundless sea
Chequered with sunbeams and with shade,   160
    Alternate to infinity,
        He fell into a dream.

    He dreamed that all he loved
Across the shoreless wastes were voyaging
    By that unpitying landsman piloted,   165
    And that at length they came
    To a black and barren island rock.
    Barren the isle ... no egg
Which sea mews leave upon the wildest shore.
    Barren the isle .. no blade   170
Of grass, no seaweed, not the vilest thing
    For human nutriment. ...

He struggled with the pitiless landsman then
    But nerved tho' his frame with love,
    Quenchless, despairing love,   175
It nought availed. .. strong Power
Truth, love and courage vanquished.
A rock was piled upon his feeble breast.
    All was subdued, but that
Which is immortal, unsubduable.   180

He still continued dreaming . . . .
>The rock upon his bosom quenched not
>The frenzy and defiance of his eye,
But the strong and coward landsman laughed to scorn
>His unprevailing fortitude, 185
>And in security of malice stabbed
>One who accompanied his voyagings.
>The blood gushed forth. The eye grew dim,
>The nerve relaxed, the life was gone.
>His smile of dastardly revenge 190
>>Glared upon dead frame.
Then back the Victim flung his head
>In horror insupportable
>Upon the jagged rock whereon he lay,
>And human Nature paused awhile 195
>>In pity to his woe.

When he awaked to life
She whom he loved was bending over him.
>Haggard her sunken eye. . .
>Bloodless her quivering lips. . . 200
>She bended to bestow
The burning moisture from her feverish tongue
>To lengthen out his life
>Perhaps till succour came! . .
But more her dear soft eyes in languid love 205
When life's last gleam was flickering in decay
>The waning spark rekindled
And the faint lingering kiss of her withered lips
Mingled a rapture with his misery.
>A bleeding Sister lay 210
>>Beside this wretched pair,
And He the dastard of relentless soul
In moody malice lowered over all.

THE VOYAGE

 And this is but a dream!
For yonder—see! the port in sight!   215
 The vessel makes towards it!
 The sight of their safety then,
 And the hum of the populous town
Awakened them from a night of horror
 To a day of secure delights.   220

Lo! here a populous Town:
Two dark rocks either side defend,
The quiet water sleeps within
 Reflecting every roof and every mast.
 A populous town! it is a den   225
Where wolves keep lambs to fatten on their blood.
'Tis a distempered spot. Should there be one,
Just, dauntless, rational, he would appear
 A madman to the rest.
Yes! smooth-faced tyrants chartered by a Power   230
Called King, who in the castellated keep
Of a far distant land wears out his days
Of miserable dotage, pace the quay
And by the magic of that dreadful word,
Hated tho' dreadful, shield their impotence,   235
Their lies, their murders, and their robberies.
See, where the sailor absent many years
With Heaven in his rapture-speaking eyes
Seeks the low cot where all his wealth reposes,
To bring himself for joy, and his small store,   240
Hard earned by years of peril and of toil,
For comfort to his famine-wasted babes.
Deep in the dark blue Sea the unmoving moon
Gleams beautifully quiet... such a night
Where the last kiss from Mary's quivering lips   245
Unmanned him. To the well-known door he speeds

His faint hand pauses on the latch .. His heart
Beats eagerly. — When suddenly the gang
Dissolves his dream of rapture — no delay!
No pity! unexpostulating power 250
Deals not in human feelings . . . he is stript
By those low slaves whose master's names inflict
Curses more fell than even themselves would give;
The Indian muslins and the Chinese toys,
These for small gain, and those for boundless love, 255
Thus carefully concealed, are torn away;
The very handkerchief his Mary gave
Which in unchanging faithfulness he wore
Rent from his manly neck! his kindling eye
Beamed vengeance, and the tyrant's manacles 260
Shook on his struggling arm; "Where is my Wife?
Where are my Children?" — close beside him stood
A sleek and pampered town's man — "oh! your wife
"Died this time year in the House of Industry
"Your young ones all are dead, except one brat 265
"Stubborn as you — Parish apprentice now."
They have appropriated human life
And human happiness, but these weigh nought
In the nice balanced Politician's scale,
Who finds that murder is expedient 270
And that vile means can answer glorious ends.
Wide Nature has outstretched her fertile Earth
In commonage to all. . — but they have torn
Her dearest offspring from her bleeding breast,
Have disunited Liberty and life, 275
Severed all right from duty, and confused
Virtue with selfishness. — The grass-green hills,
The fertile vallies and the limpid streams,
The beach on the seashore, the sea itself,
The very snow-clad mountain peaks, whose height 280

THE VOYAGE

Forbids all human footstep .. the ravines
Where cataracts have roared ere Monarchs were,
Nature's fair Earth, and Heaven's untainted air
Are all apportioned out... some bloated Lord
Some priestly pilferer, or some Snake of Law,   285
Some miserable mockery of a man,
Some slave without a heart, looks over these
And calls them *Mine* — in self-approving pride.
The millionth of the produce of the vale
He sets apart for *charity*. Vain fool!   290
He gives in mercy, while stern Justice cries,
"Be thou as one of them — resign thine hall
Brilliant with murder's trophies, and the board
Loaded with surfeiting viands, and the gems
Which millions toil to bring thee. — Get thee hence   295
And dub thyself a man, then dare to throw
One act of usefulness, one thought of love
Into the balance of thy past misdeeds!"

A Dialogue

1809

DEATH

Yes! my dagger is drenched with the blood of the brave.
I have sped with Love's wings from the battlefield grave,
Where Ambition is hushed neath the peacegiving sod,
And slaves cease to tremble at Tyranny's nod.
I offer a calm habitation to thee; 5
Victim of grief, wilt thou slumber with me?
Drear and damp is my hall, but a mild Judge is there
Who steeps in oblivion the brands of Despair.
Nor a groan of regret, nor a sigh, nor a breath
Dares dispute with grim Silence the empire of Death; 10
Nor the howlings of envy resound thro' the gloom
That shrouds in its mantle the slaves of the tomb.
I offer a calm habitation to thee;
Say, Victim of grief, wilt thou slumber with me?

MORTAL

Mine eyelids are heavy, my soul seeks repose. 15
It longs in thy arms to embosom its woes;
It longs in that realm to deposit its load,
Where no longer the scorpions of perfidy goad,
Where the phantoms of Prejudice vanish away
And Bigotry's bloodhounds lose scent of their prey. 20
Yet tell me, dark Death, when thine Empire is o'er
What awaits on futurity's mist-circled shore?

DEATH

Cease, cease, wayward mortal! I dare not unveil
The shadows that float on eternity's vale.

A DIALOGUE

What thinkest thou will wait thee? A *Spirit of Love 25
That will hail thy blest advent to mansions above?
For Love, mortal! gleams thro' the gloom of my sway
And the clouds that surround me fly fast at its ray.
Hast thou *loved?* — then depart from these regions of hate
And in slumber with me quench the arrows of fate 30
That canker and burn in the wounds of a heart
That urges its sorrows with me to depart.
I offer a calm habitation to thee;
Say, victim of grief, wilt thou slumber with me?

MORTAL

Oh sweet is thy slumber, and sweeter the ray 35
Which after thy night introduces the day!
How soft, how persuasive, self-interest's breath
Tho' it floats to mine ear from the bosom of Death!
I hoped that I quite was forgotten by all,
Yet a lingering friend may be grieved at my fall, 40
And virtue forbids, tho' I languish to die,
When Departure might heave Virtue's breast with a sigh.
Yet Death! oh! my friend, snatch this form to thy shrine
And I fear, dear destroyer, I shall not repine.

---

* The author begs to be understood by this expression neither to mean the Creator of the Universe, nor the Christian Deity. When this little poem was written the line stood thus, "What waits for the good?" but he has altered it on transcription, because however his feelings may love to linger on a future state of Happiness, neither Justice, reason nor passion can reconcile to his belief that the crimes of this life, equally necessary and inevitable as its virtues, should be punished in another:
"Earth in itself
"Contains at once the evil and the cure
"And all sufficing Nature can chastize
"Those who transgress her law."

How eloquent are eyes!

1810

    How eloquent are eyes!
Not the rapt Poet's frenzied lay,
When the soul's wildest feelings stray,
    Can speak so well as they.
    How eloquent are eyes! 5
Not music's most impassioned note,
On which love's warmest fervours float,
    Like they bid rapture rise.

    Love! look thus again,
That your look may light a waste of years 10
Darting the beam that conquers cares
    Thro' the cold shower of tears!
    Love! look thus again,
That Time the victor as he flies
May pause to gaze upon thine eyes, 15
    A victor then in vain! —

Yet no! arrest not Time,
For Time, to others dear, we spurn,
When Time shall *be* no more we burn
    When Love meets full return. 20
    Ah no! arrest not Time.
Fast let him fly on eagle wing,
Nor pause till Heaven's unfading spring
    Breathes round its holy clime.

Yet quench that thrilling gaze 25
Which passionate Friendship arms with fire,

For what will eloquent eyes inspire
   But feverish, false desire?
Quench then that thrilling gaze
For age may freeze the tremulous joy;   30
But age can never *love* destroy.
   It lives to better days.

   Age cannot love destroy.
Can perfidy then blight its flower
Even when in most unwary hour   35
It blooms in fancy's bower?
   Age cannot love destroy.
Can slighted vows then rend the shrine
On which its chastened splendours shine
   Around a dream of joy?   40

Hopes that bud in youthful breasts

1810

Hopes that bud in youthful breasts
   Live not thro' the lapse of time;
Love's rose a host of thorns invest,
   And ungenial is the clime
     Where its blossoms blow.   5
Youth says—the purple flowers are mine
   That fade the while they glow.

Dear the boon to Fancy given,
   Retracted while 'tis granted.
Sweet the rose that breathes in Heaven   10
   Altho' on Earth 'tis planted,
     Where its blossoms blow,
Where by the frosts its leaves are riven
   That fade the while they glow.

The pure soul lives that heart within   15
   Which age cannot remove
If undefiled by tainting sin,—
   A sanctuary of love
     Where its blossoms blow,
Where, in this unsullied shrine,   20
   They fade not while they glow.

To the Moonbeam

September 23. 1809

Moonbeam! leave the shadowy dale
   To cool this burning brow—
Moonbeam, why art thou so pale
As thou glidest along the midnight vale
   Where dewy flowrets grow?   5
   Is it to mimic me?
   Ah, that can never be;
   For thy path is bright
   And the clouds are light
That at intervals shadow the star-studded night.   10

Now all is deathy still on Earth,
   Nature's tired frame reposes;
Yet ere the golden morning's birth
   Its radiant gates uncloses,
   Flies forth her balmy breath;   15
   But mine is the midnight of death,
   And Nature's morn
   To my bosom forlorn
Brings but a gloomier night, implants a deadlier thorn.

Wretch! suppress the glare of madness   20
   Struggling in thine haggard eye,
For the keenest throb of sadness,
   Pale despair's most sickening sigh,
   Is but to mimic me.

TO THE MOONBEAM

But that can never be
When the darkness of care
And the death of despair
Seem in my breast but joys to the pangs that rankle there. 25

Poems to Mary

ADVERTISEMENT

The few poems immediately following are selected from many written during three weeks of an entrancement caused by hearing Mary's story —— I hope that the delicate and discriminating genius of the friend who related it to me will allow the publication of the heart-breaking facts under the title of Leonora. — For myself at that time: nondum amabam, et amare amabam, quaerebam quid amarem, amans amare.*

Mary died three months before I heard her tale. —

---

*Confess. St. Augustin.

November 1810

To Mary I

Dear girl! thou art wildered by madness,
    Yet do not look so, sweet.
I could share in the sigh of thy sadness,
    Thy woe my soul could meet.

I loved a heart sincerely.   5
    Yes! dear it was to mine;
Yet, Mary, I love more dearly
    One tender look of thine.

Oh! do not say that Heaven
    Will frown on errors past;   10
Thy faults are all forgiven,
    Thy Virtues ever last.*

The cup with death o'erflowing
    I'll drink, fair girl, to thee.
For when the storm is blowing   15
    To shelter we may flee.

---

* This opinion is of all others the most deeply rooted in my conviction. The enquirer will laugh at it as a dream, the Christian will abhor it as a blasphemy — Mary, who repeatedly attempted suicide, yet was unwilling to die alone. — Nor is it probable that she would, had I instead of my friend been subjected to the trial of sitting a summer night by her side — whilst two glasses of poison stood on the table, and she folded me to her tremulous bosom in extasies of friendship and despair! — [What are the Romances of Leadenhall Str. to this of real life?]

Thou canst not bear to languish
   In this frail chain of clay,
And I am tired of anguish.
   Love! let us haste away!

Like thee, I fear to weather
   Death's darksome wave alone.
We'll take the voyage together.
   Come, Mary! let's begone.

Strange mists my woe efface, love,
   And thou art pale in Death. . . .
Give one, one last embrace, love,
   And we resign our breath.

To Mary II

Fair one! calm that bursting heart ....
   Dares then fate to frown on thee,
Lovely, spotless, as thou art,
   Tho' its worst poison lights on me?
     Then dry that tear;   5
     Thou needest not fear
These woes when thy limbs are cold on the bier.

Start not from winter's breathing, dearest,
   Tho' bleak is yonder hill ...
As perjured love the blast thou fearest   10
   Is not half so deadly chill;
     Like these winds that blow
     No remorse does it know
And colder it strikes than the driving snow.

The tomb is damp and dark and low,   15
   Yet with thee the tomb I do not dread.
There is not a place of frightful woe
   Where with thee I'd refuse to lay my head ...
     But our souls shall not sleep
     In the grave damp and deep   20
But in love and devotion their holy day keep.*

---

* The expression *devotion*, is not used in a religious sense; for which abuse of this lovely word, few have a greater horror than the Author.

To Mary III

Mary, Mary! art thou gone
   To sleep in thine earthy cell?
Presses thy breast the death-cold stone?
Pours none the tear, the sob, the groan,
Where murdered virtue sleeps alone   5
   Where its first glory fell?

Mary, Mary, past is past!
   I submit in silence to fate's decree,
Tho' the tear of distraction gushes fast
And at night when the lank reeds hiss in the blast   10
   My spirit mourns in sympathy.

Thou wert more fair in mind than are
   The fabled heavenly train,
But thine was the pang of corroding care,
Thine, cold contempt and lone despair   15
And thwarted love — more hard to bear . . .
And I — wretch! — weep that such they were,
   And I . . . . still drag my chain.

Thou wert but born to weep, to die,
To feel dissolved the dearest tie —   20
Its fragments by the pityless world
Adown the blast of fortune hurl'd
   To strive with envy's wreckful storm.
Thou wert but born to weep and die,
Nor could thy ceaseless misery,   25
Nor heavenly virtues aught avail,

Nor taintless innocence prevail
With the world's slaves thy love to spare,
Nor the magic unearthly atmosphere
   That wrapt thine eternal form.   30

Such, loveliest Mary, was thy fate,
   And such is Virtue's doom . . . .
Contempt, neglect and hatred wait
Where yawns a wide and dreary gate
   To drag its votaries to the tomb.   35
Sweet flower! that blooms amid the weeds
Where the dank serpent, interest, feeds!

To the Lover of Mary

Drink the exhaustless moonbeam where its glare
   Wanly lights murdered virtue's funeral
   And tremulous sheds on the corpse-shrouding pall
      A languid, languid flare . . . . .
Hide thee, poor Wretch, where yonder baleful yew
Sheds o'er the clay that now is tenantless —
Whose spirit once thrilled to thy warm caress —
      Its deadly, deadly dew.
The moon-ray will not quench thy misery,
But the yew's death-drops will bring peace to thee,
And yonder clay-cold grave thy bridal bed shall be.

And since the Spirit dear that breathes of Heaven
   Has burst the powerless bondage of its clay
   And soars an Angel to eternal day,
      Purged of its earthly leaven,
Thy yearnings now shall bend thee to the tomb,
Oblivion blot a life without a stain,
And death's cold hand round thy heart's ceaseless pain
      Enfold its veil of gloom.
The wounds shall close of Misery's scorpion goad
When Mary greets thee in her blest abode
And worships holy Love, in purity thy God.

O this were joy! and such as none would fear
   To purchase by a life of passing woe,
   For on this earth the sickly flowers that glow
      Breathe of perfection there.
Yet live — for others barter thine own bliss,

And living shew what towering Virtue dares
To accomplish even in this vale of tears:
  Turn Hell to Paradise,   30
And spurning selfish joy soar high above
The Heaven of Heavens, let ever eternal *love
Despised awhile, thy sense of holier *Virtue prove.

---
 * As if they were not synonimous!

Dares the Lama

1810

Dares the Lama, most fleet of the Sons of the Wind,
   The Lion to rouse from his lair?
When the tyger awakes, can the fast-fleeting hind
   Repose trust in his footsteps of air?
No—abandoned it sinks in helpless despair;   5
   The monster transfixes his prey;
   On the sand flows its life-blood away,
And the rocks and the woods to the death-yells reply,
Protracting the horrible harmony.

Yet the fowl of the desert when danger encroaches   10
   Dares dreadless to perish, defending her brood,
Tho' the fiercest of cloud-piercing tyrants approaches,
   Thirsting—aye, thirsting for blood—
And demands, like mankind, his brother for food,
   Yet more lenient, more gentle, than they;   15
   For hunger, not glory, the prey
Must perish—revenge does not howl o'er the dead,
Nor ambition with fame bind the murderer's head.

Tho' weak as the Lama that bounds on the Mountains
   And endued not with fast-fleeting footsteps of air,   20
Yet, yet will I draw from the purest of fountains,
   Tho' a fiercer than tygers is there,
Tho' more frightful than death it scatters despair,
   And its shadow, eclipsing the day,
   Spreads the darkness of deepest dismay   25

O'er the withered and withering nations around
And the war-mangled corpses that rot on the ground.

They came to the fountain to draw from its stream
    Waves too poisonously lovely for mortals to see;
They basked for awhile in the love-darting beam   30
    Then perished—and perished like me,
For in vain from the grasp of Religion I flee.
    The most tenderly loved of my soul
    Are slaves to its chilling control...
It pursues me. It blasts me. Oh! where shall I fly?   35
What remains but to curse it, to curse it and die?

I will kneel at thine altar

1809

I will kneel at thine altar, will crown thee with bays.
    Whether God, Love or Virtue thou art,
Thou shalt live ... aye! more long than these perishing lays
    Thou shalt live in this high-beating heart.
Dear love! from its life-strings thou never shall part,   5
    Tho' Prejudice clanking her chain,
    Tho' Interest groaning in gain,
May tell me thou closest to Heaven the door,
May tell me that thine is the way to be poor.

The victim of merciless tyranny's power   10
    May smile at his chains if with thee;
The most sense-enslaved loiterer in Passion's sweet bower
    Is a wretch if unhallowed by thee.
Thine, thine is the bond that alone binds the free.
    Can the free worship bondage? nay, more,   15
    What they feel not, believe not, adore —
What if felt, if believed, if existing must give
To thee to create, to eternize, to live —

For Religion more keen than the blasts of the North
    Darts its frost thro' the self-palsied soul;   20
Its slaves on the work of destruction go forth;
    The divinest emotions that roll
Submit — to the rod of its impious control.
    At the venemous blast of its breath,
    Love, concord, lies gasping in death,   25

I WILL KNEEL AT THINE ALTAR

Philanthropy utters a war-drowned cry
And selfishness, conquering, cries Victory!

Can we, then, thus tame, thus impassive behold
   That alone whence our life springs destroyed?
Shall Prejudice, Priestcraft, Opinion and Gold —   30
   Every passion with interest alloyed —
Where Love ought to reign, fill the desolate void?
   But the Avenger arises, the throne
   Of selfishness totters, its groan
Shakes the nations. — It falls, love seizes the sway;   35
The sceptre it bears unresisted away.

Fragment of a Poem
the original idea of which was suggested by the cowardly and infamous bombardment of Copenhagen

The ice mountains echo, the Baltic, the Ocean
    Where cold sits enthroned on its solium of snow:
Even Spitzbergen perceives the terrific commotion.
    The roar floats on the whirlwinds of sleet as they blow,
    Blood clots with the streams as half frozen they flow,   5
Lurid flame o'er the cities the meteors of war
And mix their deep gleam with the bright polar glare.

Yes! the arms of Britannia victorious are bearing
    Fame, triumph and terror wherever they spread.
Her Lion his crest o'er the nations is rearing,   10
    Ruin follows ... it tramples the dying and dead ...
    But her countrymen fall ... the bloodreeking bed
Of the battle-slain sends a complaint-breathing sigh;
It is mixed with the shoutings of victory.

I see the lone female. The sun is descending   15
    Dank carnage-smoke sheds an ensanguining glare.
Night its shades in the orient earlier is blending
    Yet the light faintly marks a wild maniac's stare.
    She lists to the death shrieks that came on the air,
The pride of her heart to her bosom she prest,   20
Then sunk on his form in the sleep of the blest.

On an Icicle that clung to the grass of a grave

1809

O take the pure gem to where Southernly Breezes
    Waft repose to some bosom as faithful as fair,
In which the warm current of love never freezes
    As it circulates freely and shamelessly there,
    Which, untainted by crime, unpolluted by care,   5
Might dissolve this dim ice-drop, might bid it arise,
Too pure for these regions, to gleam in the skies.

For I found the pure gem when the daybeam returning
    Ineffectual gleams on the snow-spangled plain,
When to others the longed-for arrival of morning   10
    Brings relief to long night-dreams of soul-racking pain.
    But regret is an insult. To grieve is in vain.
And why should we grieve that a spirit so fair
Sought Heaven, to meet with its Kindred there?

Yet 'twas some Angel of kindness descending   15
    To share in the load of Mortality's woe,
Who, over thy lowly-built sepulchre bending,
    Bade sympathy's tenderest tear-drops to flow
    And consigned the rich gift to the Sister of Snow;
And if Angels can weep, sure I may repine   20
And shed tear-drops, tho' frozen to ice, on thy shrine.

Cold are the blasts

1808

Cold are the Blasts when December is howling,
   Chill are the damps on a dying friend's brow,
Stern is the Ocean when tempests are rolling,
   Sad is the grave where a brother lies low,
But chillier is scorn from the false one that loved thee,   5
More stern is the sneer from the friend that has proved thee,
More sad are the tears when these sorrows have moved thee,
   That, envenomed by wildest delirium, flow.

And alas! thou, Louisa, hast felt all this horror! . .
   Full long the fallen Victim contended with fate   10
Till — a destitute outcast abandoned to sorrow —
   She sought her babe's food at her ruiner's gate.
Another had charmed the remorseless betrayer;
He turned laughing away from her anguish-fraught prayer,
She spoke not, but wringing the rain from her hair,   15
   Took the rough mountain path, tho' the hour was late.

On the cloud-shrouded summit of dark Penmanmawr
   The form of the wasted Louisa reclined,
She shrieked to the ravens loud croaking afar,
   She sighed to the gusts of the wild sweeping wind. — 20
"Ye storms o'er the peak of the lone mountain soaring,
Ye clouds with the thunder-winged tempest-shafts lowering,
Thou wrath of black Heaven, I blame not thy pouring,
   But thee, cruel Henry, I call thee unkind."

Then she wreathed a wild crown from the flowers of the
    mountain, 25
  And deliriously laughing the heath twigs entwined.
She bedewed it with tear drops, then leaned o'er the
    fountain
  And cast it a prey to the wild sweeping wind.
"Ah! go," she exclaimed, "where the tempest is yelling.
'Tis unkind to be cast on the sea that is swelling — 30
But I left, a pityless outcast, my dwelling.
  My garments are torn — so they say is my mind."

Not long lived Louisa. — And over her grave
  Waved the desolate limbs of a storm-blasted yew.
Around it no demons or ghosts dare to rave, 35
  But spirits of love steep her slumbers in dew;
Then stay thy swift steps mid the dark mountain heather,
Tho' bleak be the scene and severe be the weather,
For perfidy, traveller, cannot bereave her
  Of the tears to the tombs of the innocent due. 40

Henry and Louisa*

*a Poem
in two parts*

1809

She died for love—and he for glory

The Parting
*Part the First
Scene — England*

I

Where are the Heroes? sunk in death they lie.
    What toiled they for? titles and wealth and fame.
But the wide Heaven is now their canopy,
    And legal murderers their loftiest name.
Enshrined on brass their glory and their shame   5
    What tho' torn Peace and martyred Freedom see?
    What tho' to most remote posterity
Their names, their selfishness for ay enscrolled,
A shuddering world's blood-boltered eyes behold,
    Mocking mankind's unbettered misery?   10

---

* The stanza of this Poem is radically that of Spencer altho' I suffered myself at the time of writing it to be led into occasional deviations. These defects I do not alter now, being unwilling to offer any outrage to the living portraiture of my own mind; bad as it may be pronounced.

Can this perfection give, can valour prove
One wish for others' bliss, one throb of love . . .

II

Yet darest thou boast thyself superior. — Thou!
   Vile worm! whom lovely woman deigns to bless,
And, meanly selfish, bask in glory's glow, 15
   Rending the soul-spun ties of tenderness
Where all desires rise for thine happiness?
   Canst thou boast thus and hope to be forgiven?
Oh! when thou started'st from her last caress,
   From purest love by vulgar Glory driven, 20
Couldst thou have e'er deserved, if thou resigned'st, Heaven?

. . . .

And shadowed by affection's purple wing
Bid thee forget how Time's fast footstep sped:
Would die in peace when thou wert mingled with the dead.

VI

Had Glory's fire consumed each tender tie 25
   That links to love the Heaven-aspiring soul,
Could not that voice, quivering in agony,
   That struggling pale resolve that dared control
Passion's wild flood when wildest it did roll,
Could not impassioned tenderness that burst 30
   Cold prudery's bondage, owning all it felt —
Could not these, warrior, quench thy battle thirst,
Nought this availed thine iron-bound breast to melt,
To make thy footsteps pause where love and freedom dwelt?

VII

Yes! every soul-nerve vibrated . . . a space 35
   Enchained in speechless awe the warrior stood.

Superior reason, Virtue, manner, grace,
    Claimed for a space their rights ... in varying mood
Before her lovely eyes in thought he stood
Whilst Glory's train flashed on his mental eye   40
    Which wandered wildly where the fight's red flood,
The crash of death, the storm of Victory,
Roll round the hopes of love that only breathe to die.

VIII

Then she exclaimed as, love-nerved, sense returned,
    "Go .. mingle in thy country's battle tide ...   45
Forget that love's pale torch hath ever burned.
    Until thou meetest me clothed in Victor-pride
May guardian spirits keep thee ... far and wide
    O'er the red regions of the day-scorched zone
For glory seek .. but here thou wilt abide,   50
    Here — in this breast. Thou wilt abide alone.
I will thine empire be. My heart shall be thy throne."

IX

When Princes at fair Reason's bidding bend,
    Resigning power for Virtue's fadeless meed,
Oi Spirits of Heaven to man submission lend,   55
    The debt of gratitude is great indeed;
In vain the heart its thankfulness to prove
    Aye might attempt to do the debt away.
Yet what is this compared to Woman's love,
    Dear Woman's love, the dawn of Virtue's day,   60
The bliss-inspiring beam, the soul-illuming ray?

X

Then Henry spoke as he checked the rising tear,
    "That I have loved thee and must love for ever
Heaven is a witness — Heaven to whom are dear
    The hearts that earthly chances cannot sever,   65

Where bloom the flowers that cease to blossom never.
   Religion sanctifies the cause, I go
To execute its vengeance. Heaven will give
   To me (so whispers hope) to quell the foe.
Heaven gives the good to conquer and to live,   70
And thou shalt — next to God — his votive heart receive.

XI

Say, is not he the Tyrant of the World
   And are not we the injured and the brave?
Unmoved shall we behold his flag unfurled,
   Flouting with impious Wing Religion's grave,   75
Triumphant gleaming o'er the passive wave,
Nor raise an arm, nor one short pleasure yield
   The boon of immortality to save?
Hope is our tempered lance, faith is our shield;
Conquest or death for these wait on the gory field.   80

XII

Even at that hour when hostile myriads clash
   And terrible death shakes his resistless dart,
Mingling wild wailings with the battle crash,
   Then thou and Heaven shall share this votive heart.
When from pale dissolution's grasp I start   85
   (If Heaven so wills) even then will I be thine.
Nor can the whelming tomb have power to part
   From all it loves a heart that loves like mine,
From thee .. round whom its hopes, its joys, its fears
     entwine."

XIII

A sicklier tint crept o'er Louisa's cheek   90
   "But thou art dearer far to me than all

That fancy's visions feign, or tongue can speak.
 Yes! may I die, and be that death eternal,
When other thoughts but thee my soul enthrall.
 The joys of Heaven I prize thee far above,   95
Thee, dearest, will my Soul its Saviour call.
My faith is thine .. my faith-gained heaven, thy love;
My Hell, when cruel fates thee from these arms remove.

XIV

Farewell" . . . she spoke. The warrior's war-steeled breast,
 Quivering in feeling's agonized excess,   100
Scarce drew its breath, to sickliness oppressed
 By mingled self-reproach and tenderness;
He dared not speak, but rushed from her caress.
 The sunny glades; the little birds of spring
Twittering from every garlanded recess,   105
 Returning verdure's joy that seem'd to sing
Whilst woe with stern hand smote his every mental string;

XV

The fragrant dew-mists from the Ivied Thorn
 Whose form o'ershadowed love's most blissful bower,
Where oft would fly the tranquil time of morn,   110
 Or swifter urge its flight dear evening's power,
When purple twilight in the East would lower
 And the amorous starbeam kiss the loveliest form
That ever bruised a pleasure-fainting flower
 Whose emanative eyebeam, thrilling, warm,   115
Around her sacred presence shed a rapturing charm;

XVI

Each object so beloved, each varied tone
 Of heavenly feeling that can never die,

Each little throb his heart had ever known,
    Impetuous rushed on fainting memory.   120
Yet not alone for parted extacy,
    To which he now must bid a long adieu,
Started the bitter tear or burst the sigh;
    In all the pangs that, spite concealment, grew
    O'er his Louisa's peace, a deeper soul-pang drew.   125

XVII

The balmy breath of soul-reviving dawn
    That kissed the bosom of the waveless lake,
Scented with spring-flowers, o'er the level lawn
    Struck on his sense, to woe scarce yet awake.
He felt its still reproach, — the upland brake   130
    Rustled beneath his war-steed's eager prance,
Hastening to Egypt's shore his way to take,
    But swifter hastening to dispel the trance
Of grief, he hurried on, smothering the last sad glance.

XVIII

Sweet flower! in dereliction's solitude   135
    That scatterest perfume to the unheeding gale
And in the grove's unconscious quietude
    Murmurest (thyself scarce conscious) thy sad tale —
Sure it is subject for the Poet's wail,
    Tho' faint, that one so worthy to be prized,   140
The fairest flower of the loveliest vale,
    To withering Glory should be sacrificed,
That hides his hateful form in Virtue's garb disguised.

XIX

Religion! hated cause of all the woe
    That makes the world this wilderness. Thou spring   145

Whence terror, pride, revenge and perfidy flow,
   The curses, which thy pampered minions bring,
On thee shall Virtue's votary fear to fling?
   And thou, dear Love! thy tender ties to sever,
To drown in shouts thy bliss-fraught murmuring,   150
   Ceaseless shall selfish Prejudice endeavour?
Shall she succeed?—oh no, whilst I live, never, never!

XX

For by the wrongs that flaming deep
   Within this bosom's agony,
That dry the source whence others weep,—   155
   I swear that thou shalt die!

Henry and Louisa

The Meeting

Part Second

I

'Tis night .. No planet's brilliance dares to light
    The dim and battle-blushing scenery,
Friends, mixed with foes, urge unremitting fight
    Beneath War's suffocating canopy,   160
And, as sulphureous meteors fire the sky,
    Fast flash the deathful thunderbolts of War,
Whilst groans unite in frightful harmony
    And wakened vultures shrieking from afar
Scent their half-murdered prey amid the battle's jar.   165

II

Now had the Genius of the south, sublime
    On mighty Atlas' tempest-cinctured throne,
Looked over Afric's desolated clime,
Deep wept at slavery's everlasting moan
And his most dear-beloved nation's groan.   170
The Boreal whirlwind's shadowy wings that sweep
    The veined bosom of the northern world
That hears contending thunders on the deep,
    Sees hostile flags on Egypt's strand unfurled,
Brings Egypt's faintest groan to waste and ruin hurled.   175

III

Is this then all that sweeps the midnight sand?
    Tells the wild blast no tales of deeper woe?

Does war alone pollute the unhappy land?
   No — the low, fluttering and the hectic glow
Of hope, whose sickly flowret scarce can blow,   180
   Chilled by the ice-blast of intense despair,
Anguish that dries the big tear ere it flow,
And Maniac love, that sits by the beacon's glare
With eyes on nothing fixed, dim like a mist-clothed star.

IV

No fear save one could daunt her — Ocean's wave,   185
   Bearing Britannia's hired asassins on
To victory's shame or an unhonored grave,
   Beheld Louisa, mid an host, alone.
The womanly dress that veiled her fair form is gone,
   Gone is the timid wandering of her eye,   190
Pale firmness nerved her anguished heart to stone;
   The sense of shame, the flush of modesty,
By stern resolve were quenched or only glowed to die.

V

"Where is my love! — my Henry — is he dead?"
   Half-drowned in smothered anguish wildly burst   195
From her parched lips — "is my ador'd one dead?
   Knows none my Henry? War! thou source accurst,
In whose red blood I see these sands immerst,
   Hast thou quite whelmed compassion's tearful spring
Where thy fierce tide rolls to slake Glory's thirst?   200
   Perhaps thou, Warrior, some kind word dost bring
From my poor Henry's lips when Death its shade did fling."

VI

A tear of pity dimmed the Warrior's gaze.
   "I know him not, sweet maiden, yet the fight,

That casts on Britain's fame a brighter blaze, 205
    Should spare all yours, if ought I guess aright.
But ah! by yonder flash of sulphurous light,
    The dear loved work of battle has begun.
Fame calls her votaries." He fled. The night
    Had far advanced before the fray was done; 210
Scarce sunk the roar of war before the rising Sun.

VII

But sight of wilder grief where slept the dead
    Was witnessed by the morn's returning glow,
When frantic o'er the waste Louisa sped
    To drink her dying lover's latest vow: 215
Sighed mid her locks the sea-gales as they blew,
    Bearing along faint shrieks of dying men
As if they sympathized with her deep woe.
    Silent she paused a space, and then again
New-nerved by fear and hope sprang wild across the plain.

VIII

See where she stops again! . . . a ruin's shade
    Darkens his fading lineaments, his cheek
On which remorseful pain is deep pourtrayed
    Glares, death-convulsed and ghastly. Utterings break —
Shuddering, unformed — ; his tongue essays to speak. 225
    Thus low he lies! poor Henry! where is now
Thy dear, deserted love? Is there no friend
    To bathe with tears that anguish-burning brow,
None comfort in this fearful hour to lend,
When to remorseful grief thy parting spirits bend? 230

IX

Yes! pain had steeped each dying limb in flame,
    When, mad with mingled hope and pale dismay,

Fleet as the wild deer his Louisa came,
   Nerved by distraction.—A pale tremulous ray
Flashed on her eyes from the expiring day.   235
   Life for a space rushed to his fainting breast.
The breathing form of love-entwined clay,
   In motionless rapture, pale Louisa prest
And, stung by maddening hope, in tears her bliss exprest.

X

Yet was the transport wavering . . . the dew   240
   Of bodily pain that bathed his pallid brow,
The pangs that thro' his anguished members flew,
   Tho' half subdued by Love's returning glow,
Doubt, mixed with lingering hope, must needs bestow.
   Then she exclaimed—"Love, I have sought thee far;
Whence our own Albion's milder sea gales blow,
   To this stern scene of fame-aspiring war;
Thro' waves of danger past thou wert my polar star.

XI

Live then, dear source of life! and let the ray
   Which lights thy kindling eyebeam softly speak   250
That thou hast loved when I was far away—
   Yet thou art pale. Death's hectic lights thy cheek.
Oh! if one moment fate the chain should break
   Which binds thy soul unchangeably to mine:
Another moment's pain fate dare not wreak.   255
   Another moment . . . . . . I am ever thine!
Love, turn those eyes on me! ah, death has dimmed their
      shine."

XII

Ceased her voice. The accents mild
   In frightful stillness died away.

More sweet than Memnon's plainings wild   260
   That float upon the morning ray
      Died every sound .. save when
      At distance o'er the plain
Britannia's legions swiftly sweeping,
Glory's ensanguined harvest reaping,   265
   Mowed down the field of men,
And the silent ruins, crumbling nigh,
With echoes low prolonged the cry
Of mingled defeat and victory.

XIII

More low, more faint, yet far more dread,   270
   Arose the expiring warrior's groan,
Stretched on the sand, his bloody bed,
In agonized death was Henry laid
   But he did not fall alone . . .
      Why then that anguished sigh   275
Which seems to tear the vital tie,
Fiercer than death, more fell
   Than tyranny, contempt or hate?
   Why does that breast with horror swell
Which ought to triumph over fate?   280
   Why? ask the pallid, griefworn mien
   Of poor Louisa, let it speak:
But her firm heart would sooner break
   Than doubt the soul where love had been.

XIV

Now, now he dies! his parting breath,   285
   The sulphurous gust of battle bears.
The shriek, the groan, the gasp of death,
   Unmoved, Louisa hears,
And a smile of triumph lights her eye

With more than mortal radiancy.— 290
Sacred to Love a deed is done!—
Gleams thro' battle clouds the Sun,
Gleams it on all that's good and fair
Stretched on the Earth to moulder there.
    Shall Virtue perish? No; 295
    Superior to Religion's tie,
    Emancipate from misery,
    Despising self, their souls can know
    All the delight love can bestow
    When Glory's phantom fades away 300
    Before Affection's purer ray,
    When tyrants cease to wield the rod
    And slaves to tremble at their nod.

XV

Then near the stunted palms that shroud
    The spot from which their spirits fled 305
Shall pause the human hounds of blood
    And own a secret dread.
There shall the victor's steel-clad brow,
Tho' flushed by conquest's crimson glow,
    Be changed with inward fear; 310
There, stern and steady by long command,
The pomp-fed despot's sceptered hand
    Shall shake as if death were near,
Whilst the lone captive in his train
Feels comfort as he shakes his chain. 315

A Translation of
The Marsellois Hymn

1

Haste to battle, Patriot Band!
   A day of Glory dawns on thee!
Against thy rights is raised an hand: —
   The bloodred hand of tyranny!
See! the ferocious slaves of power
Across the wasted country scour,
And in thy very arms destroy
The pledges of thy nuptial joy —
   Thine unresisting family!

    Chorus

Then, citizens, form in battle array,
For this is the dawn of a glorious day.
March, march, fearless of danger and toil,
And the rank gore of tyrants shall water your soil!

2

What wills the coward, traitorous train
   Of Kings, whose trade is perfidy?
For whom is forged this hateful chain,
   For whom prepared this slavery?
For you. On you their vengeance rests . . .
What transports ought to thrill your breasts!
Frenchmen! this unhallowed train,
To ancient woe would bind again
   Those souls whom valour has made free!
    Chorus &c.

A TRANSLATION OF THE MARSELLOIS HYMN

3

What! shall foreign bands compel
   Us to the laws of tyranny?
Shall hired soldiers hope to quell
   The arm upraised for liberty?
Great God! by these united arms
Shall despots, their own alarms,
Pass neath the yoke made for our head!
Yea! pomp-fed Kings shall quake with dread —
   These masters of Earth's destiny!
      Chorus &c.

4

Tremble, Kings! despised of Man!
   Ye traitors to your country —
Tremble! your parricidal plan
   At length shall meet its destiny.
We all are soldiers fit for fight,
But if we sink in glory's night
Our Mother Earth will give ye new
The brilliant pathway to pursue
   That leads to Death or Victory!
      Chorus &c.

5

Frenchmen! on the guilty brave
   Pour your vengeful energy. —
Yet in your triumph, pitying save
   The unwilling slaves of tyranny;
But let the gore-stained despots bleed,
Be death fell Boullie's bloodhound-meed;
Chase those unnatural fiends away

Who on their mothers vitals prey
  With more than tyger cruelty!
    Chorus &c.

6

Sacred Patriotism! uphold 50
  The avenging bands who fight with thee;
And thou, more dear than meaner gold,
  Smile on our efforts, Liberty!
Where conquest's crimson streamers wave,
Haste thou to the happy brave, 55
Where at our feet thy dying foes
See as their failing eyes unclose
  Our glory and thy Victory!

Written in very early youth

I'll lay me down by the church-yard tree
And resign me to my destiny;
I'll bathe my brow with the poison dew
That falls from yonder deadly yew,
And, if it steal my soul away,   5
To bid it wake in realms of day,
Spring's sweetest flowers shall never be
So dear to gratitude and me!

Earthborn glory cannot breathe
Within the damp recess of death;   10
Avarice, Envy, Lust, Revenge,
Suffer there a fearful change;
All that grandeur ever gave
Moulders in the silent grave.
Oh! that I slept near yonder yew,   15
That this tired frame might moulder too!

Yet Pleasure's folly is not mine,
No votarist, I, at Glory's shrine;
The sacred gift for which I sigh
Is not to live, to feel, alone;   20
I only ask to calmly die,
That the tomb might melt this heart of stone
  To love beyond the grave!

Zeinab and Kathema

Upon the lonely beach Kathema lay;
   Against his folded arm his heart beat fast.
Thro' gathering tears, the Sun's departing ray
   In coldness o'er his shuddering spirit past,
And all unfelt the breeze of evening came 5
That fanned with quivering wing his wan cheek's feeble flame.

"Oh!" cried the mourner, "could this widowed soul
   "But fly where yonder Sun now speeds to dawn."
He paused — a thousand thoughts began to roll;
   Like waves they swept in restless tumult on, 10
Like those fast waves that quick-succeeding beat
Without one lasting shape the beach beneath his feet.

And now the beamless, broad and yellow sphere
   Half-sinking lingered on the crimson sea;
A shape of darksome distance does appear 15
   Within its semicircled radiancy.
All sense was gone to his betrothed one —
His eye fell on the form that dimmed the setting sun, —

He thought on his betrothed... for his youth
   With her that was its charm to ripeness grew. 20
All that was dear in love, or fair in truth,
   With her was shared as childhood's moments flew,
And mingled with sweet memories of her
Was life's unveiling morn with all its bliss and care —

A wild and lovely Superstition's spell.
   Love for the friend that life and freedom gave,
Youth's growing hopes that watch themselves so well,
   Passion, so prompt to blight, so strong to save,
And childhood's host of memories combine
Her life and love around his being to entwine.

And to their wishes with its joy-mixed pain,
   Just as the veil of hope began to fall,
The Christian murderers over-ran the plain,
   Ravaging, burning and polluting all.
Zeinab was reft to grace the robbers' land;
Each drop of kindred blood stained the invaders' brand.

Yes! they had come their holy book to bring,
   Which God's own son's apostles had compiled
That charity and peace and love might spring
   Within a world by God's blind ire defiled,
But rapine, war and treachery rushed before
Their hosts, and murder dyed Kathema's bower in gore.

Therefore his soul was widowed, and alone
   He stood on the world's wide and drear expanse.
No human ear could shudder at his groan,
   No heart could thrill with his unspeaking glance;
One only hope yet lingering dared to burn,
Urging to high emprize and deeds that danger spurn.

The glow has failed on Ocean's western line,
   Faded from every moveless cloud above.
The moon is up—she that was wont to shine
   And bless thy childish nights of guileless love,
Unhappy one, ere Christian rapine tore
All ties, and stain'd thy hopes in a dear mother's gore.

The form that in the setting Sun was seen 55
   Now in the moonlight slowly nears the shore,
The white sails gleaming o'er the billows green
   That sparkle into foam its prow before,
A wanderer of the deep it seems to be,
On high adventures bent, and feats of chivalry. 60

Then hope and wonder filled the mourner's mind.
   He gazed till vision even began to fail,
When to the pulses of the evening wind
   A little boat approaching gave its sail,
Rode o'er the slow-raised surges near the strand, 65
Ran up the beach and gave some stranger men to land.

"If thou wilt bear me to far England's shore
   Thine is this heap — the Christian's God!"
The chief with gloating rapture viewed the ore,
   And his pleased avarice gave the willing nod. 70
They reach the ship, the fresh'ning breezes rise
And smooth and fast they speed beneath the moonlight
   skies.

What heart e'er felt more ardent longings now?
   What eye than his e'er beamed with riper hope
As curbed impatience on his open brow 75
   There painted fancy's unsuspected scope,
As all that's fair the foreign land appeared
By ever-present love, wonder and hope endeared?

Meanwhile thro' calm and storm, thro' night and day,
   Unvarying in her aim the vessel went, 80
As if some inward spirit ruled her way
   And her tense sails were conscious of intent,

Till Albion's cliffs gleamed o'er her plunging bow
And Albion's river-floods bright sparkled round her prow.

Then on the land in joy Kathema leaped 85
    And kissed the soil in which his hopes were sown —
These even now in thought his heart has reaped.
    Elate of body and soul he journeyed on,
And the strange things of a strange land past by
Like mites and shadows prest upon his charmed eye. 90

Yet Albion's changeful skies and chilling wind
    The change from Cashmire's vale might well denote.
There, Heaven and Earth are ever bright and kind;
    Here, blights and storms and damp forever float,
Whilst hearts are more ungenial than the zone — 95
Gross, spiritless, alive to no pangs but their own.

There, flowers and fruits are ever fair and ripe;
    Autumn, there, mingles with the bloom of spring,
And forms unpinched by frost or hunger's gripe
    A natural veil o'er natural spirits fling; 100
Here, woe on all but wealth has set its foot.
Famine, disease and crime even wealth's proud gates pollute.

Unquiet death and premature decay,
    Youth tottering on the crutches of old age,
And, ere the noon of manhood's riper day, 105
    Pangs that no art of medicine can assuage,
Madness and passion ever mingling flames,
And souls that well become such miserable frames —

These are the bribes which Art to man has given
    To yield his taintless nature to her sway. 110

So might dark night with meteor tempt fair Heaven
   To blot the sunbeam and forswear the day
Till gleams of baleful light alone might shew
The pestilential mists, the darkness and the woe.

Kathema little felt the sleet and wind,   115
   He little heeded the wide-altered scene;
The flame that lived within his eager mind
   There kindled all the thoughts that once had been.
He stood alone in England's varied woe,
Safe mid the flood of crime that round his steps did flow. 120

It was an evening when the bitterest breath
   Of dark December swept the mists along
That the lone wanderer came to a wild heath.
   Courage and hope had staid his nature long;
Now cold, and unappeased hunger spent   125
His strength, sensation failed in total languishment.

When he awaked to life cold horror crept
   Even to his heart, for a damp deathy smell
Had slowly come around him while he slept.
   He started ... lo! the fitful moonbeams fell   130
Upon a dead and naked female form
That from a gibbet high swung to the sullen storm;

And wildly in the wind its dark hair swung,
   Low mingling with the clangor of the chain,
Whilst ravenous birds of prey that on it clung   135
   In the dull ear of night poured their sad strain,
And ghastlily her shapeless visage shone
In the unsteady light, half mouldered thro' the bone.

Then madness seized Kathema, and his mind
   A prophecy of horror filled. He scaled   140

The gibbet which swung slowly in the wind
   High o'er the heath. — Scarcely his strength avail'd
To grasp the chain, when by the moonlight's gleam
His palsied gaze was fixed on Zeinab's altered frame.

Yes! in those orbs once bright with life and love   145
   Now full-fed worms bask in unnatural light;
That neck on which his eyes were wont to rove
   In rapture, changed by putrefaction's blight,
Now rusts the ponderous links that creak beneath
Its weight and turns to life the frightful sport of death. 150

Then in the moonlight played Kathema's smile
   Calmly. — In peace his spirit seemed to be.
He paused, even like a man at ease awhile,
   Then spoke — "My love! I will be like to thee,
A mouldering carcase or a spirit blest,   155
With thee corruption's prey, or Heaven's happy guest."

He twined the chain around his neck, then leaped
   Forward, in haste to meet the life to come.
An iron-souled son of Europe might have wept
   To witness such a noble being's doom   160
As on the death-scene Heaven indignant frowned
And Night in horror drew her veil the dead around.

For they had torn his Zeinab from her home,
   Her innocent habits were all rudely shriven;
And, dragged to live in love's untimely tomb,   165
   To prostitution, crime and woe was driven.
The human race seemed leagued against her weal,
And indignation cased her naked heart in steel.

Therefore against them she waged ruthless war
   With their own arms of bold and bloody crime, — 170

Even like a mild and sweetly-beaming star
   Whose rays were wont to grace the matin-prime
Changed to a comet, horrible and bright,
Which wild careers awhile then sinks in dark-red night.

Thus, like its God, unjust and pityless,   175
   Crimes first are made and then avenged by man,
For where's the tender heart, whose hope can bless
   Or man's, or God's, unprofitable plan—
A universe of horror and decay,
Gibbets, disease, and wars, and hearts as hard as they.   180

The Retrospect.

Cwm Elan
1812

To trace Duration's lone career,
To check the chariot of the year,
Whose burning wheels forever sweep
The boundaries of oblivion's deep. . . .
To snatch from Time, the monster's, jaw 5
The children which she just had borne
And, ere entombed within her maw,
To drag them to the light of morn
And mark each feature with an eye
Of cold and fearless scrutiny. . . . 10
It asks a soul not formed to feel,
An eye of glass, a hand of steel,
Thoughts that have passed, and thoughts that are,
With truth and feeling to compare;
A scene which wildered fancy viewed 15
In the soul's coldest solitude,
With that same scene when peaceful love
Flings rapture's colour o'er the grove,
When mountain, meadow, wood and stream
With unalloying glory gleam 20
And to the spirit's ear and eye
Are unison and harmony.

The moonlight was my dearer day: —
Then would I wander far away
And lingering on the wild brook's shore 25

To hear its unremitting roar,
Would lose in the ideal flow
All sense of overwhelming woe;
Or at the noiseless noon of night
Would climb some heathy mountain's height 30
And listen to the mystic sound
That stole in fitful gasps around.
I joyed to see the streaks of day
Above the purple peaks decay
And watch the latest line of light 35
Just mingling with the shades of night;
For day with me, was time of woe
When even tears refused to flow;
Then would I stretch my languid frame
Beneath the wild-woods' gloomiest shade 40
And try to quench the ceaseless flame
That on my withered vitals preyed;
Would close mine eyes and dream I were
On some remote and friendless plain,
And long to leave existence there 45
If with it I might leave the pain
That with a finger cold and lean
Wrote madness on my withering mien.

It was not unrequited love
That bade my wildered spirit rove; 50
'Twas not the pride, disdaining life,
That with this mortal world at strife
Would yield to the soul's inward sense,
Then groan in human impotence,
And weep, because it is not given 55
To taste on Earth the peace of Heaven.
'Twas not, that in the narrow sphere
Where Nature fixed my wayward fate

THE RETROSPECT

There was no friend or kindred dear
Formed to become that spirit's mate, 60
Which, searching on tired pinion, found
Barren and cold repulse around. . . .
Ah no! yet each one sorrow gave
New graces to the narrow grave:

For broken vows had early quelled 65
The stainless spirit's vestal flame.
Yes! whilst the faithful bosom swelled
Then the envenomed arrow came
And apathy's unaltering eye
Beamed coldness on the misery; 70
And early I had learned to scorn
The chains of clay that bound a soul
Panting to seize the wings of morn,
And where its vital fires were born
To soar, and spurn the cold control 75
Which the vile slaves of earthly night
Would twine around its struggling flight.
O, many were the friends whom fame
Had linked with the unmeaning name
Whose magic marked among mankind 80
The casket of my unknown mind,
Which, hidden from the vulgar glare,
Imbibed no fleeting radiance there.
My darksome spirit sought. It found
A friendless solitude around. — 85
For who, that might undaunted stand
The saviour of a sinking land,
Would crawl, its ruthless tyrant's slave
And fatten upon freedom's grave,
Tho' doomed with her to perish where 90
The captive clasps abhorred despair.

THE RETROSPECT

They could not share the bosom's feeling,
Which, passion's every throb revealing,
Dared force on the world's notice cold
Thoughts of unprofitable mould, 95
Who bask in Custom's fickle ray,—
Fit sunshine of such wintry day!
They could not in a twilight walk
Weave an impassioned web of talk
Till mysteries the spirit press 100
In wild yet tender awfulness,
Then feel within our narrow sphere
How little yet how great we are!
But they might shine in courtly glare,
Attract the rabble's cheapest stare, 105
And might command where'er they move
A thing that bears the name of love;
They might be learned, witty, gay,
Foremost in fashion's gilt array,
On Fame's emblazoned pages shine, 110
Be princes' friends, but never mine!

Ye jagged peaks that frown sublime,
Mocking the blunted scythe of Time,
Whence I would watch its lustre pale
Steal from the moon o'er yonder vale! 115

Thou rock, whose bosom black and vast
Bared to the stream's unceasing flow,
Ever its giant shade doth cast
On the tumultuous surge below!

The wounded echo's melody, 120
Woods, to whose depth retires to die

THE RETROSPECT

And whither this lone spirit bent
The footstep of a wild intent —

Meadows! Whose green and spangled breast
These fevered limbs have often pressed   125
Until the watchful fiend, despair,
Slept in the soothing coolness there!
Have not your varied beauties seen
The sunken eye, the withering mien,
Sad traces of the unuttered pain   130
That froze my heart and burned my brain?

How changed since nature's summer form
Had last the power my grief to charm,
Since last ye soothed my spirit's sadness —
Strange chaos of a mingled madness!   135
Changed! — not the loathsome worm that fed
In the dark mansions of the dead,
Now soaring thro' the fields of air
And gathering purest nectar there,
A butterfly whose million hues   140
The dazzled eye of wonder views,
Long lingering on a work so strange,
Has undergone so bright a change!

How do I feel my happiness?
I cannot tell, but they may guess   145
Whose every gloomy feeling gone,
Friendship and passion feel alone;
Who see mortality's dull clouds
Before affection's murmur fly,
Whilst the mild glances of her eye   150
Pierce the thin veil of flesh that shrouds
The spirit's radiant sanctuary.

THE RETROSPECT

O thou! whose virtues latest known,
First in this heart yet claim'st a throne;
Whose downy sceptre still shall share   155
The gentle sway with virtue there;
Thou fair in form and pure in mind,
Whose ardent friendship rivets fast
The flowery band our fates that bind,
Which, incorruptible, shall last   160
When duty's hard and cold control
Had thawed around the burning soul;
The gloomiest retrospects that bind
With crowns of thorn the bleeding mind,
The prospects of most doubtful hue   165
That rise on Fancy's shuddering view,
Are gilt by the reviving ray
Which thou hast flung upon my day.

The wandering Jew's soliloquy

Is it the Eternal Triune, is it He
Who dares arrest the wheels of destiny
And plunge me in this lowest Hell of Hells?
Will not the lightning's blast destroy my frame?
Will not steel drink the blood-life where it swells? 5
No — let me hie where dark destruction dwells,
To rouse her from her deeply-caverned lair
And, taunting her curst sluggishness to ire,
Light long Oblivion's death-torch at its flame
And calmly mount Annihilation's pyre. 10

Tyrant of Earth! pale Misery's jackall thou!
Are there no stores of vengeful violent fate
Within the magazines of thy fierce hate?
No poison in thy clouds to bathe a brow
That lowers on thee with desperate contempt? 15
Where is the noonday pestilence that slew
The myriad sons of Israel's favoured nation?
Where the destroying minister that flew
Pouring the fiery tide of desolation
Upon the leagued Assyrian's attempt? 20
Where the dark Earthquake demon who ingorged
At thy dread word Korah's unconscious crew?
Or the Angel's two-edged sword of fire that urged
Our primal parents from their bower of bliss
(Reared by thine hand) for errors not their own, 25
By thine omniscient mind foredoomed, foreknown?

THE WANDERING JEW'S SOLILOQUY

Yes! I would court a ruin such as this,
Almighty Tyrant! and give thanks to thee. —
Drink deeply — drain the cup of hate — remit; then I may die.

To Ianthe.

Sept.ʳ 1813

I love thee, Baby! for thine own sweet sake;
Those azure eyes, that faintly dimpled cheek,
Thy tender frame so eloquently weak,
Love in the sternest heart of hate might wake;
But more, when o'er thy fitful slumber bending   5
Thy mother folds thee to her wakeful heart,
Whilst love and pity in her glances blending,
All that thy passive eyes can feel, impart;
More, when some feeble lineaments of her
Who bore thy weight beneath her spotless bosom,   10
As with deep love I read thy face, recur,
More dear art thou, O fair and fragile blossom,
Dearest, when most thy tender traits express
The image of thy Mother's loveliness.—

Evening—to Harriet.

Sep. 1813

O thou bright Sun! beneath the dark blue line
Of western distance that sublime descendest,
And gleaming lovelier as thy beams decline,
Thy million hues to every vapour lendest,
And over cobweb lawn and grove and stream   5
Sheddest the liquid magic of thy light,
Till calm Earth with the parting splendor bright
Shews like the vision of a beauteous dream;
What gazer now with astronomic eye
Could coldly count the spots within thy sphere?   10
Such were thy lover, Harriet, could he fly
The thoughts of all that makes his passion dear,
And, turning senseless from thy warm caress,
Pick flaws in our close-woven happiness.

                        July 31st 1813.

To Harriett

Thy look of love has power to calm
    The stormiest passion of my Soul;
Thy gentle words are drops of balm
    In life's too bitter bowl.
No grief is mine but that alone   5
These choicest blessings I have known.

Harriett! if all who long to live
    In the warm sunshine of thine eye,
That price beyond all pain must give,—
    Beneath thy scorn to die;   10
Then hear thy chosen own, too late,
His heart most worthy of thy hate.

Be thou, then, one among mankind
    Whose heart is harder not for state—
Thou only, virtuous, gentle, kind,   15
    Amid a world of hate
And by a slight endurance seal
A fellow being's lasting weal.

For pale with anguish is his cheek,
    His breath comes fast, his eyes are dim;   20
Thy name is struggling ere he speak;
    Weak is each trembling limb.
In mercy let him not endure
The misery of a fatal cure.

O, trust for once no erring guide!   25
    Bid the remorseless feeling flee;

TO HARRIETT

'Tis malice, 'tis revenge, 'tis pride,
  'Tis any thing but thee.
O, deign a nobler pride to prove,
And pity if thou canst not love!   30

            Cook's Hotel
            May 1814

Full many a mind

Full many a mind with radiant genius fraught
Is taught the dark scowl of misery to bear;
How many a great soul has often sought
To stem the sad torrent of wild despair!

'T'would not be Earth's laws were given 5
To stand between Man, God and Heaven,
To teach him where to seek and truly find
That lasting comfort, peace of mind.

                      Stanmore.   1815

To Harriet

May 1813

Oh Harriet, love like mine that glows,
What rolling years can e'er destroy?
Without thee, can I tell my woes?
And with thee, can I speak my grief?

Ah no, past all the futile power 5
Of words to tell is love like mine.
My love is not the fading flower
That fleets ere it attains its prime;
A moment of delight with thee
Would pay me for an age of pain. 10

I'll tell not of Rapture and Joy
Which swells thro' the Libertine's frame;
That breast must feel bliss with alloy
That is scorched by so selfish a flame.

It were pleasure to die for my love, 15
It were rapture to sink in the grave
My eternal affection to prove,
My ever dear Harriet to save.

Without thee all pleasure were gloom,
And with thee all sorrow were joy. 20
Ere I knew thee, my Harriet, each year
Passed in mournful rotation away;
No friend to my bosom was dear,
Slow rolled the unvarying day.

TO HARRIET

Shall I wake then those horrors anew 25
That swelled in my desperate brain
When to death's darkened portals I flew
And sought misery's relief to my pain?

That hour which tears thee from me
Leaves nothing but death and despair, 30
And that, Harriet, never could be
Were thy mind less enchantingly fair.

'Tis not for the charms of thy form,
Which decay with the swift rolling year,
Ah no, Heaven expands to my sight 35
For Elysium with Harriet must be.

Adieu, my love; good night.

Cum Elam

Late was the night

Late was the night, the moon shone bright;
It teinted the walls with a silver light
And threw its wide, uncertain beam
Upon its rolling mountain stream.

That stream so swift that rushes along 5
Has oft been dyed by the murderer's song;
It oft has heard the exulting wave
Of one who oft the murderer braved.

The Alpine summits, which, raised on high,
Peacefully frown on the Valley beneath 10
And lift their Huge forms to the Sky,
Oft have heard the voice of death.

Now not a murmur floats on the air
Save the distant rounds of the torrent's tide,
Not a cloud obscures the moors so fair, 15
Not a shade is seen on the rocks to glide.

See that fair form that he can save,
Her garments are tattered, her bosom so bare?
She shrinks from the yawning watery grave,
And, shivering, around her enwraps her dark hair. 20

Poor Emma has toiled o'er many a mile —
The victim of misery's own sad child.
Pale is her cheek, all trembling awhile,
She totters and falls on the cold-striken wild.

1815

To St Irvyne

Feb^{ry} 28th 1805

O'er thy turrets, St Irvyne, the winter winds roar,
   The long grass of thy Towers streams to the blast.
Must I never, St Irvyne, then visit thee more?
   Are those visions of transient happiness past —

When with Harriet I sat on the mouldering height,   5
   When with Harriet I gazed on the star-spangled sky,
And the August Moon shone thro' the dimness of night?
   How swiftly the moment of pleasure fled by!

How swift is a fleeting smile chased by a sigh!
   This breast, this poor sorrow-torn breast must confess: 10
Oh Harriet, loved Harriet, tho' thou art not nigh,
   Think not thy lover thinks of thee less.

How oft have we roamed thro' the stillness of Eve
   Through St Irvyne's old rooms that so fast fade away.
That these pleasure-winged moments were transient
     I grieve;   15
   My Soul like those turrets falls fast to decay.

My Harriet is fled like a fast-fading dream,
   Which fades ere the vision is fixed on the mind,
But has left a firm love and a lasting esteem,
   That my soul to her soul must eternally bind.   20

TO ST IRVYNE

When my mouldering bones lie in the cold, chilling grave,
    When my last groans are borne o'er Strood's wide Lea,
And over my Tomb the chill night-tempests rave,
    Then, loved Harriet, bestow one poor thought on me.

To H Grove

COMMENTARIES

PUBLICATION HISTORY

BIBLIOGRAPHICAL DESCRIPTION

TEXTUAL NOTES

REFERENCE SOURCES

Commentaries

Page 37. To Harriet ("Whose is the love")

SHELLEY, as we have noted, also used this poem — with changes — as the dedication to *Queen Mab*.[1] In regard to the curious unrhymed stanzaic form, Edward Dowden, in his manuscript copybook,[2] has the following note: "The form of the stanza adopted from Southey e.g. 'Ode written on 1st of Jan 1794' (in Poems 1797). Wm Taylor & Amelia Opie had used this stanza in Annual Anthology 1799."

---

[1] See above, p. 29.

[2] Through Richard Garnett, Dowden obtained access to the Shelley family holdings in the possession of Sir Percy Florence Shelley. But he decided also to contact the other branch of Shelley's descendants, and sometime in 1884 got in touch with the Esdaile family. The rest of the story can be followed in the Dowden-Garnett correspondence in *Letters about Shelley*.

On July 9, 1884, Richard Garnett (at the British Museum) wrote to Dowden (at Trinity College, Dublin) that he found Dowden's comments on "the early poetry indeed interesting." That the reference is to the poetry in the Esdaile Notebook is indicated by a letter from Dowden to Garnett on November 21: "Mr. Esdaile's book is still in my hands." As Dowden had intended to visit Garnett on a trip to London on April 26, presumably he had then shown him the notebook. On November 21 also Dowden told Garnett that he intended to "make a copy" of the notebook. (*Letters about Shelley*, pp. 104, 106-7, 102.) On the title page of the first volume of the copybook (see above, p. 32), under the title "Shelley/Esdaile MS./vol i.," Dowden has written the following note: "The MS was copied for the purposes of my *Life of Shelley*, in which, by the kind permission of Mr Esdaile some poems & passages of poems were printed.

Southey's poem "Written on the First of January" opens as follows:

> Come, melancholy Moralizer, come!
> Gather with me the dark and wintry wreath;
>   With me engarland now
>   The Sepulchre of Time.

The garland image may indicate that Shelley (see line 12) not only had the stanzaic form in mind but also had some remembrance of content.

Below his comment on the form of the stanza Dowden has another (written in pencil): "Note that these Southean rimeless pieces come in a group & are placed first." There are four such "rimeless pieces" following this dedicatory poem.

Page 38. A sabbath Walk

DOWDEN in his manuscript copybook made the following comments: "Unrimed stanza. Southey's influence Compare 'Written on Sunday Morning' in Southey's vol of 1797. ? Written at Keswick 1811-12." Then he added in pencil: "or at *Tremadoc* 1812-13?"

Dowden does not give his reasoning for these possible datings but it is clear enough. The poem was written on a "winter's day" (line 28) among mountains (line 5). In the period during which these poems were being written, Shelley was only twice in mountainous country in winter:

I was not forbidden to make a copy. But of course these two MS volumes must be kept absolutely private & no copies must be taken. Edward Dowden."

Dowden informed Garnett in his letter of November 21 that he would send him the copybooks. These were returned by Garnett the following June. (*Ibid.*, pp. 129, 130.) Volume I has a few notations by Garnett in pencil.

at Keswick, in the English Lake District, between November 1811 and February 1812 (where he met Southey); at Tremadoc, in Wales, between November 1812 and March 1813.

Of the two, the evidence favors Keswick and the winter of 1811-1812 rather than Tremadoc and the winter of 1812-1813. We learn, for instance, from a letter to Elizabeth Hitchener that Shelley was in the habit of taking walks of this kind at Keswick: "I have taken a long *solitary* ramble to-day. These gigantic mountains piled on each other, these water-falls, these million-shaped clouds tinted by the varying colors of innumerable rainbows hanging between yourself and a lake as smooth and dark as a plain of polished jet — oh, these are sights attunable to the contemplation."[3]

In another Keswick letter to her we find sentiments very similar to those in the poem: "You talk of religion, — the influence human depravity gained over your mind towards acceding to it. — But, for this purpose, the Religion of the Deist, or the worshipper of virtue would suffice, without involving the persecution, battles, bloodshed, which countenancing Christianity countenances. — I think, my friend, *we* are the devoutest professors of *true* religion I know, — if the perverted and prostituted name of 'Religion' is applicable to the idea of Devotion to Virtue."[4]

The letter goes on to discuss the crisis in Shelley's relationship with Hogg because of Hogg's attempt to seduce Harriet. The confrontation had taken place but shortly before: "I sought him, and we walked to the fields beyond York. I desired to know fully the account of this affair.

---

[3] November 23, 1811, Shelley, *Complete Works*, VIII, 197-8.

[4] November 17-18, 1811, *ibid.*, pp. 195-6. The letter is undated but the London postmark is November 20. It took two or three days for mail to go from Keswick to London.

I heard it *from him*, and I believe he was sincere. All I can recollect of that terrible day was that I said I pardoned him, freely, fully pardoned him, that I would still be a friend to him."[5] After Shelley arrived at Keswick a series of agonized letters passed between him and Hogg (with Hogg threatening suicide): "I have just finished reading your long letter to Harriett it is late, as the post is so. Therefore I may not say all I wish, indeed that is *not* probable. words cannot express half my reasonings the thousandth of my feeling. . . . *Can* I not feel? are not those throbbing temples that bursting heart chained to mine . . do they not sympathize."[6]

We know of no other crisis in Shelley's life in these years to which the following lines (lines 6-8) could apply:

> even when the frost has torn
> All save the ivy clinging to the rocks
> Like friendship to a friend's adversity!

And here it might be well to interpolate a point which will come up many times, namely, that references of this kind in Shelley's poetry, which may at first seem to be general in nature, almost always turn out to be specific and autobiographical. This penchant, indeed at times almost obsession, for the autobiographical was to continue throughout Shelley's poetry—in *Rosalind and Helen, Julian and Maddalo, Epipsychidion.*

Shelley's indebtedness to Southey's "Written on Sunday Morning," noted by Dowden, is clear enough. Southey's poem opens:

> Go thou and seek the House of Prayer!
> I to the woodlands wend, and there
> In lovely Nature see the God of Love.

---

[5] November 14, 1811, *ibid.*, p. 187.
[6] November 13, 1811. From the original manuscript in The Carl H. Pforzheimer Library.

But Southey's mild deism is far removed from Shelley's militant anti-clericalism:

> 'Tis not the fabled cause that framed
> The everlasting orbs of Heaven.

Shelley, at first impressed by Southey, grew disillusioned:

> Southey, the poet, whose principles were pure and elevated once, is now the paid champion of every abuse and absurdity. I have had much conversation with him. He says, "You will think as I do when you are as old." I do not feel the least disposition to be Mr. S's proselyte.[7]

Page 40. *The Crisis*

THE TITLE apparently does not refer to any particular event but to the general historical period, which Shelley believed was mounting to a crisis:

> the consummating hour
> Dreadfully, sweetly, swiftly is arriving.

The theme anticipates *Queen Mab*:

> Man, like these passive things,
> Thy will unconsciously fulfilleth:
> Like theirs, his age of endless peace,
> Which time is fast maturing,
> Will swiftly, surely come.[8]

---

[7] To William Godwin, January 16, 1812, Shelley, *Complete Works*, VIII, 244. But Shelley continued to use the unrhymed stanza form of Southey. He used it in *Queen Mab;* and he was conscious of its origin: "The didactic is in blank heroic verse, and the descriptive in blank lyrical measure. If an authority is of any weight in support of this singularity, Milton's 'Samson Agonistes,' the Greek Choruses, and (you will laugh) Southey's 'Thalaba' may be adduced." (To Hogg, February 7, 1813, Shelley, *Complete Works*, IX, 44.)

[8] *Queen Mab*, III, 233-7.

So far as the general references to the despotism and corruption of the English and European monarchies are concerned, the poem could have been written at any time between 1809 and the period of the compilation of the Notebook. Later composition, however, is indicated by the poem's stark directness, which contrasts with the earlier *Original Poetry* manner (with its echoes from Gray, Scott, Campbell, and Monk Lewis). The only specific reference, that to mother and child murder, may be paralleled in a letter to Elizabeth Hitchener from Keswick on January 7, 1812, which like the poem comments on political and social matters:

> Popular insurrections and revolutions I look upon with discountenance. *If such things must be,* I will take the side of the People . . . Keswick seems more like a suburb of London than a village of Cumberland. Children are frequently found in the River, which the unfortunate women employed at the manufactory destroy.[9]

The Southeyan unrhymed stanzas also point to compostion at Keswick.

Page 41. Passion

DOWDEN in his manuscript copybook has the following note: "? To the *deadly nightshade* only that Shelley c^d hardly have failed to insert this name. Again unrimed stanza." Dowden's view receives support from the following lines in *Queen Mab*:

> Like passion's fruit, the nightshade's tempting bane
> Poisons no more the pleasure it bestows.[1]

[9] Shelley, *Complete Works*, VIII, 234, 235.
[1] *Queen Mab*, VIII, 129-30. We might also note *Prometheus Unbound*, III, iv, 79-83.

This might, in fact, be taken as settling the matter if it were not for a passage in a letter from Keswick to Hogg in which Shelley argues against Hogg's joining them at Keswick:

> "Absence extinguishes small passions and kindles great ones" but *presence* without fullest satiation will kindle the passions to an inextinguishable flame. how have I heard you talk of the infinite progression of Love. — It is strange to me that you who know the human mind so well should think so lightly of sensation If you have *loved* I can believe that you have not felt it lightly —. Harriet has written to you — What she has said I know not. *I* have not been able to write for this day or two to you owing to having been ill from the poison of laurel-leaves.[2]

The connection of passion both in the poem and in the letter with a poisonous plant is unlikely to be coincidental. It would seem, however, that the plant described in the poem was neither the deadly nightshade nor the laurel. The description seems best to fit the plant known as *Arum maculatum*, popularly known as adder's root, a plant with a mottled stem and poisonous berries.[3] Perhaps Shelley did not insert the name in the title because he was not really sure what the plant was.

As this letter to Hogg can be dated about November 17-18, 1811, and the letter to Elizabeth Hitchener paralleling "A sabbath Walk" was written on November 17, it may be that both poems were written at about the same time.

---

[2] November 17-18, 1811. From the original manuscript in The Carl H. Pforzheimer Library.

[3] Information supplied by Miss Elizabeth C. Hall, Research Librarian, New York Botanical Garden, the Bronx, New York.

Page 43. To Harriet ("Never, O never")

As this poem is also in unrhymed Southeyan stanzas and is placed at the end of what appears to be a Keswick sequence, presumably it, too, was written at Keswick. If so, the poem may have its origin not in Harriet's jealousy of another woman—as one might at first think—but in jealousy of Hogg. That this could well have been so is clear from a reading of Shelley's letters to Hogg from Keswick. Hogg, in a frenzy of guilt, was threatening suicide and Shelley in the midst of his own agitation was trying at once to calm him, point out his errors, and affirm both past friendship and present regard. It is an easy correspondence to misread and one should not take a sentence or two out of context, but perhaps the following might give some indication of the moods that could have inspired the poem. "Oh how I haved loved you. I was even ashamed to tell you how! & now to leave you *forever*. . . .—no not forever . . Night comes . . . Death comes . . Cold calm death almost I would it were tomorrow there is another life. . . . . are you not to be the first there. . . . Assuredly . . ."[4] Harriet, reading these lines or hearing Shelley express similar sentiments, might well have felt that he had gone a little far in his efforts to soothe Hogg's ruffled feathers, and her protest could have produced just such a poem. Both poem and letter, we might note, contain death-wish fantasies.

Shelley's sister, Hellen, remembered Harriet as having "hair quite like a poet's dream."[5] Peacock described it as

---

[4] November 7-9, 1811. From the original manuscript in The Carl H. Pforzheimer Library.
[5] Hogg, *Shelley*, I, 32.

"light brown."[6] Shelley here calls it auburn. Perhaps Shelley and Peacock saw it in a different light.

Page 44. *Falshood and Vice*

SHELLEY included this poem in the Notes to *Queen Mab* with the following introductory comment: "I will here subjoin a little poem, so strongly expressive of my abhorrence of despotism and falshood, that I fear lest it never again may be depictured so vividly. This opportunity is perhaps the only one that ever will occur of rescuing it from oblivion." The two versions, however, are not identical. There are a number of word changes, and two canceled lines in the Esdaile Notebook (lines 81-82) do not appear in the *Queen Mab* version. The Notebook version was not, of course, itself a composition draft but was copied from another manuscript. In fact, Shelley himself perhaps miscopied "with" for "wields" in line 7. In any case, there must have been at least three manuscripts: a composition draft, the Esdaile Notebook, and one used for *Queen Mab*.

In general style and content the poem is similar to Shelley's 1810-1811 radical verse, resembling, for instance, "War" in *Posthumous Fragments of Margaret Nicholson*, published in November 1810. But there is at least one piece of evidence which seems to place it after Shelley's first meeting with Southey at Keswick in December 1811.

C. D. Locock noted in his edition of Shelley's poems that "Coleridge's 'War Eclogue,' *Fire, Famine and Slaughter*, is, no doubt, the inspiration of this Dialogue."[7] When we

---

[6] Peacock, *Memoirs*, p. 95.

[7] C. D. Locock, *The Poems of Percy Bysshe Shelley* (London, 1911), II, 553.

turn to Coleridge's poem the influence is indeed clear. Furthermore, *Fire, Famine and Slaughter* obviously made a deep impression on Shelley. Its influence on the first part of the Furies episode in *Prometheus Unbound* (Act I, lines 495-538) is unmistakable. The Carl H. Pforzheimer Library contains a copy of the poem in Mary Shelley's hand, presumably copied out for Shelley.

One problem, however, Locock fails to note. *Fire, Famine and Slaughter*, one of Coleridge's early, revolutionary poems, was first published (anonymously) in the *Morning Post* in 1798; then in 1800 in the *Annual Anthology* (again anonymously). Coleridge did not publish it again until 1817, in his volume *Sibylline Leaves*, and then with an apologetic preface. He would not, in all probability, have included it in this book if Leigh Hunt had not published it the previous year in *The Examiner* ("to his annoyance," commented Crabb Robinson).[8] If, then, the poem was not published between 1800 and 1816, how did Shelley obtain access to it in the meantime? He would not normally have encountered either the *Morning Post* of 1798 or the *Annual Anthology* of 1800; and even if he had, in neither instance was the poem identified as Coleridge's. When we recall, however, that Southey was the editor of the *Annual Anthology*, an explanation presents itself; namely, that Southey showed it to Shelley and told him that the poem was by Coleridge. Southey would almost certainly have had the *Annual Anthology* volumes in his extensive library at Keswick (a library that Shelley visited).

Shelley informed Elizabeth Hitchener on December 15, 1811, that he expected to meet Southey "soon"; on December 26 he wrote: "I have also been much engaged

---

[8] *Henry Crabb Robinson on Books and Their Writers*, ed. Edith J. Morley (London, 1938), I, 198.

in talking with Southey."⁹ In a letter of about January 17 (undated but bearing a London postmark of January 20), also to Elizabeth Hitchener, he included his poem *The Devil's Walk*. As this poem imitated similar poems by Coleridge and Southey, it is apparent that Southey had been showing him his own and perhaps also Coleridge's writings.

"Falshood and Vice," then, was almost certainly written later that the middle of December 1811. It is possible that it was written in Dublin or at Keswick just before he left for Dublin. The comments on the "unhappy land" (line 12) sound rather like Ireland and a line in *The Devil's Walk* (the first draft of which was written at Keswick), "Fat — as the death-birds on Erin's shore," may echo the same scene.

In spite of its title the poem is social rather than moral in purport. By "Falshood" Shelley means essentially religion (and his tenor here is similar to that of Paine or Holbach) and by "Vice," war and despotism. War-Despotism claims that it has done more harm than religion; Religion answers that if its lies had not first weakened the mind of Man he would not have accepted such evils. Although some references are to history in general, the main emphasis is on Shelley's own age, especially the Napoleonic Wars:

> I have extinguished the noonday sun
> In the carnage smoke of battles won.

The "bloated wretch" (line 70) is most likely the Prince Regent, whose fatness is made much of in *The Devil's Walk*.

---

⁹ Shelley, *Complete Works*, VIII, 223.

Page 48. *To the Emperors of Russia and Austria*

THE POEM gives the impression of having been written shortly after the battle (December 2, 1805), but the radical and pacifist sentiments point to at least late 1809 and such skilled turns of phrase as

> on yonder plain
> The game, if lost, begins again

to 1810 or, more probably, 1811.

In spite of the partiality to Napoleon implied in the title, Shelley did not share the admiration for him that we find in such other English radicals of the time as Hazlitt or Byron, for he regarded war itself with such abhorrence that he hated all its practitioners. In December 1812, he wrote of him to Hogg as "a hateful and despicable being."[1] In "Lines Written on Hearing the News of the Death of Napoleon" (1821), he writes:

> Napoleon's fierce spirit rolled,
> In terror, and blood, and gold,
> A torrent of ruin to death from his birth.[2]

But much as he abhorred Napoleon, Shelley still put him above such petty tyrants as the Austrian Emperor and the Russian Czar, whom he considered "slaves" (line 44) of the great "tyrant."

The lines (29-30)

> Till from the ruin of the storm
> Ariseth Freedom's awful form

---

[1] December 27, 1812, Shelley, *Complete Works*, IX, 37.
[2] See also "Feelings of a Republican on the Fall of Bonaparte"; *A Philosophical View of Reform* (1820), Shelley, *Complete Works*, VII, 14; *The Triumph of Life* (1822), lines 215-27.

anticipate the conclusion of "Sonnet: England in 1819":

> from which a glorious Phantom may
> Burst, to illumine our tempestuous day.

The "glorious Phantom" is freedom or liberty.

Page 50. To November

THE "My Harriet" of line 12 indicates that the poem was written to Harriet (Westbrook Shelley and not to Shelley's boyhood sweetheart, Harriet Grove.[3] Shelley does not refer to Harriet Grove as "my Harriet," and could not appropriately have done so. But he did call his wife "my Harriet"; for instance, when writing to Hogg on his Irish travels: "My Harriet insisted on accompanying me."[4] As Shelley eloped with Harriet Westbrook in the summer of 1811 and the Notebook poems had been compiled and rejected for publication by the spring of 1813, "November" is obviously either November 1811 or November 1812. Of the two, 1811 seems the more likely.

On November 6, 1811, Shelley and Harriet arrived in Keswick; the first part of November 1812 they spent in London, the second at Tremadoc in Wales. At Tremadoc, Shelley worked on *Queen Mab*, which is much more mature in style than "To November" and appears to have absorbed all his energies.

The unhappy May of stanza four was probably the May of 1811, when Shelley was alone at Field Place after having been with Harriet Westbrook in London.

---

[3] For an account of Harriet Grove and the Grove family, see Frederick L. Jones, "Introduction to the Diary of Harriet Grove," *Shelley and his Circle*, II, 475-506.

[4] March 31, 1813, Shelley, *Complete Works*, IX, 61.

Page 52. *Written on a beautiful day in Spring*

THE Wordsworthian tone points to a "Spring" following Shelley's stay at Keswick in the winter of 1811-1812, when he apparently was introduced to Wordsworth's poems by Southey. If so, the "Spring" was that of 1812, for the Notebook poems had been compiled for publication by the spring of 1813. In the spring of 1812 Shelley was in Wales, having just returned from his first visit to Ireland. Late in June he left Wales for Devon. We find similar Wordsworthian influence in a poem apparently written shortly after he arrived in Devon, "To Harriet ('It is not blasphemy')."

Shelley's use of the words "God" and "Heaven" (see line 10) in his poetry has caused confusion, leading some critics to ascribe orthodox Christian beliefs to him.[5] The problem occurs several times in the Esdaile Notebook poems.

Shelley's views on God and immortality during these early years are best expressed in his letters to Elizabeth Hitchener:

> What then is a "God"? It is a name which expresses the unknown cause, the supposititious origin of all existence. When we speak of the soul of man, we mean that unknown cause which produces the observable effect evinced by his intelligence and bodily animation, which are in their nature conjoined, and, as we suppose, as we observe, inseparable. The word God then, in the sense which you take it analogises with the *universe*, as the soul of man to

---

[5] For an interesting discussion of the point, see C. E. Pulos, *The Deep Truth* (University of Nebraska Press, 1954), pp. 101-4.

his body, as the vegetative power to vegetables, the stony power to stones.[6]

... is then soul annihilable? Yet one of the properties of animal soul is consciousness of identity. If this is destroyed, in consequence the *soul* whose essence this is must perish; but as I conceive and as is certainly capable of demonstration that nothing can be annihilated, but that everything appertaining to nature, consisting of constituent parts infinitely divisible, is in a continual change, then do I suppose, and I think I have a right to draw this inference, that neither will soul perish; that in a future existence it will lose all consciousness of having formerly lived elsewhere, will begin life anew, possibly under a shape of which we have now no idea.[7]

"God," then, Shelley used as a synonym for the essence of existence. He does not believe in a personal immortality, but (as in *Adonais*) the return of the soul to "the burning fountain whence it came." Presumably he had the same idea in mind with regard to "Heaven" in this poem. The situation, however, is complicated by the fact that Shelley, in his poetry, felt free to express ideas which he did not believe to be capable of rational proof, if they were "exalting." As he later put it in a note to *Hellas*:

The received hypothesis of a Being resembling men in the moral attributes of his nature, having called us out of non-existence, and after inflicting on us the misery of the commission of error, should superadd that of the punishment and the privations consequent upon it, still would remain inexplicable and incredible. That there is a true solution of the riddle, and that in our present state the solution is unattainable by us, are propositions which may be regarded as equally certain; meanwhile, as it is the province of the poet to attach himself to those ideas which exalt and ennoble humanity, let him be permitted

[6] June 11, 1811, Shelley, *Complete Works*, VIII, 102.
[7] June 20, 1811, *ibid.*, p. 108.

to have conjectured the condition of that futurity towards which we are all impelled by an inextinguishable thirst for immortality. Until better arguments can be produced than sophisms which disgrace the cause, this desire itself must remain the strongest and the only presumption that eternity is the inheritance of every thinking being.

Even while Shelley was writing of immortality to Elizabeth Hitchener, he considered himself, as he informed her, to be an atheist.[8]

Page 53. *On leaving London for Wales*

DOWDEN, attempting to date this poem, wrote in his copybook: "date ?Nov 1812 or Summer of 1811. I think Nov 1812." And to this Richard Garnett has added in pencil: "Yes. RG." The reason for the selection of the two dates is that Shelley only twice left London for Wales, once in July 1811, when he went to Cwm Elan prior to eloping with Harriet Westbrook, and once in October 1812, when he returned to Tremadoc.

Dowden gives one of his reasons for favoring the latter date in a note opposite "Snowdon's" (line 30): "Snowdon—Shelley describes in a letter to Hogg the beauty of the road under Snowdon from Capel Cerig to Tremadoc." The letter was written on February 7, 1813, to Hogg in London. In it Shelley, urging Hogg to visit him at Tremadoc, informs him that the coach from London "passes at the foot of Snowdon."[9] So that Shelley himself expected to pass the mountain on his way from London to Tremadoc. He would not, however, have passed Snowdon on

---

[8] October 8, 1811, Shelley, *Complete Works*, VIII, 152: "You will enquire how *I* an *Atheist* chose to subject myself to the ceremony of *marriage*."

[9] Shelley, *Complete Works*, IX, 44.

his way to Cwm Elan, which was much further south (near Rhayader).

The poem, in fact, can be understood only against the background of Shelley's visit to London in October and November 1812. The main purpose of the visit was to raise money for an embankment at Tremadoc which a liberal Member of Parliament, William Madocks (after whom the town was named), had begun in order to rescue land from the sea. Shelley had worked on this project briefly in September. The enthusiasm with which he threw himself into it is conveyed in a speech he made before the town corporation at Beaumaris shortly before leaving for London (as reported in the *North Wales Gazette*).

From London, Shelley went to his native Sussex hoping to raise money—and failed: "In Sussex I meet with no encouragement. They are a parcel of cold, selfish, and calculating animals, who seem to have no other aim or business, on earth, but to eat, drink, and sleep; but in the mean while my fervid hopes, my ardent desires, my unremitting personal exertions (so far as my health will allow), are all engaged in that cause, which I will desert but *with my life*."[1] His last hope was the Duke of Norfolk. But the Duke "regretted that he had no funds at his immediate disposal."[2] That this experience must have been bitter—"we submitted to a galling yet unappealable necessity"[3]—has been clear but how deeply Shelley had been shaken by it has not been realized by his biographers.

Let us take, for instance, the following lines (51-54):

The storm fleets by and calmer thoughts succeed,
Feelings once more mild reason's voice obey.

---

[1] To John Williams, November 7, 1812, Shelley, *Complete Works*, IX, 23.
[2] Hogg, *Shelley*, I, 368.
[3] To Fanny Imlay, December 10, 1812, Shelley, *Complete Works*, IX, 31.

Woe be the tyrants' and murderers' meed,
But Nature's wound alone should make their Conscience bleed.

In terms of the total stanza what Shelley is saying is that one should not be tempted to use violence against "tyrants" and "murderers," but should let "Nature's wound alone" "make their Conscience bleed." "Nature's wound," here, really does not make sense unless it is taken as a reference to the embankment; failure to complete it would keep land under the sea and prevent it from being cultivated. Similarly in the previous stanza the "rocks to ruin hurled" (line 42) must refer to the rocks that are being rolled down the mountains in order to build the embankment, a project which would create a triumph for "Reason." "Tyrants" and "murderers" (and those bound by "Custom's obduracies" — line 24) must be aimed primarily at those who, like the Duke of Norfolk, had refused to assist the project. The "storm" refers to Shelley's initial rage at this refusal.

Although so much of the poem is personal, it is not entirely so. During Shelley's stay in London the British government declared war on the United States, a general election was waged in which the Tories slandered the reform Whigs, and Moscow was burned, an event which Shelley, back in his mountain fastness, turned into verse:

> Hark to that roar, whose swift and deaf'ning peals
> In countless echoes through the mountains ring.
> Startling pale midnight on her starry throne![4]

Similarly Shelley's attack on London no doubt received added bite from his recent experiences there, but Shelley, raised in the country, never did have much use for the city:

[4] *Queen Mab*, IV, 38-40.

> Hell is a city much like London —
> A populous and smoky city.[5]

On the other hand, he was under no illusion that those living in the mountains were more enlightened than those in the city: "The society in Wales is very stupid. They are all aristocrats or saints."[6] "Mountain Liberty" (line 23) is a natural, not a social, phenomenon. Nature may or may not affect the mind. To those responsive to its magnificence, Snowdon (and Shelley here anticipates "Mont Blanc") makes human evil seem small and dim ("Lethe").

The stanza form of the poem, we may note, is the Spenserian, previously used in "Henry and Louisa" and later in *The Revolt of Islam*. To judge from the archaism of line 27 — "Blots out the unholiest rede of worldly witnessing" — Shelley had recently been reading Spenser.[7]

Page 56. A winter's day

DOWDEN notes in his copybook: "1811-12 Keswick or 1812-13 Tanyrallt." "Tanyrallt" was the name of the house that Shelley rented at Tremadoc. So Dowden assumed that we have once more a choice between the two winters spent in the mountains — a reasonable assumption, for the verse, spotty though it is, is still rather smoother than most of Shelley's writing in 1809 or 1810. Of the two win-

---

[5] *Peter Bell the Third*, III, i.

[6] To T. J. Hogg, December 3, 1812, Shelley, *Complete Works*, IX, 28.

[7] *Ibid.*, p. 34. After returning to Wales from London, Shelley ordered a list of books from Hookham. In it he included Spenser's "Works Fairy Queen &c. (Cheapest poss. Edit.)." Perhaps he had been reading Spenser in London and wished to continue his studies. Possibly the line was added after Spenser's "Works" arrived. See the Textual Note on this line.

ters, Dowden appears to have favored that of 1812-1813, for he added in reference to the "cascade" of line 4: "Hogg says that Shelley was enthusiastic about the Welsh waterfalls."

Dowden perhaps also had in mind that the previous poem was written either at Tremadoc or in London just before Shelley left for Tremadoc in October 1812. Shelley, however, is not using a rigid chronological sequencing. The next two poems were probably written at Dublin in the spring of 1812, and after that we are back at Keswick in January 1812.

So far as the waterfalls are concerned, there were also waterfalls near Keswick, and perhaps more likely to be "murmuring" ones than those in the Welsh mountains. "The moor" (line 12), however, definitely tips the balance toward Keswick. There are no moors in the rugged mountains around Tremadoc, but there are moors to the east of the Lake District and Shelley passed through them when in November he had traveled on the coach road from York to Keswick. We might note also that the style of "A winter's day" is similar to that of "To November," the death theme to that of "To Harriet ('Never, O never')," and the "passion" reference to that in "Passion."

It is interesting to note in some of these poems Shelley's echoings of eighteenth-century poetic diction, for instance, "peals of vernal music." Shelley — unlike Byron — later moved so far from these Augustan roots that we are apt to forget that they existed.

Page 58. *To Liberty*

A POEM by Shelley on liberty could, of course, have been written any time between late 1809 and the compilation of the Notebook. But Shelley usually dates the earlier poems, and there are parallels with *Queen Mab* in this poem which indicate a later date.[8] The final stanzas on the downfall of monarchies and their thrones and prisons is a kind of summary of the first half of the final canto of *Queen Mab*. In *Queen Mab* the "palace of the monarch-slave" becomes a "heap of crumbling ruins";[9] the "ponderous chains" of the "prison's mouldering courts" have "rusted amid heaps of broken stone."[1] The line "The pyramids shall fall" appears as "Those pyramids shall fall,"[2] and the final lines anticipate the opening of Canto IX: "O happy Earth! reality of Heaven!" The general sentiments of the second stanza and others are echoed in:

> Yon monarch, in his solitary pomp,
> Was but the mushroom of a summer day,
> That his [Time's] light-wingèd footstep pressed to dust:
> Time was the king of earth: all things gave way
> Before him, but the fixed and virtuous will,
> The sacred sympathies of soul and sense,
> That mocked his fury and prepared his fall.[3]

The poem, then, was almost certainly written between the late fall of 1811 and the period of composition of *Queen Mab*. There is some indication also that it might have been written either during Shelley's Irish expedition in 1812 (as was the next poem) or shortly thereafter. In a letter from Dublin, Shelley included other material that went into *Queen Mab*,[4] and he is much concerned with

---

[8] The concept for *Queen Mab* first appeared in a letter to Elizabeth Hitchener: December 11, 1811, Shelley, *Complete Works*, VIII, 213.
[9] *Queen Mab*, IX, 94, 96.
[1] *Ibid.*, 119, 114, 120.
[2] *Ibid.*, II, 129; see also IX, 26-30.
[3] *Ibid.*, IX, 31-7.
[4] To Elizabeth Hitchener, February 14, 1812, Shelley, *Complete Works*, VIII, 271.

having some American children (pupils of Elizabeth Hitchener) visit him; Harriet's sentiments in a letter to Elizabeth Hitchener in March 1812 doubtless echo Shelley's: "Do we not find tyranny and oppression everywhere? have you not plenty of it, even in your peaceful village? 'tis everywhere. —Yes! there is one spot where it is not—America. We know an Am[erican]: he says he has not seen a beggar there for this 8 years."[5] With this we might compare lines 26-30. The note of defiance in the poem and its assertion of future victory seem to have a deeper and more personal tone than in "The Crisis." In the "free and fearless soul" (line 16) who is considering defiance of tyranny with its prison and slander, Shelley doubtless has himself partly in mind (as he did later in Lionel of *Rosalind and Helen*), and this mood accords with that engendered by his Irish experience. Before he went to Ireland poverty and tyranny were abstractions; in Ireland they became realities.

Page 60. On Robert Emmet's Tomb

EMMET's execution (in 1803) by the British authorities, following his abortive rebellion, so moved Southey that he immediately sat down to write a poem on the subject. Shelley had doubtless long admired Emmet[6] but his interest may have been further stimulated by Southey. When he left Keswick for Ireland he had a letter of introduction from Godwin to John Philpot Curran and met him several times. As Curran's daughter Sarah had been Emmet's sweetheart (the story inspired Moore's "She is far from the

---

[5] March 10, 1812, *ibid.*, p. 293.
[6] See Commentary to "The Monarch's funeral," below p. 200.

land"), Shelley perhaps heard a good deal about him from Curran.[7]

From the poem itself it appears that Shelley visited Emmet's tomb. Apparently he composed it just before or just after leaving Ireland on April 4, for in a letter to Elizabeth Hitchener shortly after his return he commented: "I have written some verses on Robert Emmett, which you shall see, and which I will insert in my book of Poems."[8]

When Hogg visited the Shelleys in London some six months later, he found that they had brought back from Ireland a broadside on Emmet's trial, which Harriet showed him with some emotion.[9]

Emmet's burial place is something of a mystery. He was first buried in the burial grounds known as Bully's Acre or Hospital Fields, where executed criminals and paupers were interred. But a short time later, according to R. R. Madden, the body was "removed with great privacy and buried in Dublin."[1] Madden, who was the leading authority on the Irish revolutionaries of this period, found that there were two conflicting stories on where the body was buried after its removal, one favoring Michan's Churchyard — where "a large stone without any writing on it was laid over the grave" — and the other favoring St. Anne's Churchyard, where Emmet's parents were buried. Of the two, Madden inclines toward Michan's Churchyard, where he found the stone in question. This is apparently the burial ground visited by Shelley:

> No trump tells thy virtues — the grave where they rest
> With thy dust shall remain unpolluted by fame.

[7] Perhaps not all of it favorable. See Leslie Hale, *John Philpot Curran* (London, 1958), p. 232.
[8] Shelley, *Complete Works*, VIII, 309.
[9] Hogg, *Shelley*, I, 366.
[1] R. R. Madden, *The Life and Times of Robert Emmet* (New York, 1857), p. 230.

The reason for the lack of writing on the stone is to be found in Emmet's final speech at his trial:

> Let no man write my epitaph; for as no man who knows my motives dares now vindicate them, let not prejudice or ignorance asperse them. Let them rest in obscurity and peace; my memory be left in oblivion and my tomb remain uninscribed, until other times and other men can do justice to my character. When my country takes her place among the nations of the earth, then, and not till then, let my epitaph be written. I have done.[2]

Page 62. a Tale of Society as it is

SHELLEY included the first 78 lines of this poem in a letter to Elizabeth Hitchener from Keswick on January 7, 1812, with the introductory comment: "I now send you some Poetry: the subject is not fictitious. It is the overflowings of the mind this morning." Following the poem he added: "The facts are real: that recorded in the last fragment of a stanza is literally true. The poor man said: 'None of my family ever came *to parish,* and I w[oul]d starve first. I am a poor man; but I could never hold my head up after that.' —Adieu, my dearest friend. Think of the Poetry which I have inserted as a picture of my feelings, not a specimen of my art."[3]

That Shelley had, as he stated, just written the poem is indicated by the fact that it is incomplete in the letter; if he had finished it he would presumably have sent all of it to Elizabeth Hitchener. It may be, too, that he had actually written the first 78 lines in one morning, for he composed rapidly. After sending those lines to Elizabeth Hitchener he

---

[2] Hale, *op. cit.,* p. 229.
[3] Shelley, *Complete Works,* VIII, 238.

finished the poem and made some minor changes in wording.

The genre of the poem is that established by Wordsworth in "The Cumberland Beggar" and similar poems, namely, the tale of "humble" life told in deliberately unadorned style. This genre had been used by Southey and Coleridge to spread radical social views, for instance, in "The Soldier's Wife":

> Woe-begone mother, half anger, half agony,
> As over thy shoulder thou lookest to hush the babe,
> Bleakly the blinding snow beats in thy haggard face.
>
> Ne'er will thy husband return from the war again,
> Cold is thy heart, and as frozen as Charity!
> Cold are thy children. — Now God be thy comforter!

The first of these stanzas, Southey informs us, was written by Coleridge, and if Southey told Shelley this at Keswick it would have impressed the poem on his mind.

Just when Shelley finished his poem we do not know, but the additional material seems to be superior to the preceding stanzas, for instance, lines 89-90:

> The same kind light feeds every living thing
> That spreads its blossoms to the breath of spring.

Page 67. *The solitary*

SHELLEY himself dates this poem "1810." In the early months of 1810 he was at Eton, in the summer at Field Place, in the fall at Oxford, and in the winter back at Field Place for the Christmas vacation (which began about

December 10).⁴ As he also seems to have hesitated about the date, apparently first writing 1811 and then changing it to 1810, there is some reason for favoring Field Place and the Christmas vacation as the place and time of composition. The gloomy mood of the poet in contrast to the "genial bowl" of line 15 is similar to that expressed in his letters to Hogg during this vacation, for example: "Oh here we are in the midst of all the uncongenial jollities of Xmass, when you are compelled to contribute to the merriment of others."⁵

The poem is one of several in this book which anticipate *Alastor*, not, of course, in style or merit but in theme: the "isolated" poet who "cannot, cannot love" and contemplates suicide.

This is the first also of two poems in the Notebook which were published either in whole or in part by W. M. Rossetti in his 1870 edition of Shelley's poems from manuscripts in the "command" of Richard Garnett.⁶

Page 68. The Monarch's funeral

SHELLEY also dated this poem "1810" and the probability is, as with the previous poem, that it was written late in the year. The monarch whose death is anticipated was, of course, George III; and George became seriously ill after the death of his favorite daughter, Amelia, on November 2, 1810. In January 1811 his condition was so serious that Parliament passed the Regency Act.

---

⁴ *Shelley and his Circle*, II, 659. ⁵ *Ibid.*, p. 676.
⁶ Shelley, Rossetti ed., 1870, I, xvii; see *ibid.*, II, 507-8, 599. See also below, pp. 218, 238.

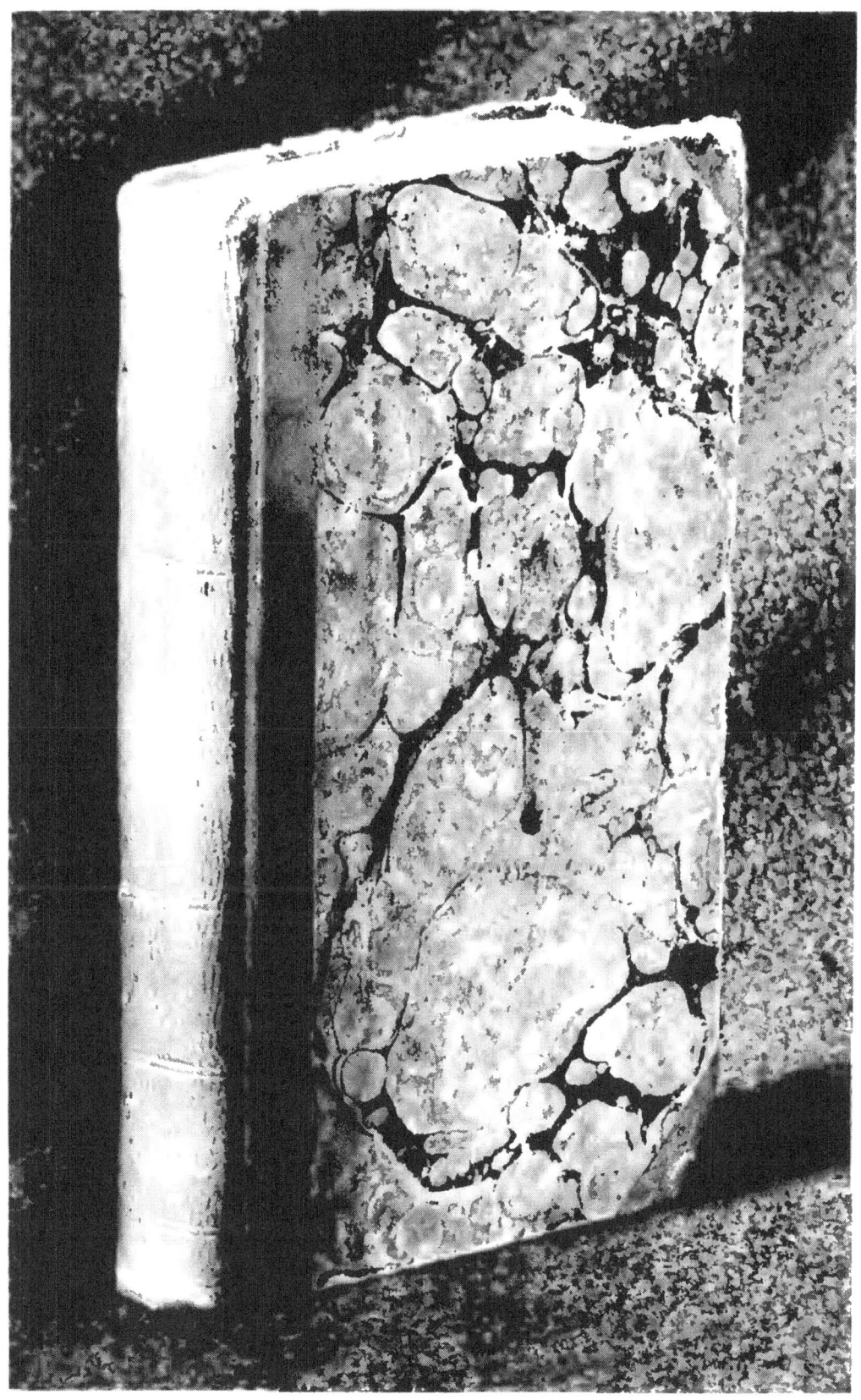

1 The Esdaile Notebook

11 "Field Place," a recent photograph. With the exception of the pillared portico (added in 1846) the house appears essentially as it did in Shelley's day. Shelley was born in the upper room of the right wing, which has two windows facing front and one, partly obscured by the chimney, facing to the side.

To Harriet

Whose is the love that gleaming thro' the world
Wards off the poisonous arrow of its scorn?
Whose is the warm & partial praise
Virtues most sweet reward?

Whose looks gave grace to the majestic theme
The sacred, free & fearless theme of truth
Whose form did I gaze fondly on
And love mankind the more?

Harriet! on thine — thou wert my purer soul
Thou wert the inspiration to my song
Thine are these early wilding flowers
Tho' garlanded by me.

Then twine the withering wreath-buds round thy brow
Its bloom may deck thy pale & faded prime
Can they survive without thy love
Their wild & mossy birth?

III The dedicatory poem, with the title in Harriet's hand

And wait in still hope for thy better end
1287

The Voyage
~~The I~~
A Fragment
Devonshire – August 1812
Quenched is the ——— rage
Each passant wave that flung
its neck that writhed beneath the tempest,
Indignant up to Heaven
Now breathes in its sweet slumber
To mingle with the day
A spirit of tranquillity
Beneath the cloudless sun
The gently swelling main
Scatters a thousand colourings

The present day –

IV The last line of "A retrospect of Times of Old," with Shelley's line count following it; the opening of "The Voyage"; the conclusion of the final footnote of "A retrospect of Times of Old"

1809
Henry & Louisa*
a Poem
in two parts

———

She died for love —, & he for glory

The Parting
Part the First.
Scene — England

I

Where are the Heroes? sunk in death they lie·
 What toiled they for? titles & wealth & fame —

---

* The stanza of this Poem is radically that of Spencer
although I suffered myself at the time of writing
it to be led into occasional deviations.
These defects I do not alter now, being unwilling to offer any outrage to the living production of my own mind; bad as it may
be pronounced.

v The first page of "Henry and Louisa"

For they had torn his Zeinab from her home
  Her innocent habits were all rudely shriven
And dragged to hide in woe's untimely tomb
  To prostitution, crime & woe was driven
The human race seemed leagued against her weal
And indignation cased her naked heart in steel

Therefore against them she waged ruthless war
  With their own arms of hate & bloody crime
Even like a mild & sweetly-beaming star
  whose rays were wont to grace the matin prime
  Changed to
  ~~Even like~~ a comet horrible & bright
Which with cancers unkindling sinks in dark-red night

Thus, like its god, unjust & pitiless
  Crimes first are made & then revenged by man
For where's the tender heart, whose hope can bless
  Or man's, or god's, unprofitable plan
A universe of horror & decay
Gibbets, disease, & wars & hearts as cold as they
                                              2640.

vi The final page of "Zeinab and Kathema," showing Shelley's corrections

VII The first page of "To Harriett ('Thy look of love')," in Harriet Shelley's hand

VIII Shelley's "St. Irvyne," where he and Harriet Grove went for moonlight walks (actually "Hill Place," owned first by Lady Irvine and then by the Duke of Norfolk)

COMMENTARIES

The Irish patriot whose death is mourned (line 21-31) is perhaps Robert Emmet,[7] to whom Southey, Moore, and other poets wrote tributes (possibly the "lays" of line 25). Shelley had been interested in the Irish cause at least since October 1809, which is the date he appended to "The Irishman's Song" in *Original Poetry*.

Line 38 may be paraphrased as follows: "Who [now] exploits the poor so that he may dine off gold plate?" In lines 57-8 "dross" is the subject of "supplies" and "earth" its object.

Page 71. *To the Republicans of North America*

SHELLEY enclosed this poem, except for the fourth stanza, in a letter to Elizabeth Hitchener from Dublin on February 14, 1812, with the introductory comment: "Have you heard [that] a new republic is set up in Mexico? I have just written the following short tribute to its success."[8] On March 10 he wrote: "The Republic of Mexico proceeds and extends. I have seen American papers, but have not had time to read them. I only know that the spirit of Republicanism extends in South America, and that the prevailing opinion is that there will soon be no province which will recognize the ancient dynasty of Spain."[9]

The reference is to the revolution in Mexico led first by Father Miguel Hidalgo y Costilla, who in 1810 gathered an army of some 80,000 peasants and captured several cities (a rebellion still celebrated by a national holiday in Mex-

---

[7] See Commentary to "On Robert Emmet's tomb," above, p. 196.
[8] Shelley, *Complete Works*, VIII, 272.
[9] *Ibid.*, p. 292.

ico). The following year he was defeated in battle and executed by the Spanish authorities. But the struggle was continued by another member of the lower clergy, Father José María Morelos y Pavón. In 1812 Morelos and his peasant army seized considerable territory, capturing Oaxaca in November; in September 1813 a congress was convened and in November Mexican independence was proclaimed. Two years later, however, Morelos was executed and the revolutionary congress dissolved.

As the poem was first written in February 1812 and independence was not proclaimed until November 1813, presumably Shelley had seen in the "American papers" a manifesto of liberty issued during the course of the struggle.

The title, as the Textual Notes indicate, is puzzling. In the letter the poem has no title. In the Notebook Shelley first wrote "To the Republicans of New Spain" (the Viceroyalty of New Spain being the official name for all the Spanish colonies of Central and North America). He then wrote "outh" through part of "New Spain," but neglected to change the long sweeping capital "N." This gives us "Nouth," and an opportunity to try to guess whether Shelley meant North or South. Of the two "North" seems preferable: if Shelley had finally settled on "South" he would surely have changed the initial capital "N"; "New Spain" indicates that he was still thinking primarily of North America (the Spanish possessions in South America were the Viceroyalties of New Granada, Peru, and La Plata). However, as his letter of March 10 shows, he was interested also in the revolutions in South America, and this interest, too, is expressed in the poem: Mount Cotopaxi (line 21) is not in Mexico but in South America (Ecuador). The curious hybrid "Nouth" probably reflects this dual interest. Mount Cotopaxi, we might note, is an active volcano, and, hence, makes a fitting revolutionary symbol.[1]

Why did Shelley change the title from "New Spain" to "North America"? Perhaps because he objected to using the official Spanish title as implying colonial domination. But another factor may have entered in. Between the time of writing the poem and compiling the Notebook, the British-American War of 1812 had broken out. It may be that Shelley intended his title to hint at seditious support for North American republicans in the United States.

Lines 35-6:

> Blood may fertilize the tree
> Of new bursting Liberty

seem to echo the close of Barère de Vieuzac's speech before the French National Convention (at the trial of Louis XVI) in which he demanded the death penalty: "The tree of liberty grows only when watered by the blood of tyrants."[2] The fourth stanza, which contains these lines, may have been composed later than the rest. The first three stanzas are written with fairly thick ink strokes, the last two with thin ones. Shelley may, of course, simply have stopped to sharpen his pen or pick up a new one as he copied, but it is curious that this fourth stanza is omitted in the letter to Elizabeth Hitchener. The striking line "Slow to Peace and swift to blood" could serve as the epitaph of many a

---

[1] And possibly it inspired a passage in *The Revolt of Islam* (II, xiv); see G. M. Matthews, "A Volcano's Voice in Shelley," *A Journal of English Literary History*, XXIV (September 1957), 199-200.

[2] The same thought had been expressed by Thomas Jefferson in a letter to W. S. Smith, November 13, 1787: "The tree of liberty must be refreshed from time to time with the blood of patriots and tyrants. It is its natural manure."

"tyrant." The "desolated world" of the final stanza is perhaps echoed in the fall of Jupiter in *Prometheus Unbound:*

> This desolated world, and thee, and me,
> The conqueror and the conquered, and the wreck
> Of that for which they combated.[3]

Page 73. Written at Cwm Ellan[4]

"CWM ELAN," near Rhayader in southern Wales, was the ten-thousand-acre estate of Shelley's cousin Thomas Grove. Shelley was at Cwm Elan on two occasions, in the summer of 1811, without Harriet, and in the spring of 1812, with Harriet. That this poem was written on the first of these visits can be seen by comparing it with a poem which was written on the second, "The Retrospect."

In "The Retrospect," as its title implies, Shelley is looking back on his first visit. In it he describes, for instance, that aversion to daylight and love for night expressed in "Written at Cwm Ellan":

> For day with me, was time of woe
> When even tears refused to flow.

Something of both the mood and the natural background of "Written at Cwm Ellan" appears in a comment in a letter to Elizabeth Hitchener from Cwm Elan on July 26, 1811:

> Nature is here marked with the most impressive character of loveliness and grandeur, *once* I was tremulously alive to tones and scenes . . . the habit of analysing feelings I fear does not agree with this . . . Rocks, piled on

---

[3] *Prometheus Unbound,* III, i, 77-9.
[4] In his letters Shelley spells the word "Elan"; so, too, do the road guides of the time. In other sources it is sometimes spelled "Elian."

each other to an immense height, and clouds intersecting them, in other places waterfalls midst the umbrage of a thousand shadowy trees form the principal features of the scenery. I am not wholly uninfluenced by its magic in my lonely walks, but I long for a thunderstorm —[5]

"Written at Cwm Ellan" has to be considered in conjunction with "Dark Spirit of the desert rude" and "Death-spurning rocks!"

Page 74. To Death

WHILE Shelley and Hogg were at Oxford, Shelley presented him with five short manuscripts, two of prose pieces (one of them a translation), three of poems.[6] Among the poetry was a manuscript of the first 48 lines of "To Death." This manuscript (which is now in The Carl H. Pforzheimer Library)[7] is on a single sheet, written on both sides, and its final line ("To that mysterious strand") is at the bottom of the second page. Presumably there was a second sheet which contained the final 20 lines; but, if so, Hogg never possessed it, for he comments: "The following *unfinished* verses were written at Oxford; they have never been published."[8] Thus there were at least two early manuscripts of the poem, one that Shelley gave to Hogg (with a page missing) and one that he kept. Apparently the version that he kept did not have all the changes he made in the copy given to Hogg, for of these changes only one ("ebon wing" in line 3 for "hand of fate") appears in the Notebook version. In lines 19 and 44 he retained his original wording.

---

[5] Shelley, *Complete Works*, VIII, 133.
[6] *Shelley and his Circle*, II, 644, 665-6. See also above, p. 235.
[7] *Ibid.*, pp. 641-3.
[8] Hogg, *Shelley*, I, 124. My italics (K.N.C.).

The manuscript that he kept may, then, have been an earlier version. And this appears to be so for other poems also.

Shelley and Hogg were together at Oxford from the opening of the fall term in 1810 until they were expelled on March 25, 1811, with the exception of the Christmas vacation, which ran from about December 10 to about January 22.[9] The poem would have fitted well in *The Posthumous Fragments of Margaret Nicholson*, which appeared about the middle of November, but it is not in that volume. It was, then, perhaps written later than September or October. It is not, despite Ingpen's indication, dated "1810" in the Esdaile Notebook.[1]

As the poem begins with an echo from Pope's "The Dying Christian to His Soul,"[2] it is difficult to tell who is speaking. At first the poem sounds rather like a monologue by a historical or fictional character, but further reading — in the light of Shelley's penchant for the autobiographical — shows it to be a personal poem. The "I" is Shelley and the "death" being contemplated is his own. Although a number of his early poems have a gloomy, almost suicidal note, this is particularly marked in his letters of late December 1810 and January 1811, when the final crisis in his relations with Harriet Grove took place. He apparently went to London and perhaps to Fern (in Wiltshire) in search of her. He may have been informed by her brothers of her engagement. Whatever happened, he went into a deep depression: "I have wandered in the snow for I am cold we[t] — & mad."[3] "Is suicide wrong? I slept with a loaded pis-tol & some poison last night but did not die . . .

[9] *Shelley and his Circle*, II, 659.
[1] Shelley, *Complete Works*, III, 73.
[2] Pope himself, of course, was echoing the Bible (I Corinthians: XV, 55, a passage included in the Church of England burial service).
[3] To T. J. Hogg, January 1, 1811, *Shelley and his Circle*, II, 679.

But can the dead feel.   dawns any daybeam on the night of dissolution?"[4]

In these comments (in letters to Hogg) he speaks only of his own death; in the poem he writes also of the slaughter of war (again, the Napoleonic wars), a pacifist theme with which Hogg had no sympathy.

The thought in the tangled and compressed lines from 49 to 52 seems to run somewhat as follows: It is well that Vice (vicious people) should know no pain except ("but") that of the sting of conscience ("memory"), for (the unspoken thought apparently runs) this is the worst of all; the joy of Virtue (the virtuous person) comes also from conscience.

Page 77. Dark Spirit of the desart rude

"ELLAN's foamy course" (line 10) informs us that this poem was written at Cwm Elan. Parallels with "The Retrospect" show that, like "Written at Cwm Ellan," it was a product of the 1811 visit. In "The Retrospect," Shelley tells of his former loneliness and depression and contrasts it with his present (1812) happiness with Harriet beside him:

> My darksome spirit sought. It found
> A friendless solitude around. . . .
>
> Have not your varied beauties seen
> The sunken eye, the withering mien,
> Sad traces of the unuttered pain
> That froze my heart and burned my brain?

---

[4] To T. J. Hogg, January 3, 1811, *ibid.*, p. 684. Shelley, as usual, is more affirmative about immortality in his poetry than in his letters or other prose. In the poem (lines 18-21) he exempts "love" from the power of death.

> How changed since nature's summer form
> Had last the power my grief to charm,
> Since last ye soothed my spirit's sadness —
> Strange chaos of a mingled madness![5]

Considered in this light, "Dark Spirit of the desert rude" is seen to be another precursor of *Alastor*. In *Alastor* the "spirit of solitude" is depicted as a destructive power, the young poet-hero following it helplessly to his death. The theme clearly had a powerful hold on Shelley's mind.

Shelley as a boy on the family estate had apparently led a rather lonely life, and at Eton he liked to go off for long walks either alone or with one companion. Solitude is a theme, although not a major one, in his juvenile novels. When he was left alone in London, following his expulsion from Oxford, he wrote to Hogg: "I cannot endure the horror the evil which comes to *self* in solitude."[6] But although Shelley had long had a dread of solitude, the concept of it as a destructive agent, an "alastor," perhaps first grew during these weeks at Cwm Elan in the summer of 1811.

In "Written at Cwm Ellan" and "Dark Spirit of the desert rude" Shelley is too close to this experience and insufficiently advanced as a poet to render a coherent picture. He is tormented by a spirit of solitude which he hunts but is unable to find. Looking around he sees only a "desolate Oak" (line 35). This oak was perhaps a product of the poetic imagination. Hogg wrote a poem on an oak being strangled by ivy, and sent it to Shelley, who commented on it in a letter on January 12, 1811, taking the oak as a reference to himself and the ivy to Harriet Grove.[7] Perhaps

---

[5] See above, pp. 157-8, lines 84-5, 128-35.
[6] May 8, 1811, *Shelley and his Circle*, II, 770.
[7] *Ibid.*, pp. 696-9, 705-6.

these associations came into his mind when, some seven months later, he wrote "Dark Spirit of the desart rude." The matter is further complicated by the fact that Hogg's poem (and perhaps Shelley's also) was influenced by an earlier (1798) poem by Robert Southey, "The Oak of our Fathers."[8] In his final lines Shelley gives the poem an antimonarchical twist not present in either Southey or Hogg.

Page 79. *The pale, the cold and the moony smile*

EXCEPT FOR "Falshood and Vice" and the other lines in the *Queen Mab* volume,[9] this is the only one of the Esdaile Notebook poems that Shelley himself published. And it is the only one that he published in a volume later than the period during which he compiled the Notebook, namely, in *Alastor, or The Spirit of Solitude, and Other Poems* (1816). This does not necessarily signify that he later felt it was the only poem in the Notebook worth publishing. For most of them he apparently retained no other manuscript, and those on Harriet he would have hesitated to publish after the break-up of their marriage. But the fact that he did keep another manuscript of this poem and later published it perhaps indicates special regard for it. Such regard would certainly have been justified, for of all the poems in the book this one foreshadows most surely Shelley's lyric gifts (in spite of "moony" in line 1).

When the poem appeared in the *Alastor* volume it con-

---

[8] Hogg's dependence on Southey is clear; for instance, both have images of the ivy drinking the sap of the tree. I fail, however, to note any verbal echoes from Southey in Shelley although the general concept is similar.

[9] The dedication "To Harriet ('Whose is the love')" and lines 58-69 of "To Harriet ('It is not blasphemy')."

tained a good many changes — nearly all of them for the better. For instance, the new third stanza reads as follows:

> This world is the nurse of all we know,
>   This world is the mother of all we feel,
> And the coming of death is a fearful blow,
>   To a brain unencompassed with nerves of steel;
> When all that we know, or feel, or see,
> Shall pass like an unreal mystery.

The weak first two lines are changed entirely (except for the rhyme words), the awkward and overlong "nerve-strings" is changed to "nerves," the loose and dragging "we feel and we see" is tightened into "or feel, or see," and the whole line is given a firm beat, the trite "fleet by," for instance, being changed to the simple but strong "pass." The poem is, in fact, immeasurably improved, and a study of the two texts reveals a good deal about Shelley's critical insights as well as his poetic development.

In the *Alastor* volume, the poem has no title, but it is headed thus: "There is no work, nor device, nor knowledge, nor wisdom, in the grave, whither thou goest. — ECCLESIASTES." The quotation (*Ecclesiastes,* IX, 10), however, is a taking-off point for the poem rather than an explanation of it. Shelley was not in complete agreement with the materialistic pessimism of Ecclesiastes. His view, as we have seen, was expressed in a letter to Elizabeth Hitchener on June 20, 1811: "I think I have a right to draw this inference, that neither will soul perish; that in a future existence it will lose all consciousness of having formerly lived elsewhere . . ."[1]

It is apparently this concept that Shelley has in mind in the difficult lines:

[1] Shelley, *Complete Works,* VIII, 108.

COMMENTARIES

> The secret things of the grave are there
> Where all but this body must surely be.

The body decays but the mind or soul becomes part of "the secret things" of death, that is, of those forces which preserve soul, not individually but as part of a general spirit substance existing in (line 10) "the calm of eternal day."

There is no indication in the manuscript of the date of the poem, but to judge by its merits it was probably one of the later ones. And this is supported by the fact that it is undated. (The only "later" poem which is dated is "The Voyage," 1812.) We might note also that Shelley made use of Ecclesiastes in *Queen Mab* (the opening of Canto V and its note).[2]

Page 81. Death-spurning rocks!

OPPOSITE this poem, in his copybook, Dowden makes the notation: "[?Cwm Elan Spring of 1812]," and after this Richard Garnett has written in pencil: "Probably." That Dowden and Garnett are right in linking the poem with Wales in indicated by the "jagged" rocks of the setting. But it sounds more like Shelley's first visit to Cwm Elan (1811) than his second (1812).[3] And this, as with "Written at Cwm Ellan" and "Dark Spirit of the desert rude," is supported by the similarity between the situation in the

---

[2] Ecclesiastes seems later to have been something of a favorite with Shelley; see Bennett Weaver, *Toward the Understanding of Shelley* (University of Michigan Press, 1932), pp. 21-2, 138-44; *Mary Shelley's Journal*, p. 128, January 21, 1820.

[3] See Commentary to "Dark Spirit of the desert rude," p. 207.

poem and that described the following year in looking back on the 1811 visit in "The Retrospect." For instance, lines 11-13 of this poem are similar (in content though not in style) to lines 120-4 in "The Retrospect":

> Woods, to whose depth retires to die
> The wounded echo's melody,
> And whither this lone spirit bent
> The footstep of a wild intent —

In the later poem, the "lone spirit" (the "maniac sufferer" of the earlier poem, who, in both cases, is Shelley) remembers the retreat in the woods and his impulse to suicide, and even echoes the words, "wild intent," to describe this impulse.

In looking back on this crisis Shelley assigned to it not one but a number of causes. It was not only "unrequited love," nor hurt "pride," nor loneliness, nor "broken vows," but a combination of them all. What probably happened is that the shattering events of the previous months — the breaking off of their "engagement" by Harriet Grove, the expulsion from Oxford, the conflict with his family, the involvement in London with Harriet Westbrook — all of which he had suppressed by keeping continually active — burst upon him at once amid the quiet of Cwm Elan. (We find a similar phenomenon in *Alastor*, which reflects delayed reaction to the Harriet-Mary crisis of the previous year.) But of all the factors which Shelley lists as causing the crisis, the break with Harriet Grove seems to be the most important:

> For broken vows had early quelled
> The stainless spirit's vestal flame.
> Yes! whilst the faithful bosom swelled
> Then the envenomed arrow came
> And apathy's unaltering eye
> Beamed coldness on the misery.

Harriet Grove, Shelley seems to be saying, broke off their relationship just when they were becoming most intimate. Her brother, Charles Grove, describes the break as follows: "But she became uneasy at the tone of his letters on speculative subjects, at first consulting my mother, and subsequently my father also on the subject. This led at last, though I cannot exactly tell how, to the dissolution of an engagement between Bysshe and my sister, which had previously been permitted, both by his father and mine."[4]

It was, then, not only that Harriet made the break but the manner in which she made it (in the fall of 1810) that so wounded Shelley. Her discussing his letters with her parents he regarded as a betrayal, her conformity a retreat from a principled existence. Even then, however, he did not give up hope. The worst blow apparently came in December 1810 or January 1811, when he heard that she was engaged to a young landowner, William Helyar. His suffering was clearly acute. "She is gone, she is lost to me forever," he laments to Hogg;[5] and his sister followed him when he went hunting for fear he would kill himself. During this whole critical period, from the autumn until the new year, he apparentlly felt nothing but "apathy" and "coldness" in his family and perhaps in Harriet herself. In March came the expulsion and then (in early July) a few days with the second Harriet before leaving London, followed by the "short but violent nervous illness" he informed Elizabeth Hitchener of during his first days at Cwm Elan.[6]

Shelley may have thought that his "illness" was over,

---

[4] Hogg, *Shelley*, II, 155.
[5] January 11, 1811, *Shelley and his Circle*, II, 701.
[6] To Elizabeth Hitchener, [postmark: July 15, 1811], Shelley, *Complete Works*, VIII, 124.

but as the "Retrospect" indicates, it returned and persisted, in one degree or another, throughout his stay (of about one month). And how intense it was at times the present poem bears witness. As in the "Retrospect," one has the impression that the break with Harriet Grove was the bitterest blow. What else could the "snares" of "memory" (line 14) that so torture him refer to? The "vain and bitter tears" seem to echo the letters he wrote to Hogg in January about the break: walking in the snow "cold, we[t] — & mad," sleeping with a loaded pistol,[7] and so on. We find the same suicidal despair in the poem: "why need he live to weep who does not fear to die?"

It is apparent from these poems that Shelley's attachment to Harriet Grove was deeper than has been generally realized. Peacock deprecated it,[8] but he never met Harriet Grove and did not not know Shelley at the time. Nor did Shelley (as Peacock himself makes clear) confide in him later. It may be objected that if he was still brooding over Harriet Grove in July he could not have been in love with Harriet Westbrook when he eloped with her in August. But to a young man of eighteen much is possible. Furthermore, we do not know how much of the brooding in July was caused by the loss of love and how much by hurt pride and jealousy. Shelley tended to react violently whenever his will was blocked. "To Harriet ('It is not blasphemy')" indicates that by July his actual love for Harriet Grove was fading under the glow of his new interest in Harriet Westbrook.

Shelley's feelings are so overwhelming that the poem is hardly a polished performance; but for all its lack of dis-

---

[7] To Hogg, January 1, 1811, *Shelley and his Circle*, II, 679; to Hogg, January 3, 1811, *ibid.*, p. 684.
[8] Peacock, *Memoirs*, p. 60.

(line 23) and the burning of the hearts of dead revolutionaries, must however, refer not to Emmet's small and abortive *Putsch* but to the rebellion of the United Irishmen, led by Wolfe Tone, in 1798. Shelley felt a special kinship with the United Irishmen, for many of them were not only nationalists but anti-clerical revolutionaries, and he made a special effort in Dublin to find those who were still alive. He doubtless received many firsthand accounts of the rebellion from his Irish friend Catherine Nugent, of whom Harriet wrote: "She has felt most severely the miseries of her country, in which she has been a very active member. She visited all the Prisons in the time of the Rebellion, to exhort the people to have courage and hope. She says it was a most dreadful task; but it was her duty, and she would not shrink from the performance of it."[2] The bloody suppression of this rebellion, by Castlereagh, was notorious:

> Cold-blooded, smooth-faced, placid miscreant!
> Dabbling its sleek young hands in Erin's gore.[3]

"The Tombs" is written in the Southeyan irregular blank verse which Shelley, as we have noted, apparently first used at Keswick, that is, in the months immediately preceding his trip to Ireland. The "phantasmal world" (line 20) with its "brute and morbid" shapes expresses a theory of the transitory nature of social evil which we find in Shelley's later poetry (for instance, in *Hellas*). It is most clearly expressed in his fragmentary novel *The Assassins* (1814): "The perverse, and vile, and vicious — what were they? Shapes of some unholy vision, moulded by the spirit of Evil, which the sword of the merciful destroyer should sweep from this beautiful world. Dreamy nothings; phantasms of misery and mischief, that hold their death-like

[2] March 18, 1812, *ibid.*, p. 299.   [3] Byron, *Don Juan*, Dedication, XII.

cipline it has a kind of jagged power, conveying a sense of wild, adolescent suffering.

The initial image of the rocks gives more of a picture of geological vistas than was usual at the time. The work and theories of Leibniz, Whiston, Cuvier, and others were providing the first clues to the immense age of the earth, and Shelley was an avid follower of the latest scientific theories.[9]

The reference to the blasted and decaying oak tree both in this poem (lines 6-7) and in "Dark Spirit of the desert rude" (lines 34-7) perhaps indicates that both poems were composed in the same period. It may also, as we have seen, have had associations in Shelley's mind with his rejection by Harriet Grove.

"Way-worn wanderer" (line 23) is apparently an echo from Southey's "The Soldier's Wife," which begins: "Weary way-wanderer, languid and sick at heart." "Weary, way-worn wanderer" appears in Edgar Allan Poe's "To Helen."

Page 83. The Tombs

THE REFERENCE to Erin in line 22 indicates that this poem was written in Dublin in 1812. Perhaps it is a kind of companion piece to "On Robert Emmet's tomb," which Shelley referred to in a letter to Elizabeth Hitchener shortly after he left Ireland.[1]

The line "When blood and chains defiled the land"

---

[9] King-Hele, *Shelley*, p. 158; Grabo, *A Newton among Poets*, pp. 175-80; Cameron, *The Young Shelley*, pp. 247-8, 393-4.

[1] [?April 16, 1812], Shelley, *Complete Works*, VIII, 309. See also Commentary, p. 196, above.

state on glittering thrones, and in the loathsome dens of poverty."[4] He considered social evil "phantasmal" because it rests ultimately on the ideas — Opinion — which holds the social structure together:

> Opinion is more frail
> Than yon dim cloud now fading on the moon
> Even while we gaze, though it awhile avail
> To hide the orb of truth — and every throne
> Of Earth or Heaven, though shadow, rests thereon.[5]

If people could see through the falsity of these ideas society would be renovated:

> it is our will
> That thus enchains us to permitted ill.[6]

Evidently Shelley had the seeds of these concepts by 1812 (some of them, as we shall see, by 1809).

Page 85. *To Harriet* ("It is not blasphemy")

DOWDEN in his copybook makes the following notes on this poem:

> ?1812 8 lines have been pub^d from W Garnett's transcript of a Boscombe MS.
> Note the traces of Wordsworths *Tintern Abbey*
> Perhaps when Shelley came by Chepstow from Cwm Elan to Lynmouth, summer of 1812 he saw Tintern Abbey & was impressed by Wordsworths poem.
> I think this is a Lynmouth poem: its tone is like that of the Sonnet on Aug. 1. 1812.

He then lists several parallels with "Tintern Abbey."

---

[4] Shelley, *Complete Works*, VI, 164.
[5] *The Revolt of Islam*, VIII, ix. See below, p. 253.
[6] *Julian and Maddalo*, lines 170-1.

That Southey showed Shelley a copy of *Lyrical Ballads* at Keswick is most probable; and *Paterson's Roads* (1811) shows that the coach road to Chepstow passed near Tintern Abbey.[7] From Chepstow, Shelley went to Lynmouth, arriving there late in June 1812. Moreover, as the next poem in this volume is also to Harriet and is dated August 1, 1812, it is probable that "To Harriet ('It is not blasphemy')" was written at about the same time, that is, in the summer of 1812 in Devon.

Twelve of the final lines (lines 58-69) Shelley published in one of the Notes to *Queen Mab* as a separate poem on time.[8] In these lines Shelley, as he indicates in his note, is indebted to a passage in William Godwin's *Political Justice*: "The indolent man reclines for hours in the shade; and, though his mind be perpetually at work, the silent progress of time is unobserved. But, when acute pain, or uneasy expectation, obliges consciousness to recur with unusual force, the time appears insupportably long."[9]

Dowden notes that eight lines (lines 5-13) had been published from Richard Garnett's "transcript of a Boscombe MS." "A Boscombe MS," as we have seen, refers to a manuscript in the possession of Shelley's son, Sir Percy Florence Shelley, who lived at Boscombe Manor, near Bournemouth. The Boscombe text for these lines is identical with that in the Esdaile Notebook.[1]

---

[7] We might note also that when William Godwin went through Chepstow on his way to see Shelley he visited Tintern Abbey. (Journal entries for Sept. 11, 12, 1812, Paul, *Godwin*, II, 209.)

[8] Shelley, *Complete Works*, I, 157. Note to VIII, 203.

[9] Godwin, *Political Justice*, I, 412.

[1] See Commentary to "The solitary," above, p. 199, and to "How eloquent are eyes!," below, p. 238. The Boscombe manuscript lines were published by H. B. Forman (Shelley, Forman ed., 1877, p. 359) with the following note: "These lines were given by Mr. Rossetti from a transcript of Mr. Garnett's, taken from one of the Boscombe MSS. The date affixed by Mr. Rossetti is 1811."

COMMENTARIES

Compared with Shelley's other verse of this period, the poem is technically quite skillful, its echoes of Wordsworth (foreshadowing those in the opening lines of *Alastor*) no more than the usual dependence of the forming poetic mind upon models. It does, however, seem a curiously low-keyed poem for a young husband to write to a young wife, especially a husband capable of such intensity as Shelley. One has the impression of an immature relationship, one of "friendship" (line 42) rather than passion,[2] and accompanied by some condescension:

> when some years have added judgement's store
> To all thy woman sweetness, all the fire
> Which throbs in thine enthusiast heart . . .

It seems also that the poem was written after a quarrel or misunderstanding, although not a serious one, and that Shelley was trying to make up:

>   wilt thou not turn
> Those spirit-beaming eyes and look on me . . .
>   but to feel
> *One* soul-reviving kiss . . .

Perhaps the most interesting lines biographically (and philosophically) come at the beginning:

>   O Thou,
> Whose dear love gleamed upon the gloomy path
> Which this lone spirit travelled, drear and cold,
> Yet swiftly leading to those awful limits
> Which mark the bounds of Time and of the space
> When Time shall be no more . . .

If we compare this with the poetry that reflects Shelley's feelings at Cwm Elan in July 1811 and his joyous letter

---

[2] For a different view, see White, *Shelley*, I, 244-5.

on August 3 to Hogg announcing that Harriet had "thrown herself upon *my* protection,"[3] Shelley seems in these lines to be saying that he was rescued from a state of suicidal gloom by Harriet's love.

Shelley in some of his early poems, as Bennett Weaver has commented, "seems to have fixed his mind upon intimations of eternity."[4] It is, however, not always easy to grasp his concept of the relation between time and eternity. "The space / When Time shall be no more" in the above lines is perhaps as close as he comes to a definition. ("Space" is used in a temporal sense, that is, the space of time after which time shall be no more.) But even this does not help us much when confronted with the image in a letter from Ireland, in which Time is called on to "burst the barriers of Eternity."[5] The difficulty continues throughout Shelley's later works as well, culminating in the much-discussed passage in *Prometheus Unbound* where the "past hours" "bear Time to his tomb in eternity."

Page 88. Sonnet. *To Harriet on her birth day*

HARRIET WESTBROOK was born on August 1, 1795.[6] This sonnet, then, was written for her seventeenth birthday. "Somewhat" in line 2 is used in a substantive sense. One would gather from the final line, as from the beginning of

---

[3] *Shelley and his Circle*, II, 856.

[4] "Shelley: The First Beginnings," *Philological Quarterly*, XXXII (April 1953), 186. We find a similar obsession with eternity also in Blake and the young Coleridge.

[5] To Elizabeth Hitchener, February 14, 1812, Shelley, *Complete Works*, VIII, 271. In some of these concepts — and others in these poems — Shelley might have been indebted to the early poems of Coleridge, particularly "Religious Musings."

[6] Ingpen, *Shelley in England*, p. 265 n.

the previous poem, that Harriet (and Eliza) had been pressing Shelley on his anti-religious views.

Page 89. Sonnet. *To a balloon, laden with Knowledge*

SEE Commentary to the next poem, "Sonnet. On launching some bottles."

Page 90. Sonnet. *On launching some bottles*

FROM Ireland, Shelley, as we have seen, went to Wales, and from Wales to Devon. He arrived in Devon on about June 24, 1812, and settled (until late August) at the seaside village of Lynmouth near Linton on the west coast. There he worked on his *Letter to Lord Ellenborough* (a defense of the imprisoned republican journalist Daniel Isaac Eaton) and *Queen Mab*. But he did not devote all his time to writing.

On August 19 his Irish servant, Daniel Healey, was arrested and sentenced to six months' imprisonment for circulating the broadside *Declaration of Rights*, which Shelley had written in Dublin. On the same day, Henry Drake, Town Clerk of nearby Barnstaple, wrote an agitated letter to Lord Sidmouth, the Home Secretary:

> The Mayor has also been informed that Mr. Shelley has been seen frequently to go out in a Boat a short distance from Land and drop some Bottles into the Sea, and that at one time he was observed to wade into the Water and drop a Bottle which afterwards drifting ashore was picked up, and on being broken was found to contain a seditious

Paper, the Contents of which the Mayor has not yet been able to ascertan but will apprize your Lordship immediately on learning further particulars.[7]

The "seditious paper" turned out to be "The Devil's Walk" (imitated from similar verses by Southey and Coleridge) Shelley's *jeu d'esprit* on the Prince Regent and other matters. The Home Secretary endorsed Drake's letter: "Recommend that Mr. Shelley's proceedings be watched if he is still at Linton. It would also be desirable to procure the address of his different correspondents, to whom he writes, from the post-office."[8]

In September, the Home Secretary, whose office presided over a network of informers worthy of a Persian satrap, received a second communication, this one from John Hopkins, Inspecting Commander of Revenue Cruisers, Western District, enclosing a copy of Shelley's *Declaration of Rights,* one of his ships "having found the same in a Sealed Wine Bottle, floating near the Entrance of Milford Haven on the 10th Inst." The Inspecting Commander, after making inquiries, found that a similar bottle with similarly explosive contents had been picked up a few weeks previously near Lynmouth by one of his ships.[9]

The "knowledge," then, with which the bottles celebrated in this sonnet were freighted, was presumably that to be garnered from *Declaration of Rights* and *The Devil's Walk.* So far as we know Shelley had no other printed works at the time small enough to place in a bottle. The balloon, if big enough, could also have carried the *Letter to Lord Ellenborough* (which was printed by August 4).

---

[7] Peck, *Shelley,* I, 271.
[8] William Michael Rossetti, "Shelley in 1812-13," *Fortnightly Review,* n.s., IX (January 1871), 77.
[9] Hughes, *The Nascent Mind of Shelley,* p. 156.

COMMENTARIES

The "knowledge" in the bottles apparently traveled far and wide. Milford Haven is in Wales across the Bristol Channel from Lynmouth. The balloon presumably was wafted inland.

Page 91. Sonnet. On waiting for a wind

A SECOND letter from Henry Drake, Town Clerk of Barnstaple, to Lord Sidmouth, of September 9, 1812, opens as follows:

> Referring your Lordship to my letter of 20th ult., and in addition to the information therein contained, I beg to inform your Lordship that, not being enabled to obtain here sufficient information respecting Mr. Shelley, I went to Lymouth, where he resided, and returned yesterday. On my arrival there, I found he, with his family, after attempting in vain to cross the Channel to Swansea from that place, had lately left Lymouth for Ilfracombe; and, on my following him there, found he had gone to Swansea, where I imagine he at present is.[1]

If Shelley wished to sail from the village of Lynmouth to Wales he must have intended to hire a fishing boat or similar craft. From Ilfracombe, however, he would have had no trouble, for according to *Paterson's Roads* (1811), packet-boats sailed from Ilfracomb to Swansea every Monday and Thursday.

Whether this sonnet was written during the first attempts to leave from Lynmouth or later at Ilfracombe we do not know (although Lynmouth seems more likely), but it must, in either case, have been written during the last

---

[1] William Michael Rossetti, "Shelley in 1812-13," *Fortnightly Review*, n.s., IX (January, 1871), 78.

(223)

days of Shelley's stay in Devon. And these dates we know fairly accurately.

On Saturday, September 19, William Godwin, arriving at Lynmouth to stay with the Shelleys, received a shock. "The Shelleys," he wrote in dismay to his wife, "have gone! have been gone these three weeks."[2] Now, Godwin was a precise man about dates; for instance, he also informs us that the Shelleys "had lived here nine weeks and three days." "These three weeks," then, is probably pretty close to the mark; and when we note that he wrote on a Saturday and that the packets for Swansea sailed on Mondays and Thursdays, the probability is that the Shelleys left for Swansea on Thursday, August 27. If we go back a further nine weeks and three days we can set the date of their arrival at Lynmouth at about June 22.

This sonnet, then, was probably written between, say, August 24 and 27, 1812.

That Shelley's activities in Devon were not so impractical as some observers have thought is shown by the seriousness with which they were taken by the authorities. The situation in England in 1812 was explosive; there were outbreaks of frame breaking and food riots (including some in west Devon) and miners' strikes in Cornwall.

Page 92. *To Harriet ("Harriet! thy kiss to my soul is dear")*

THERE SEEMS to be no specific indication of date in this poem. It is, however, placed with the Devon poems, and the final stanza could refer most appropriately to Shelley's

[2] Paul, *Godwin*, II, 211.

anti-government activities in Devon. Perhaps these had even frightened the "enthusiast" Harriet (certainly they must have frightened Eliza) and she may have remonstrated with Shelley. That there was trouble developing with Eliza may be implied in the "with me to live" of line 24, which is perhaps a hint — made specific in "To Harriet ('Oh Harriet, love like mine')" — that Eliza might leave the household.

Shelley's later violent hatred of Eliza, then, may have had roots that went back almost to the beginning of the marriage. From at least the summer of 1812 on, there may have been considerable discord in the household.

Although some of the phrasing is trite, the poem has a musical lilt that anticipates the later lyrics (for instance, some in *Prometheus Unbound*) and indicates 1812 rather than 1811 as the date of composition. So, too, does its placing in the volume; it comes in what is apparently a run of 1812 (Devon) poems. It seems to show more genuine and spontaneous feeling for Harriet than the more elaborate "To Harriet ('It is not blasphemy')."

Page 94. Mary to the Sea-Wind

DOWDEN in his copybook comment first suggested that this might be "one of the Oxford poems to Mary"; then, below this, he wrote, in darker ink and perhaps some time later: "or Lynmouth 1812." Of the two, the second suggestion is the more likely. The story told in the Oxford poems (of betrayal and suicide) does not agree either in situation or in mood with this poem; the Mary of the Oxford poems is not near the sea. The sea and the "sea-wind" suggest Devon. There is a Mary in "The Voyage," which was written in Devon in August 1812. This Mary's husband is at sea, as is the lover of "Mary to the Sea-Wind."

Page 95. *A retrospect of Times of Old*

THIS POEM, strange though it may sound to modern ears, is part of a genre popular in Shelley's day as a result of the archaeological discoveries which followed European conquests in Asia and Africa. Shelley, as one might expect, is not satisfied with sentimental moralizing on past glories but gives the genre a political twist.

Dowden, for some reason, made no general comment about the poem in his copybook, but he did in his biography of Shelley:

> Here also on the Devon coast was probably written "A Retrospect of Times of Old" — a rhymed piece, also unpublished, having much in common with those earlier pages of "Queen Mab," which picture the fall of empires, and celebrate the oblivion that has overtaken the old rulers of men and lords of the earth."[3]

Dowden's reasoning here is certainly sound. When we turn to the second canto of *Queen Mab,* in which Shelley begins his survey of the past ("The Past, the Present, and the Future are the grand and comprehensive topics of this Poem," he informed Hookham[4]), the general parallel with this "retrospect" is unmistakable even though the style is different and no notable specific parallels appear, for example:

> Behold, the Fairy cried,
> Palmyra's ruined palaces! . . .

---

[3] Dowden, *Shelley*, I, 285.
[4] To Hookham, August 18, [1812], Shelley, *Complete Works*, IX, 19.

COMMENTARIES

> Monarchs and conquerors there
> Proud o'er prostrate millions trod—
> The earthquakes of the human race;
> Like them, forgotten when the ruin
> That marks their shock is past.[5]

On August 18, 1812, Shelley informed Hookham that he did not begin *Queen Mab* until he arrived in England—on or about June 22. As he also informed him that he was then on "the Present," he must have completed "the Past." He left Devon at the end of August.

There is one other piece of evidence which indicates that "A retrospect of Times of Old" was composed during these weeks on the "Devon coast." In his letter of August 18 Shelley thanks Hookham for having sent him Peacock's *The Genius of the Thames, Palmyra and other Poems*. "The conclusion of 'Palmyra,'" he felt, was "the finest piece of poetry I ever read." In the later stanzas of *Palmyra* we find such passages as:

> These arches, dim in parting day,
> These dust-defiled entablatures,
> These shafts, whose prostrate pride around
> The desert-weed entwines its wreath,
> These capitals that strew the ground,
> Their shattered colonnades beneath,
> These pillars, white in lengthening files,
> Grey tombs, and broken peristyles,
> May yet, through many an age, retain
> The pomp of Thedmor's wasted reign:
> But Time still shakes, with giant-tread,
> The marble city of the dead,
> That crushed at last, a shapeless heap,
> Beneath the drifted sands shall sleep.

[5] *Queen Mab*, II, 109-10, 121-5.

In *Queen Mab*, Shelley writes of the ruins of Palmyra. One source of information about Palmyra available both to him and to Peacock was Count Volney's *Les Ruines* (1791), the influence of which on *Queen Mab* was established as long ago as 1896 by the German scholar L. Kellner.[6] Its influence on the "retrospect" also seems probable; for example:

> Here, said I to myself, an opulent city once flourished; this was the seat of a powerful empire. Yes, these places, now so desert, a living multitude formerly animated, and an active crowd went here and there about streets which at present are so solitary. Within these walls, where a mournful silence reigns, the noise of the arts and the shouts of joy and festivity continually resounded. These heaps of marble formed regular palaces; these prostrate pillars were the majestic ornaments of temples; these crumbling galleries present the outlines of public squares.[7]

Although Peacock and Volney concern themselves with the ruins of Palmyra (in Syria), Shelley does not appear to be discussing any particular ruined city or its history; rather, he seems to be giving a composite picture. True, he mentions Persepolis in his first footnote, but the "Simoon" of line 25 (the same as the "tainted blast" of line 8) is a supposedly harmful desert wind, whereas Persepolis is on the Iranian high plateau. Furthermore, as Shelley indicates in his footnote, the story of the king who murders his brother and commits suicide is not based on an actual historical episode (although it seems generally similar to the story of Cambyses). His objective is to show

---

[6] L. Kellner, "Shelley's Queen Mab and Volney's Les Ruines," *Englische Studien*, XXII (1896), 9-40.

[7] C. F. Volney, *The Ruins, or A Survey of the Revolutions of Empires* (London, 1921), p. 3.

COMMENTARIES

modern "conquerors" the vanity of their conquests by revealing the downfall of past kings and empires. He wishes also to emphasize the greater corruption of the modern representatives of the species (who have no "compunction"). What would have immediately caught his readers' attention (and perhaps the Attorney General's) if the poem had been published is the inclusion of the British national heroes "Wellington and Nelson" among the "legal murderers" and "scourges of mankind." Wellington's Spanish campaign was assailed in *The Devil's Walk*. Nelson he abhorred particularly for his bombardment of Copenhagen. (See above, page 127.)

Page 98. The Voyage

As THIS POEM is not easy to follow, it might be well to outline the narrative. The poem opens with a small ship (line 18), which has come through a storm, moving along a rocky shore toward a port. The ship is carrying four passengers: two old sailors, who have gone through many hardships together (lines 70-111); a "landsman" (line 114) of unnamed occupation, but apparently connected with business; and a young idealist (line 149). The first 220 lines of the poem deal with the voyage and the life stories of these passengers. At line 221, what is, in effect, a second poem begins; it centers on the seizure of a sailor by the press gang in the port after the vessel has docked.

The first 69 lines of the poem are introductory. They refer back to the storm (which, we later learn — line 219 — was "a night of horror") and discuss the thoughts of the passengers in general as they sail along the shore (lines 18-21):

> That little vessel's company
> Beheld the sight of loveliness—
> The dark grey rocks that towered
> Above the slumbering sea.

The "young and happy spirits" (line 40) who "Along the world are voyaging" does not refer to the ship's passengers but is a general reference to people on the voyage of life (as in *Alastor*). The life stories of the four passengers begin at line 70:

> Two honest souls were they
> And oft had braved in fellowship the storm.

That the "two honest souls" were sailors appears both from the nature of their adventures together and from Shelley's note (to line 109) on the moral superiority of "old sailors" from small ships to navy men. "The storm" is not the storm of the night before, nor is the "fragile bark" (line 81) the ship on which the passengers are sailing; both refer to an earlier incident in the lives of the two sailors.

The "landsman" (line 114) is a man who once had some idealism, or at least human, selfless feeling, but who married for money and became corrupted (lines 133-7):

> He bound himself to an unhappy woman;
> Not of those pure and heavenly links that Love
>   'Twines round a feeling to Freedom dear,
> But of vile gold, cank'ring the breast it binds,
> Corroding and inflaming every thought.

The young idealist (line 149), gazing out at the bright sea, falls asleep and has a dream (lines 162-213). He dreams that he and his beloved (line 198) and a "Sister" (line 210) are in a boat which is piloted by the evil landsman to a barren island (line 167). In the dream he is ill and the landsman piles a large rock upon his "feeble breast" (line 178). But like the Wandering Jew he does not die. He faints. When he regains consciousness — all still within the dream — his beloved, who is also enfeebled, is bending over him (line 198). Beside them (line 210) is the body of the "Sister" (whether his or hers is not stated), stabbed by the evil landsman (lines 186-8). The young idealist awakes and sees that the ship is coming into port (line 215).

The port is described as a "populous town" with "two dark rocks" on either side of the harbor; and the second part of the poem opens. On the quayside is the press gang. A sailor "absent many years" (line 237) is hurrying to join his wife, Mary, and his children. As he reaches his door they seize him to force him into service in the army or navy (lines 248-61). A "sleek and pampered town's man" (line 263) standing by tells him that his wife and all his children but one are dead; that one is now a "parish apprentice." The poem ends with 31 lines attacking "Politicians," rich landlords,[8] and others responsible for such injustices.

This second part, one might suspect, was originally a separate poem. It is in a different verse form, and the content, after a rather tacked-on introduction, has no relationship to the first part. Moreover, the boat puts into port in the morning (lines 215-20), but when the press gang seizes the sailor, apparently but shortly afterward, it is night (lines 243-4).

Shelley does not specify a definite locale. He seems, in fact, to be attempting, in the first part, to create a dreamlike atmosphere, which might have been dispelled by realistic detail. It seems clear, however, that some of his experiences in the preceding months entered into the poem.

---

[8] See also *Queen Mab*, III, 106-17. Lines 290-98 may contain some echo of the story of Jesus and the rich young man. (*Matthew*, XIX, 16-24.)

On their voyage to Dublin from Whitehaven (in February), Shelley informed Godwin: "We were driven by a storm completely to the North of Ireland, in our passage from the Isle of Man. Harriet (my wife) and Eliza (my sister-in-law) were very much fatigued, after twenty-eight hours' tossing in a galliot during a violent gale."[9]

On the return trip, Shelley, Harriet, and Eliza left Dublin for Holyhead on April 4. Owing to adverse winds — Harriet informed Catherine Nugent — a voyage which should have taken twelve hours took thirty-six: "We did not arrive at Holyhead till near 2 o'clock on Monday morning. Then we had above a mile to walk over rock and stone in a pouring rain before we could get to the inn. The night was dark and stormy; but the sailors had lanterns, or else I think it would have been better to have remained on board. As soon as we could get supper we did. We did not eat anything for 36 hours, all the time we were on board, and immediately began *upon meat*; you will think this very extraordinary, but Percy and my sister suffered so much by the voyage, and we were so weakened by the vegetable system, that had they still continued it would have been seeking a premature grave."[1] From Holyhead they went to Barmouth, and then — to take up the story with Shelley: "We came from Barmouth to Aberystwyth, thirty miles, in an open boat."[2]

Much of this sounds like raw material for the poem. The picture of the young idealist, with a wife, and sister (or sister-in-law), on a ship following a stormy voyage perhaps is telescoped from the stormy night crossing from Dublin to Holyhead and the following trip in the small

---

[9] To Godwin, February 24, 1812, Shelley, *Complete Works*, VIII, 279. See also to Elizabeth Hitchener, February 13, 1812, *ibid.*, p. 269.
[1] April 16, [1812], *ibid.*, p. 310.
[2] To Elizabeth Hitchener, ?April 16, 1812, *ibid.*, p. 307.

ship down the coast (the ship in "The Voyage" appears to be small). The harbor into which the ship enters is generally similar to that at Aberystwyth, which has mountains towering behind it. And some of it may have come from the more severe storm in February—which is probably also the source for the vivid description of the storm endured by the two old sailors (lines 74-81).

Shelley had, as we saw in "a Tale of Society as it is," long deprecated the activities of the press gang. In Dublin he had been interested in the case of one Redfern, who had been impressed into the British Army in Portugal.

> An Irishman has been torn from his wife and family in Lisbon, because he was an expatriat[e], and compelled to serve as a common soldier in the Portuguese Army, by that monster of antipatriotic inhumanity *Beresford*, the idol of the belligerents. You will soon see a copy of his letter, and soon hear of my or Sir F. Burdett's exertions in his favor. He *shall* be free. This nation shall awaken. It is attended with circumstances singularly characteristic of cowardice and tyranny. My blood boils to madness to think of it.[3]

A letter from Redfern had been printed (perhaps by Shelley himself), and Shelley took copies to England for distribution. He apparently also attempted to get Sir Francis Burdett, the Reform leader, to take up the case in Parliament.

There seems little doubt that Shelley's experiences in this case wove their way into his treatment of the sailor and the press gang. In fact, the reference (lines 230-3) to the king in his "dotage" who controls the press gang from his "distant land" may have been suggested by the arrest of Redfern by the subjects of George III in Portugal.

Shelley dated the poem August 1812. It was in that

---

[3] To Elizabeth Hitchener, March 10, 1812, *ibid.*, p. 290.

month also that he sent *Queen Mab* to Hookham.[4] The similarity is most marked, both in style and in content, between "The Voyage" and *Queen Mab*: in style, the same mixture of Southeyan unrhymed lyrical measure and regular blank verse; in content, the attack on the press gang and political corruption.

The reference to Necessity in the note to line 109 is the first in Shelley's works to a doctrine that was to become central to much of his greatest poetry, including *Prometheus Unbound* and *The Triumph of Life*; his definition of it here is the most succinct he ever made:

> the soul of Nature...
> Blind, changeless, and eternal in her paths.

In a Note to *Queen Mab* he elaborates:

> He who asserts the doctrine of Necessity means that, contemplating the events which compose the moral and material universe, he beholds only an immense and uninterrupted chain of causes and effects, no one of which could occupy any other place than it does occupy, or act in any other place than it does act.

The attack in the same note on the "habits of coercion and subjection imbued" into the sailors on the "King's ships" is a reflection of a campaign at the time against brutality in the navy. Part of the regeneration of society envisaged in *Prometheus Unbound* was the abolition of this brutality; ships are seen as

> Tracking their path no more by blood and groans,
> And desolation, and the mingled voice
> Of slavery and command.

The theory of the complementary evils of "coercion and subjection," "slavery and command," are embodied also in the lines (129-32):

---

[4] To Thomas Hookham, August 18, [1812], *ibid.*, IX, 19.

> Yes! in the dawn of life,
> When guileless confidence and unthinking love
> Dilate all hearts but those
> Which servitude or power has cased in steel.

Shelley's argument is that the natural channels of love are dammed up among the upper classes by power, among the lower by oppression.

Page 108. A Dialogue

THIS POEM was among five manuscripts that Shelley apparently gave in a group to Hogg at Oxford.[5] Four were kept by Hogg and retained after his death by the Hogg family. They are now in The Carl H. Pforzheimer Library.[6] The fifth, that of "A Dialogue," was given or sold by Hogg to the book and manuscript collector Dawson Turner in 1834. In a letter accompanying the manuscript Hogg wrote: "I now send you a poem, or rather a rough draft of part of a poem, by his hand, and from his head and heart. The papers amongst which it was found, and other circumstances, lead me to believe that it was written in 1810, when the young poet was but seventeen or eighteen years old. It is doubtless unpublished, and of a more early date than any of his published poems; on all accounts, therefore, it is most interesting."[7] In the sales catalogue of Dawson Turner's library in 1859 we find the following notation: "Shelley, P.B., 2 A.L.s. and 8 pages 4to. of Aut. Poems, etc. 1810-1815." As Turner is unlikely to have had any other

---

[5] See Commentary to "To Death," above, p. 205.
[6] *Shelley and his Circle*, SC 114, 120, 123, 124.
[7] Hogg, *Shelley*, I, 123.

manuscript by Shelley as early as one of 1810, we can take it that this item included Hogg's manuscript of "A Dialogue." Who bought it or where it is at present does not appear to be known.

Shelley did not give Hogg his sole copy, for he obviously had one when he was compiling this volume of poems. And that the manuscript Shelley kept contained a similar text, although not exactly the same as that given to Hogg, is shown by Shelley's footnote, in which he tells us that when the poem was originally written the first part of line 25 read "What waits for the good?" Hogg, in his life of Shelley, prints: "Nought waits for the good." "What" in our manuscript is quite clear. It is possible, of course, that Hogg misread "Nought" for "What" in his manuscript, but this seems unlikely, for Hogg was quite skilled in reading Shelley's hand.

By "the papers among which it was found," Hogg doubtless means the other four manuscripts given to him by Shelley at the same time. Shelley, it would seem, gave them to him in January 1811 when they returned to Oxford after the Christmas holidays.[8] Hogg apparently assumed that all the manuscripts were written in 1810. But of the two dates given for "A Dialogue"—1809 by Shelley, 1810 by Hogg—Shelley's is preferable. In style the poem is rather like "The Irishman's Song" in *Original Poetry*, which is dated October 1809, and this style, in turn, reflects the influence of Scott ("Young Lochinvar") and Campbell ("Lochiel's Warning") on Shelley's earliest poetry. If 1809 is correct, the poem can hardly have been written before the latter months of the year, for it was apparently in these months that Shelley's anti-war and anti-monarchical feelings first

---

[8] *Shelley and his Circle*, II, 629-30, 657-9, 665-6.

began to take form,[9] such sentiments as those expressed in line 4:

> And slaves cease to tremble at Tyranny's nod.

We might note, too, that "scorpions of perfidy" and "Bigotry's bloodhounds" sound like references to those members of the Shelley and Grove families who tried to break up Shelley's engagement to Harriet Grove, a first attempt at which apparently took place in the fall of 1809.

Some of the changes Shelley made in the poem are revealing. For instance, in the version given to Hogg lines 2-3 read: "I come, care-worn tenant of life, from the grave,/ Where Innocence sleeps 'neath the peace-giving sod." In revising the poem for the Notebook, Shelley changes these lines to: "I have sped with Love's wings from the battlefield grave,/Where Ambition is hushed neath the peace-giving sod." He thus changes a personal, philosophical reference to a social, anti-war reference.

The lines that Shelley quotes in his footnote are from his own *Queen Mab*, III, 80-3, where they appear as follows:

> earth in itself
> Contains at once the evil and the cure;
> And all-sufficing nature can chastise
> Those who transgress her law.

As "A Dialogue" was written in either 1809 or 1810 and *Queen Mab* was not begun until the summer of 1812, this footnote must have been written when Shelley was "preparing" his poems for Hookham.

---

[9] See Commentaries to "I will kneel at thine altar" and "Henry and Louisa," below, pp. 250, 260.

Page 110. How eloquent are eyes!

As the fortunes of this poem and the next ("Hopes that bud in youthful breasts") have been joined by Shelley's editors, it seems best to treat the two together.

Shelley's works contain a poem called "Eyes: A Fragment" and another called "Love's Rose." "Eyes: A Fragment" consists of the first thirteen lines of "How eloquent are eyes!" These thirteen lines were first published by W. M. Rossetti (in his edition of Shelley's poems in 1870) from a copy made by Richard Garnett of a manuscript in the possession of Shelley's son, Sir Percy Florence Shelley.[1]

The source for "Love's Rose" is a letter from Shelley to Hogg of June 18-19, 1811. Shelley gives the first two stanzas, then places four large X's below them, and then gives the third. In editing this letter for *Shelley and his Circle,* I commented that, although Shelley's editors have assumed that all three stanzas comprise one poem, it did not seem clear that the final stanza belonged with the other two. Now, with the full text of both poems before us for the first time, the mystery can be solved. The stanza which has been represented as the third stanza of "Love's Rose" is in reality the final stanza of "How eloquent are eyes!" (which was arbitrarily given the title "Eyes: A Fragment" by Rossetti).

Shelley, in including these lines (and some others) in his letter to Hogg, introduces them with the coment: "I transcribe for you a strange melange of maddened stuff which I wrote by the midnight moon last night."[2] When editing

---

[1] Shelley, Rossetti ed., 1870, II, 601; see also above, pp. 200, 218.
[2] June 18-19, 1811, *Shelley and his Circle,* II, 810.

this letter I felt that this claim should perhaps not be taken literally; and my skepticism is now strengthened. Some of the lines in the letter may have been written "by the midnight moon last night," but it is unlikely that any lines of either "How eloquent are eyes!" or "Hopes that bud in youthful breasts" were written then, for in the Notebook both are dated 1810.

Apparently, when Shelley wrote to Hogg he had some manuscripts of earlier poems beside him and included snatches from these poems in the letter to give an impression of spontaneous creativity. Such a procedure is perhaps indicated by a variant reading in line 5 of "Hopes that bud in youthful breasts." Hogg, when publishing the letter that contained the poems, printed "honours" for "blossoms." It might be assumed that this was a misreading by Hogg. But the manuscript that Hogg used (now in The Carl H. Pforzheimer Library) shows "honours" quite clearly. This is a puzzling reading. "Honours" appears to make no sense. However, if Shelley was copying the poem from a manuscript as he hastily and excitedly composed his letter, he could have made such an error; but when copying the poems into the Notebook, a more methodical task, he would be more likely to transcribe correctly. Looking at the words in print or in a neat script it might seem impossible to read "blossoms" as "honours." But in Shelley's script the two are not so far apart as one might imagine. In the manuscript of the letter, "nours" is rather similar in appearance to "ossoms." If the writing was messy and the "l" of "bl" very short (as it sometimes was in Shelley's script) "bl" could be misread for "h." In the Pforzheimer manuscript of the letter, however, the "h" is clear; it occurs twice, and both times is followed by the "bl" of "blow," which provides a basis for comparison.

Lines 16-20 are obscure. Apparently Shelley is again contrasting time with eternity and saying, in effect, that "our love will be fully realized in eternity."

Page 112. Hopes that bud in youthful breasts

SEE Commentary to the preceding poem, "How eloquent are eyes!"

Page 113. To the Moonbeam

THIS POEM, like the two preceding ones, was included in a letter to Hogg in 1811 (this one on May 17)—with the title "To the Moonbeam." At this time the letters to Hogg were sprinkled with tantalizing romantic hints about Harriet and Eliza Westbrook, and Shelley seems to be implying that the poem was somehow connected with them, but it, too, was an earlier poem. In fact, almost two years earlier.

Shelley himself simply used the date "September 23, 1809" as the title. The date and the romantic content indicate that the poem concerns Harriet Grove; the gloomy note—which we find in other 1809 poems—shows that the course of love was not running smooth; the use of the date alone as a title must have significance. Shelley also specifically dated another poem on Harriet Grove, which seems to have reference to a particular event.[3]

That there was a break in the romance in the fall of 1809 was suggested by Newman White: "In September of 1809, however, the correspondence between Bysshe and Harriet practically ceased. For fifteen months Harriet recorded only one letter from Shelley and two letters to him. It would look as though someone had decided already that

---

[3] See Commentary to "To St Irvyne," below, p. 305.

it would be as well not to allow matters to proceed too far."[4] Harriet's diary, with its brief entries, does not give indication of a crisis on September 23, but she records receiving "a most affec^t letter" from Shelley's sister Elizabeth on September 19 and another on September 27, both of which she answered immediately.[5]

The major crisis, which broke up the romance, came a year later. The reason for it, Charles Grove stated, lay in Shelley's anti-religious views.[6] Charles, we might note, had been away in the navy in the fall of 1809 and either knew of no difficulties in that year or did not consider them important. But the reason he gives for the break in 1810 could have been operative also in 1809. Both *Zastrozzi* and "Henry and Louisa" show that Shelley's anti-religious views had developed in 1809; and Shelley was hardly one not to discuss them.

As a poem, "To the Moonbeam" has no more merit than Shelley's other juvenile efforts. We might note, however, the unusual musical effect that he obtains with the skipping short lines followed by the long leaping rhythm of the last line. This verse form anticipates that of some of the Choruses of *Prometheus Unbound* — for instance, on the colonization of the planets:

>   We'll pass the eyes
>   Of the starry skies
> Into the hoar deep to colonize:
>   Death, Chaos, and Night,
>   From the sound of our flight,
> Shall flee, like mist from a tempest's might.

[4] White, *Shelley*, I, 63.
[5] *Shelley and his Circle*, II, 530, 531. Both entries have crossed-out, illegible words following the notation of receiving the letters. Crossed-out words in Harriet's journal — as we can tell from the legible ones — usually have reference to Shelley.
[6] See Commentary to "Death-spurning rocks!," above, p. 211.

Page 115. Poems to Mary

As SHELLEY tells us in his "Advertisement," these four poems on "Mary" are but a "few" "selected from many." At least one other has survived; it was included in a letter to Elizabeth Hitchener on November 23, 1811, from Keswick:

> To Mary
> Who died in this opinion
>
> Maiden, quench the glare of sorrow
>   Struggling in thine haggard eye:
> Firmness dare to borrow
>   From the wreck of destiny;
> For the ray morn's bloom revealing
>   Can never boast so bright an hue
> As that which mocks concealing,
>   And sheds its loveliest light on you.
>
> Yet is the tie departed
>   Which bound thy lovely soul to bliss?
> Has it left thee broken-hearted
>   In a world so cold as this?
> Yet, though, fainting fair one,
>   Sorrow's self thy cup has given,
> Dream thou'lt meet thy dear one,
>   Never more to part, in Heaven.
>
> Existence w[oul]d I barter
>   For a dream so dear as thine,
> And smile to die a martyr
>   On affection's bloodless shrine.
> Nor *would* I change for *pleasure*
>   That withered hand and ashy cheek,
> If my heart enshrined a treasure
>   [Such as] forces thine to break.

Shelley introduces the poem as follows: "I transcribe a little Poem I found this morning. It was written some time ago; but, as it appears to shew what I then thought of eternal life, I send it."[7]

That this poem is from the same "Mary" group as those in the Notebook is indicated by the similarity of theme and the fact that it was "written some time ago." (They are dated "November 1810.") Apparently it would have come before "Mary III," which tells us that Mary is dead, for Mary in this poem, although in a bad way (with "haggard eye" and "ashy cheek"), is still alive. The "opinion" in which Mary died is a belief in immortality, a theme also in the Notebook poems.

Who Mary was, we do not know; and almost nothing is known of her "story" beyond what Shelley tells us in these poems. We can, however, fill in a part of the background.

The "friend" who told Shelley the story can be identified as Thomas Jefferson Hogg, for *Leonora*, referred to in the "Advertisement," was a novel (now apparently lost) written by Hogg. In 1811 Shelley wrote several letters to Hogg urging him to publish *Leonora*; and in one of them he linked Leonora and Mary: "Pray publish Leonora. demand 100 £ for it from Robinson, he will give it in the event. It is divine, is delightful   not that I like y^r heroine, but the poor Mary is a character worthy of Heaven. I adore it."[8]

From Shelley's "Advertisement" one might gather that *Leonora* was primarily the story of Mary, but the letter indicates that Mary was a subsidiary character; Leonora was the heroine. In fact, the novel does not at all appear to have been the kind of sentimental tale that the "Mary" poems relate; rather it was a sophisticated, anti-religious

---

[7] Shelley, *Complete Works*, VIII, 198-9.
[8] January 3, 1811, *Shelley and his Circle*, II, 684.

novel: "... the printers refused to proceed with it, in consequence of discovering that he had interwoven his free notions throughout the work, and at the same time strongly endeavoured to dissuade him from its publication altogether."[9]

Just how Mary and her story fitted into such a work is not clear. Mary was obviously very religious; perhaps her misfortunes were somehow linked to her beliefs.

In addition to the poems we have only one comment in Shelley's letters that adds anything to the "story": "I think were I compelled to associate with Shakespeare's Caliban with any wretch, with the exception of Lord Courtney, my father, B^p Warburton or the vile female who destroyed Mary that I should find something to admire."[1] What part the "vile female" played in the Mary story is not clear. To judge from the poems and their notes, Mary seems to have been deserted by a lover and then committed suicide. Perhaps the "vile female" enticed her lover away from her or spread gossip about her. But if so, the gossip must have been false, for we are assured that Mary was "taintless" and "spotless."

Hogg must have told Shelley the story of Mary shortly after they first met, for the poems are dated "November 1810" and Shelley and Hogg met in October when the fall term opened at Oxford. As the Advertisement tells us that Mary died "three months" before Shelley heard her story, her death must have occurred during the summer of 1810. If, then, Hogg knew her, as Shelley implies in the Advertisement (page 115), she probably lived near his home town of Stockton-on-Tees (County Durham), where he had spent the summer. Even if Hogg did know her, however,

---

[9] John Slatter, quoted in White, *Shelley*, I, 95.
[1] To T. J. Hogg, May 8, 1811, *Shelley and his Circle*, II, 770; on the "wretches," see *ibid.*, p. 774.

the story of his sitting up with her on a "summer night" enfolded in her "tremulous bosom" with two glasses of poison ready on the table sounds more like Monk Lewis than life. On the other hand, it may be that Mary did commit suicide, for Shelley—eighteen at the time—was deeply moved by her story: an "entrancement" of "three weeks" duration during which he wrote "many" poems on Mary. In view of Shelley's susceptibility in such matters (for instance, in regard to Emilia Viviani), this probably means that he was obsessed by Mary's story day and night.

We do not know when he wrote the "Advertisement." Possibly it was written at the time of the compilation of the Notebook; but "Advertisements" were usually written only for complete volumes, not for parts of volumes; hence, Shelley sometime after hearing Mary's story, may have decided to publish a small volume of poems on the subject, of which this "Advertisement," the Esdaile Notebook poems, and one other poem have survived. The implication in the lines quoted from St. Augustine—which may be translated: "I loved not yet, yet I loved to love . . . I sought what I might love, in love with loving"—seems to be that Shelley's obsession with Mary's story was due to the fact that he then had no one to love and did not know what love was, but that these omissions have now been rectified. If so, the "Advertisement," was written after his marriage to Harriet.

The quotation from St. Augustine was used later as a motto for *Alastor*, whose immature poet-hero was also "in love with love." The admission in the "Advertisement" that the state applied to Shelley himself at an earlier age provides further confirmation of the autobiographical nature of *Alastor*.

Of the poems, the first, "To Mary I," is so poor, running at times into doggerel, that one wonders why

Shelley chose it from the "many" available. The one in the letter to Elizabeth Hitchener is a better poem. The final poem, "To the Lover of Mary," is the best and the most interesting, for, if taken in conjunction with the poem in the letter to Elizabeth Hitchener, it gives us further insight into Shelley's views on immortality in these years. In the poem in the letter Shelley tells us that Mary believes that she will meet her lover in Heaven. But Shelley himself, although envying such a belief, is skeptical:

> Existence w[ould] I barter
> For a dream so dear as thine.

The second stanza of "To the Lover of Mary" depicts the same kind of vision. At first it seems as though this were the poet's own belief, but the following stanza (added later)[2] redresses the balance. Such a vision would indeed be a "joy"; one would suffer a life of "woe" on earth in such a hope; but it is better to work (as Shelley thought of himself as doing) to make this world a better place:

> And living shew what towering Virtue dares
> To accomplish even in this vale of tears.[3]

---

[2] As indicated in the Textual Notes. The quality of the verse suggests early composition; so perhaps the stanza was on a page of the manuscript which Shelley found after he had copied the earlier stanzas.

[3] The phrase "vale of tears" appeared later in the well-known lines in "Hymn to Intellectual Beauty":
> Why dost thou pass away and leave our state,
> This dim vast vale of tears, vacant and desolate?

Strangely enough none of Shelley's editors seem to have attempted to trace the origin of this famous phrase. It originated in the Eighty-fourth Psalm and first appeared in the Bishops' Bible in 1568. It was repeated in the Douay Version of the Old Testament in 1609-1610 (there, due to a difference in numbering, in the Eighty-third Psalm). The King James Version translates the phrase not as "vale of tears" but "valley of Baca" (weeping). It is recorded by the NED in the works of Sir Walter Raleigh, and we find it also in various seventeenth- and eighteenth-century poets. Keats commented in a letter to his brother and sister-in-law in April 1819: "The common cognomen of this world among the misguided and superstitious

COMMENTARIES

We might note that although Shelley does not express a belief in immortality in these poems he does not renounce it either. He is opposed to the theological concept of rewards and punishments (as the note to "To Mary I" informs us), but he does not absolutely reject immortality as such. This is consistent with the mingling of hope and skepticism on the subject that we find in his letters to Hogg and Elizabeth Hitchener in these years.[4]

The comment in the footnote to "To Mary I" on "the Romances of Leadenhall S^{tr}" refers to the Minerva Press on Leadenhall Street, which published trashy "novels of real life."[5]

The syntax in line 20 in "To the Lover of Mary" is complex. The meaning is: "The wounds caused by Misery's scorpion goad shall close."

Page 116. To Mary   I

SEE Commentary to "Poems to Mary."

Page 118. To Mary   II

SEE Commentary to "Poems to Mary."

---

is 'vale of tears' from which we are to be redeemed by a certain arbitary [sic] interposition of God and taken to Heaven." (*The Letters of John Keats.* ed. Hyder Edward Rollins, Harvard University Press, 1958, II, 101-2.) Rollins, in his note, refers to "Hymn to Intellectual Beauty" but obviously Keats had some religious source in mind.

[4] See Commentary to "Written on a beautiful day in Spring," above, p. 188.

[5] See William A. Wheeler and Charles G. Wheeler, *Familiar Allusions, A Handbook of Miscellaneous Information*, Boston, 1882; and Dorothy Blakey, *The Minerva Press, 1790-1820*, London, 1939.

Page 119. To Mary III

SEE Commentary to "Poems to Mary."

Page 121. To the Lover of Mary

SEE Commentary to "Poems to Mary."

Page 123. Dares the Lama

WHEN Shelley met Hogg at Oxford in the fall of 1810, he told him of his talented sister Elizabeth, whereupon Hogg fell in love with her (sight unseen). In their letters during the Christmas vacation in December and January, we hear much about Shelley's loss of Harriet Grove because of his anti-religious views and Hogg's "love" for Elizabeth. Later, after the expulsion from Oxford in March, Shelley became alarmed at Hogg's eagerness and began to emphasize Elizabeth's shortcomings, particularly her tendency to conformity in religious and social matters. This poem, "Dares the Lama," was included in a letter of April 20, 1811,[6] with the comment: "There it is — a mad effusion of this morning!"

We are faced once more, however, with a disagreement between the Notebook and a letter, for the poem is dated 1810 in the Notebook. That 1810 is the correct date is indicated by the fact that the poem almost certainly refers to the break-up of Shelley's engagement to Harriet Grove, which occurred in the fall of that year and precipitated just such anti-clerical feelings as we find in the poem: "Oh! I burn with impatience for the moment of xtianity's dissolution it has injured me; I swear on the altar of

[6] Shelley, *Complete Works*, VIII, 78-9, where (p. 76) it is wrongly dated April 28. For dating, see *Shelley and his Circle*, II, 757.

perjured love to avenge myself on the hated cause of the effect which even now I can scarcely help deploring . . . On *one* subject I am cool, (religion) yet that coolness alone possesses me that I may with more certainty guide the spear to the breast of my adversary, with more certainty ensanguine it with the hearts blood of Xt's hated name."[7] By April 1811 Shelley—to judge by his letters—does not seem excited enough about this issue to write poetry on it.

Whether the poem was written in late 1810 or in April 1811, however, the reference in the lines

> For in vain from the grasp of Religion I flee.
> The most tenderly loved of my soul
> Are slaves to its chilling control

is to Harriet Grove and Elizabeth Shelley. If it was written in 1810, as it almost certainly was, the main reference is to Harriet Grove. But that Shelley intended Hogg to believe that he was thinking primarily of Elizabeth is indicated in the following paragraph from the letter of April 20, 1811:

> My sister does not come to town, nor will she ever, at least I can see no chance of it. I will not deceive myself; she is lost, lost to everything; Intolerance has tainted her — she talks cant and twaddle. I would not venture thus to prophesy without being most perfectly convinced in my own mind of the truth of what I say. It *may* not be irretrievable; but, yes, it is! A young female, who only once, only for a short time, asserted her claim to an unfettered use of reason, bred up with bigots, having before her eyes examples of the consequences of scepticism, or even of philosophy, which she must now see to lead directly to the former. A mother, who is mild and tolerant, yet narrow-minded; how, I ask, *is she* to be rescued from its influence?[8]

---

[7] December 20, 1810, Abinger Manuscripts, Pforzheimer microfilm, reel VII.

[8] To Hogg, April 28, 1811, Shelley, *Complete Works*, VIII, 77.

The indication, then, is that Shelley wrote the poem in 1810 on himself and Harriet Grove (with incidental reference to Elizabeth, who apparently agreed with some of Harriet's objections to Shelley's views) and then later included it in a letter to Hogg with the implication that it was primarily on Elizabeth's backsliding from enlightenment—which rendered her an unsuitable mate for Hogg.

The tenor of the poem is mainly anti-clerical. The spirit "fiercer than tygers" of line 22 is religion. It is religion whose shadow has spread "the darkness of deepest dismay" over the battlefield (presumably by its visions of hell, which are "more frightful than death"). Religion is the poison in the waves of the fountain (of life?) which has corrupted those the poet loves and which has injured the poet himself.

The poem, like others of the same period, is often melodramatic and juvenile, but it would be a mistake to allow this to obscure the fact that it was born of a deep shock and expresses a fiercely held conviction. Shelley at the time simply lacked the skill to depict intense emotion with controlled power.

Page 125. I will kneel at thine altar

WHEN Shelley was "yet a boy," as he tells us in "Hymn to Intellectual Beauty," he had a spiritual experience one spring day which changed his life:

> I called on poisonous names with which our youth is fed:
>   I was not heard: I saw them not:
>   When musing deeply on the lot
> Of life, at that sweet time when winds are wooing
>   All vital things that wake to bring
>   News of birds and blossoming,
>   Sudden, thy shadow fell on me;
> I shrieked, and clasped my hands in extacy!

> I vowed that I would dedicate my powers
> To thee and thine: have I not kept the vow?

The same experience is referred to in the autobiographical Dedication to *The Revolt of Islam,* in which Shelley tells us that it occurred outdoors one May morning within sound of "school-room voices." And it is referred to again, as Newman I. White suggested, in *Julian and Maddalo* in a passage in which Shelley tells us that "when a boy" he dedicated his life to "justice and love."[9]

The present poem, "I will kneel at thine altar," has a similar theme. As in the Hymn, the poet rejects the "poisonous names" of orthodox religion, and his dedication, as in *Julian and Maddalo,* is to love. Love and intellectual beauty were closely associated in Shelley's thinking, and in his later poetry the personifications of both have much in common. Both were ideals for which one should strive and which the existing society tended to thwart. The dedication, in all these poems, is fundamentally to humanity.

Both in "Hymn to Intellectual Beauty" and in the Dedication to *The Revolt of Islam* Shelley refers to a particular experience on a particular day. Is this poem, "I will kneel at thine altar," a contemporary account of the same experience, perhaps written only shortly after it? If so, the experience must have taken place in May, 1809, for the Dedication to *The Revolt of Islam* places it in May and this poem is dated 1809 by Shelley. In fact, Shelley seems to place a particular emphasis on the date. He gives "1809" as sole title and puts a design under it.

It is difficult, however, to accept so early a date as May 1809 for this experience. In January 1812 Shelley wrote to William Godwin:

---

[9] *The Best of Shelley,* ed. Newman I. White (New York, 1932), p. 473.

> It is now a period of more than two years since first I saw your inestimable book on "Political Justice"; it opened to my mind fresh and more extensive views; it materially influenced my character, and I rose from its perusal a wiser and a better man. I was no longer the votary of romance; till then I had existed in an ideal world — now I found that in this universe of ours was enough to excite the interest of the heart, enough to employ the discussions of reason; I beheld, in short, that I had duties to perform.[1]

These comments to Godwin, one would assume, refer to the same period as that in which the experience referred to in the Dedication occurred; and "more than two years" prior to January 1812 would indicate that he first read *Political Justice* not later than the fall of 1809. To this we must add another comment to Godwin a few months later in reference to Shelley's final period at Eton:

> My fondness for natural magic and ghosts abated, as my age increased. I read Locke, Hume, Reid, and whatever metaphysics came in my way, without, however, renouncing poetry, an attachment to which has characterized all my wanderings and changes. I did not truly *think* and *feel*, however, until I read "Political Justice," though my thoughts and feelings, after this period, have been more painful, anxious and vivid — more inclined to action and less to theory. Before I was a republican: Athens appeared to me the model of governments; but afterwards, Athens bore in mind the same relation to perfection that Great Britain did to Athens.[2]

Shelley, in other words, had radical tendencies before he read Godwin; he had read Hume's anti-religious philosophy (there is, in fact, anti-religious sentiment in his horror novel *Zastrozzi*, written earlier in the year); and he was a "republican," which means that he was opposed to

---
[1] January 10, 1812, Shelley, *Complete Works*, VIII, 240.
[2] June 3, 1812, *ibid.*, p. 331.

the monarchy and the House of Lords. Mixed with this, no doubt, was the Whig anti-war sentiment he had long been exposed to. But if Shelley did not really begin to "think and feel" about these things — that is, to become emotionally and intellectually involved in them — until he read Godwin, then "I will kneel at thine altar" must have been written after he read *Political Justice*. Furthermore, although some of the language — "tyranny's power," "Priestcraft" — is as much republican as it is Godwinian, the concept implied in "Opinion" (line 30) is specifically Godwinian. In *Political Justice* Godwin has many discussions on the pernicious effects of "Opinion,"[3] by which he means the ideas implanted by a reactionary society in its own interests (a doctrine Shelley embodied in *The Revolt of Islam*.[4]

It is probable, then, that the poem was written in the latter months of 1809, and that it does not deal with the experience referred to in "Hymn to Intellectual Beauty" but was preliminary to it.

Shelley's dating of this poem "1809" and its Godwinian echoes also indicate that Shelley first read *Political Justice* in 1809 and not in 1810. And this would have to be — on the basis of Shelley's comments to Godwin — late in 1809. This dating, as we shall see, is strengthened by the evidence of "Henry and Louisa," and it agrees with Hogg's statement that Shelley first read *Political Justice* in Dr. Lind's copy,[5] for Shelley's association with Lind came during his Eton days. It would seem that Lind lent him the book in the fall term of his last year there (1809-1810).[6]

---

[3] Godwin, *Political Justice*, I, xlvi (Index).
[4] *The Revolt of Islam*, VIII, ix-x. See above, p. 217.
[5] Hogg, I, 313-14.
[6] There is, however, one piece of evidence which seems to indicate the spring of 1810 for the first reading of *Political Justice*. In a letter of January 16, 1812, Shelley informed Godwin that his romances, *Zastrozzi* and

Although the poem is influenced by Godwin, its central theme, love — love as the motive power for the young revolutionary, and love as the essential ingredient in the higher order of society which is to succeed the old — is not Godwinian. (Godwin placed the emphasis on Necessity, not on love.) It was, however, to become the central theme of much of Shelley's greatest poetry. The final lines

> But the Avenger arises, the throne
> Of selfishness totters, its groan
> Shakes the nations. — It falls, love seizes the sway;
> The sceptre it bears unresisted away.

form a kind of crude epitome of the message of *Prometheus Unbound*.

Shelley is not, that is to say, in this poem — or in any other — simply reflecting Godwin's doctrines. He had his own social philosophy into which he integrated those parts of Godwin's which he felt were relevant. In this early period, what apparently happened was that the reading of *Political Justice* pulled together his previous views on war, religion, and government and gave them new meaning.

For the general sense of lines 16-18 we might compare the conclusion of *A Defence of Poetry*, for example: "But even whilst they deny and abjure, they are yet compelled to serve, the Power which is seated upon the throne of their own soul."

St. Irvyne, were written before he had read any of Godwin's works except *St. Leon. Zastrozzi,* we know, was being written in the spring of 1809 and Shelley intended to complete it by July. We do not know when he began *St. Irvyne,* but on April 1, 1810, he wrote to his friend Edward Fergus Graham of "my new Romance," which must be *St. Irvyne.* It may be that most of *St. Irvyne* had been written by the late fall of 1809, or perhaps Shelley is stretching a point in his January 16 letter to flatter Godwin. Whatever the explanation, the main weight of evidence points to a reading of *Political Justice* in late 1809.

Page 127. Fragment ... bombardment of Copenhagen

SHELLEY enclosed a version of this poem in a letter to Hogg on January 11, 1811.[7] Below the poem he placed a line of X's across the page and then wrote the following stanza:

> All are Bretheren, — the   African bending
>   To the stroke of the hard hearted Englishmans rod
> The courtier at Luxury's Palace attending
> The Senator trembling at Tyranny's nod
> Each nation wch kneels at the footstool of God
> All are Bretheen [sic]; then banish Distinction afar
> Let concord & Love heal the miseries of War.

As this stanza is the same in form and meter as those preceding it, presumably it is a conclusion to the Copenhagen poem. Following this final stanza Shelley writes: "These are Eliza's. she has written many more, & I will shew you at some future time the whole of the composition. I like it very much. if a Brother may be allowed to praise a sister."

The implication seems to be that all the lines quoted are by Elizabeth, that they are part of one poem, and that the line of X's means that the middle stanzas have been omitted or have not yet been written. It is possible, of course, that Shelley meant that only the final stanza (quoted above) below the row of X's was by Elizabeth. It may also be that the second stanza of the poetry quoted in the letter was by Elizabeth, for neither it nor the final stanza appear in the Esdaile Notebook version. If Shelley and his sister wrote the poem together, each doing some stanzas, the collaboration is remarkable, for the stanzas are identical in style and

---

[7] *Shelley and his Circle*, II, 700-3.

sentiment. It is more likely that the whole poem, in both versions, was by Shelley and that he was representing the letter version as Elizabeth's in order to stimulate Hogg's interest in her (as he did also with "Cold are the blasts").[8] The only extant poems by Elizabeth are not at all in this radical vein but are personal narratives or lyrics.

If, however, the second stanza and the final ("All are Bretheren") stanza in the letter version are Shelley's, why do they not appear in the Notebook? It may be that Shelley, when he came to compile the Notebook, thought them inferior, or, more probably, that they were not in the manuscript from which he was copying. That Shelley was aware that the poem was not complete is indicated both by the word "Fragment" in the title and the row of X's below it. There is, indeed, some indication that it was planned as a rather long poem, in, say, eight to ten stanzas. The final stanza in the Notebook version on the "lone female" seems somewhat tacked on. Perhaps it was originally part of a series of examples on the horrors of the British bombardment (in 1801, by a fleet under Nelson's command). The "All are Bretheren" stanza of the letter version with its general moralistic tone sounds like a true final stanza.

Shelley does not date the poem in the Notebook, as he usually does with earlier poems. It may be, then, that it was written but shortly before the letter of January 11, 1811, in which it was included.

We might note that the change in the Esdaile text in line 5 from "tinges" to "clots with" is apparently an example of a creative addition Shelley made as he copied.

---

[8] See Commentary, below, p. 258.

COMMENTARIES

Page 128. On an Icicle

SHELLEY enclosed this poem (with two additional stanzas) in a letter to Hogg on January 6, 1811, with the comment: "You see the subject of the foregoing. I send because I think it may amuse you."[9] This comment, as I noted in editing the letter,[1] implies that the poem deals with some "subject" discussed in previous letters to Hogg. The most likely of these subjects is Hogg's hopeless "love" for Elizabeth Shelley. The poem, however, is here dated 1809, and was doubtless a product of the crisis in Shelley's romance with Harriet Grove in the fall of that year. (The anti-war and other radical sentiments in the poem also point to the latter part of the year.) So that, as with "Dares the Lama," Shelley in 1811 is sending Hogg an 1809 poem which grew out of his own romance, with the implication that it has just been written and refers to Hogg and Elizabeth.[2]

That Shelley was again using an early manuscript for the Notebook may be indicated by one textual matter. In the letter version "And" in line 13 is crossed out and "Say" substituted; in the Esdaile version "And" is retained. On the other hand, some of the Esdaile readings are superior to those in the letter. For instance, the rather fine line "And consigned the rich gift to the sister of Snow" is not in the letter. It would seem that Shelley revised an 1809 manuscript when preparing the poem for

---

[9] *Shelley and his Circle*, II, 690.

[1] *Ibid.*, pp. 692-3.

[2] In editing the letter, I felt that Shelley intended Hogg to take the reference as being to the 1810-1811 break with Harriet Grove. This is possible, but it seems to me now that it was more likely part of Shelley's bedevilment of Hogg on his "love" for Elizabeth. In the letter version line 19 reads: "Not for *thee* soft compassion celestials did know." Shelley's underlining of "thee" seems to imply a reference to Hogg (partly humorously, as his comment indicates: "I think it may amuse you").

(257)

publication and did not have a copy of the 1811 letter version with him.

Page 129. Cold are the blasts

FOR THIS poem we are fortunate (or unfortunate) in possessing two other texts. It was published first in *Original Poetry* by Victor (Shelley) and Cazire (his sister Elizabeth), and it is there dated "July, 1810." It was next published by Hogg in his biography of Shelley in 1858 along with fragments of two other poems. Below the poems Hogg commented: "Bysshe wrote down these verses for me at Oxford from memory. I was to have a complete and more correct copy of them some day. They were the composition of his sister Elizabeth, and he valued them highly as well as their author."[3]

The manuscript which Shelley gave to Hogg is now in The Carl H. Pforzheimer Library.[4] An examination of it shows that Hogg was telling the truth, for the paper of the manuscript is the same as that of two letters written by Shelley from Oxford and different from the paper he was using at the family home, Field Place, during the same months. These verses were presumably written down for Hogg shortly after Shelley and he got together again at Oxford after the Christmas vacation in January 1811.

But if Hogg is reliable obviously Shelley is not. He told Hogg that the poem was by Elizabeth,[5] but its presence in the Esdaile Notebook shows that he intended to include it in his projected book of poems. As he would hardly

---

[3] Hogg, *Shelley*, I, 126.
[4] SC 114, *Shelley and his Circle*, II, 625-7.
[5] Hogg believed him, and so, too, alas, did the present editor; see *Shelley and his Circle*, II, 629-31.

have included it if he had not written it, we must assume that, as with the poem on the bombardment of Copenhagen, it was Shelley's and not Elizabeth's. As with the Copenhagen poem, however, it is possible that some of it was by Elizabeth, or that the other verses he wrote down for Hogg with it were composed by her. It is more likely, however, that Shelley was simply pulling Hogg's leg on all occasions and that none of these poems or any part of them was by Elizabeth.

The problem is further complicated by the fact that the poem is dated in the Notebook "1808," and in *Original Poetry* "July, 1810." Possibly the latter date refers to a revised version. We might note also that the second "8" in 1808 is considerably larger than the first, which might mean that Shelley hesitated on it or added it later. Perhaps he was not sure whether the poem was written late in 1808 or early in 1809. But if 1808 is correct, "Cold are the blasts" may be the earliest poem in the Notebook. (The only other contenders seem to be "Written in very early youth" and "Late was the night.")

We run into similar complications in regard to text. When Shelley wrote down these verses for Hogg at Oxford, Hogg did not know — or gives no indication of knowing — that they had already been published in *Original Poetry*. That this Oxford transcription was based ultimately either on the *Original Poetry* text or on one very similar to it, however, is shown by the fact that both it and Hogg's omit one line in stanza three, which is seven and not the usual eight lines in length. On the other hand, Shelley was not simply copying from *Original Poetry;* for instance, in line 14, *Original Poetry* reads: "He turned laughing aside";[6] Hogg's manuscript: "He turned callous aside"; line 17 in

---

[6] Shelley, *Complete Works*, I, 9.

Hogg's manuscript has the reading "dark summit," *Original Poetry* reads "wild height."[7] These changes also support Hogg's statement that Shelley was writing the verses down "from memory" and not copying them.

If we now examine the three texts, the Esdaile, the *Original Poetry* and Hogg's, we find that although the *Original Poetry* and Hogg's are close to each other, the Esdaile has many readings that they do not. Whole lines are changed: 8, 17, 21-3, and 38. The Esdaile manuscript also corrects the third stanza, previously only seven lines long, by bringing it to the eight-line form. In order to do so, however, Shelley changed two lines completely (lines 21-2) and added the rhyming line "Thou wrath of black Heaven, I blame not thy pouring." Apparently he was making revisions when preparing the poem for new publication.

Perhaps Shelley had a source for this tale of horror, but if so, no one has yet found it. When the poem was printed in *Original Poetry* the names, Henry and Louisa, were left blank, perhaps to suggest a contemporary story which might be recognized if names were given. Henry and Louisa are also the names of the hero and heroine of the next poem in the book, but there appears to be no connection between the two works.

Page 131. Henry and Louisa

"Henry and Louisa" was Shelley's first attempt at a long poem, the predecessor of the now lost *Poetical Essay on the*

---

[7] There is no evidence that Shelley had a copy of *Original Poetry* with him when he was compiling the Esdaile Notebook, and some indication that he did not in the fact that he does not include more of its poems in the Notebook, for instance, "The Irishman's Song," which would have fitted in rather well.

Existing State of Things and of *Queen Mab*. It shows that both Shelley's radical social philosophy and his technical skills had developed earlier than had been thought. He was himself, as his note informs us, aware of the juvenile character of the poem — it was written when he was sixteen or seventeen — but he also seems to have felt that it had a special importance in the history of the development of his mind: "These defects I do not alter now, being unwilling to offer any outrage to the living portraiture of my own mind; bad as it may be pronounced."

The opening lines of the poem indicate its main purpose:

> Where are the Heroes? sunk in death they lie.
> What toiled they for? titles and wealth and fame

namely, an attack on war, specifically the Napoleonic Wars. This purpose is pursued by means of a story of two lovers, Henry and Louisa. In "Part the First" the scene is England; the two lovers are meeting in a country house (presumably Louisa's) for the last time before Henry, who is in the cavalry (a horse appears in stanza XVII), leaves for battle in Egypt. In "Part Second" the scene is Egypt. Henry has been mortally wounded; Louisa appears, searching for him (how she got to Egypt is not quite clear); she finds him lying on the sands beside a ruin near the sea; he is able to recognize her but is too badly injured to speak; when he dies she commits suicide.

Such is the bare outline of the story. Let us fill in some of the particulars.

The theme of the first stanza is the futility of war. All that comes of war is that the generals and kings have their "glory and their shame" "enshrined on brass"; the "misery" of mankind remains "unbettered." Stanza II is an attack on the soldier — a "vile worm" seeking only "vulgar glory." Stanzas III and IV and all but the last three lines of V are missing,[8] but as the attack on the soldier is still sustained in VI, presumably it continued in III, IV, and V. In VII we are told that, coarsened though he has been by war and army discipline, even the soldier—now specifically one "warrior"—can respond momentarily to love (though his "mental eye" is occupied by visions of "the fight's red flood"). Louisa, too, is obsessed by chauvinistic concepts (VIII), and approves her lover's search for glory; his vision will live and dominate in her breast while he is away: "I will thine empire be" (an image later to appear in the opening lines of *Epipsychidion*).

Henry is religious as well as chauvinistic. "Religion," he informs Louisa, "sanctifies the cause. I go/To execute its vengeance." The flag of the tyrant he is to fight flouts "with impious wing religion's grave." Like Mary of the Mary poems, he has an almost beatific belief in immortality (XII):

> Then thou and Heaven shall share this votive heart.
> When from pale dissolution's grasp I start.

Louisa, however, has her doubts:

> But thou art dearer far to me than all
> That fancy's visions feign, or tongue can speak.

---

[8] Shelley has included the missing lines in his line count. The count before "Henry and Louisa" is 1985; after it, 2326; as there are 315 lines in the poem as it now stands, this total should be 2300. Shelley, then, added 26 for the missing lines. The spaces left blank, however (see Textual Notes), indicate only 24 missing lines (making, with the three lines included, three Spenserian stanzas).

We might assume that Shelley had lost a page of the manuscript from which he was copying and left the spaces blank either in the hope of finding it or of composing new lines to fill the gap. This, however, brings up a problem. Did he include the missing lines in the manuscript that he sent to Hookham? If so, why did he not fill them in here? It is, of course, possible that he left them blank in the manuscript sent to Hookham and explained that he would fill them in later. If they were in the manuscript sent to Hookham, however, we can only assume that they were temporarily lost, then found again, and that Shelley forgot or neglected to copy them into the Notebook.

COMMENTARIES

Although Louisa is no Cythna, there is perhaps in her the first element of Shelley's later "new woman" heroine.

She bids Henry farewell (XIV), and overwhelmed by emotion, but still soldierly and silent, he rushes out of the house. There he appears to be in a garden where he and Louisa had often met. When he is alone it is apparent that beneath the stern exterior lies the suppressed sensitivity of a poet (not unlike Shelley himself[9]) as the "beloved" objects in the garden "rushed" with the beating of his heart "Impetuous" "on fainting memory." But there is a "deeper soul-pang" (XVI) even than memory. This, it appears from the next stanza, is the "still reproach" of nature for his war-making — the Rousseauistic theme of the contrast between nature and (evil) society.

Suppressing more such thoughts, Henry mounts his horse, which apparently has been waiting outside, and rides away, forcing himself not to look back. As he goes, his horse's hoof (symbolically) crushes a flower, a sacrifice to "withering Glory" (XVIII).

The last three stanzas of this first part are interjections by the poet himself, first on the flower thus sacrificed, then on religion, assailed as the source of "terror, pride, revenge and perfidy," an attack presaging those in *The Wandering Jew* and *Queen Mab*. In the final stanza, of only four lines, we learn that the poet himself has suffered deep "wrongs" at the hands of religion. This seems to be an extension of a charge in the previous stanza that "selfish Prejudice" was attempting to "drown in shouts" the "murmuring" of love, something which the poet swears he will thwart. Behind the anti-religious sentiments of

---

[9] Shelley had a special interest in the name Henry, perhaps even some sense of identification with it. Henry is the lover of Ianthe in *Queen Mab*. Shelley also used the name in "Cold are the blasts," for an unfaithful lover, and in the sixth song in *St. Irvyne*, for a lover who is drowned.

the poem, then, there is a personal motive, and doubtless behind other aspects of it also.

The second part opens with a rather colorful description of a night battle in Egypt. The "Genius of the south" on Mount Atlas (in Morocco), looking at Africa's "desolated clime," weeps "at slavery's everlasting moans" (one of Shelley's few references to slavery, which ceased to be a live issue in English politics after the abolition of the slave trade in the British Empire in 1807). "Hostile flags" are "unfurled" in Egypt, the Genius's "most dear-beloved" nation. Among those fighting in Egypt are "Britannia's hired assassins" (IV). Alone among the troops is Louisa, just arrived from England, seeking Henry. Seeing the actual havoc of war, it no longer seems glamorous to her:

> War! thou source accurst,
> In whose red blood I see these sands immerst.

She asks a soldier if he knows where Henry is. He does not, but hopes that "the fight/That casts on Britain's fame a brighter blaze" will spare him for her sake. As for himself, he must rush back to "the dear loved work" of war. The battle continues all night and into the dawn: "Scarce sunk the roar of war before the rising Sun." Louisa searches among the dead and wounded along the sands for her lover, the "sea-gales" carrying off the "shrieks of dying men." Then (VIII) under "a ruin's shade" she finds him in the agonies of death:

> his cheek
> On which remorseful pain is deep pourtrayed
> Glares, death-convulsed and ghastly.

Louisa presses him to her; he recognizes her amid his pain, but is unable to speak. As they regard each other in silence, they hear the distant roar of battle:

COMMENTARIES

> Britannia's legions swiftly sweeping,
> Glory's ensanguined harvest reaping,
> Mowed down the field of men,
> And the silent ruins, crumbling nigh,
> With echoes low prolonged the cry
> Of mingled defeat and victory.

Henry, dying, no longer has the bright confidence in immortality he had shown at the parting in England:

> Why does that breast with horror swell
> Which ought to triumph over fate?

Shelley's purpose is now apparent, namely, to show by two contrasting scenes that the glitter of war and the promises of religion alike are false. But he has another purpose also. Louisa's anti-religious sentiments perhaps should have prepared us for the workings of nobility in her. Now they come to the surface. Looking at the silent body of her lover, she decides to join him in death: "Sacred to Love a deed is done!" This act, because it is unselfish, is an act of "Virtue," and virtue is "superior to Religion's tie." It casts a kind of holy (although Shelley does not use the word) glow over the graves of the lovers, a glow which promises disaster to the despot but freedom to others:

> The pomp-fed despot's sceptered hand
> Shall shake as if death were near,
> Whilst the lone captive in his train
> Feels comfort as he shakes his chain.

A new order will arise from virtuous and unselfish acts.

Such, then, is the story. Shelley may have had some source for it, but more probably he invented it. He must have known many young men who had views similar to those of Henry and went off to war (Harriet Grove had two brothers in the navy). Nor is it difficult to identify the campaign about which he was writing. During Shelley's life up to this time Britain was involved in Egypt only twice. In 1801 an expedition under Sir Ralph Abercromby attacked Napoleon's forces and drove them out. In 1803 the British were themselves forced out by the Turks, and Mohammed Ali began his rise to power. In 1807 the British again invaded Egypt, with a force of 5000, this time to attack the Turks. They took Alexandria but after two defeats at Rosetta, with heavy losses, were again forced to evacuate.

Of the two campaigns there can be no doubt that Shelley had the second in mind. He was too young to remember that of 1801, but the campaign of 1807 could have made an impression on him. Henry's remarks on religion sanctifying "the cause" and the enemy's flag being "impious" also make more sense if the foes were the Turks and not the French. The battle along the shore amid ruins, then, must have been that at Rosetta (where the Rosetta stone had been found in 1799).

Although the poem deals with the events of 1807, according to Shelley's notation it was composed in 1809. This notation is almost certainly correct. Whereas Shelley might not always remember when he composed a particular short poem, he would hardly forget the date of one of this length, probably, indeed, the first such he had written. The last two stanzas of the first part, then, must refer to the attempts to break up Shelley's engagement to Harriet Grove in the fall of 1809.

If one or both of these stanzas were inspired by the 1809 crisis, something of the earlier course of the affair must be reflected in other lines. For instance, the "impassioned tenderness that burst / Cold prudery's bondage" (lines 30-1) may be a reference to a declaration of love on the part of Harriet; so too:

COMMENTARIES

> But thou art dearer far to me than all
> That fancy's visions feign, or tongue can speak.

The scene in which Henry rushes out of the house in an emotional turmoil to find the world of nature unchanged (lines 103-7) gives the impression of a personal experience. That there were such declarations and scenes is indicated in Shelley's agonized poem on the break of the following year, "A Melody to a Scene of Former Times."

It would seem, then, that the poem was written in the latter months of 1809. This dating is also supported by its general radical social content and by a specific parallel with "The Irishman's Song," which is dated (in *Original Poetry*) October 1809. The final stanza of "The Irishman's Song" begins with the line: "Ah! where are the heroes! triumphant in death." "Henry and Louisa" opens: "Where are the Heroes? sunk in death they lie."

"Henry and Louisa," "The Irishman's Song," "A Dialogue," and "I will kneel at thine altar" were apparently all written in the latter months of 1809, probably after Shelley's first reading in *Political Justice*.

The ground, however, must have been prepared for the seeds of *Political Justice*. What prepared it? To judge from "Henry and Louisa," it was largely the war itself. The year 1809 saw two campaigns which brought the war home to the British public with new force, for in both the British suffered heavy losses. On July 28 came the indecisive battle of Talavera, which forced the withdrawal of Wellington's forces from Spain into Portugal. Then came the disastrous Walcheren expedition in August, as a result of which 20,000 British dead were left on the Netherlands beaches. Shelley was particularly indignant about the second of these disasters. In 1810 he actively defended an Irish journalist, Peter Finnerty, who had been imprisoned by the government for exposing British blundering at

Walcheren, and even announced a book of poetry whose proceeds were to be used "to maintain in Prison Mr. Peter Finnerty, imprisoned for a libel."[1]

In *Political Justice* Shelley would not only have found general radical principles but also specific anti-war arguments. If, indeed, he had gone no further than page 7 he would have come across the following:

> Among the various schemes that he has formed to destroy and plague his kind, war is the most terrible. Satiated with petty mischief and the retail of insulated crimes, he rises in this instance to a project that lays nations waste, and thins the population of the world. Man directs the murderous engine against the life of his brother; he invents with indefatigable care refinements in destruction; he proceeds in the midst of gaiety and pomp to the execution of his horrid purpose; whole ranks of sensitive beings, endowed with the most admirable faculties, are mowed down in an instant; they perish by inches in the midst of agony and neglect, lacerated with every variety of method that can give torture to the frame.

If, interested by this, he had consulted Godwin's index at the front of the volume and followed the entries on war, he would have found this devastating attack on the soldier:

> The man that is merely a soldier, ceases to be, in the same sense as his neighbours, a citizen. . . . It cannot be a matter of indifference, for the human mind to be systematically familiarised to thoughts of murder and desolation.[2]

The effect of such writing upon the mind of a young and sensitive intellectual already moving in a radical direction can well be imagined. The characters of Henry and the soldier to whom Louisa speaks in Egypt seem to be

---

[1] Cameron, *The Young Shelley*, p. 50. It is not certain that the book was published.
[2] Godwin, *Political Justice*, II, 168-9.

fictional renderings of Godwin's comments on the soldier. In the notes to *Queen Mab* he quotes Godwin's similar comments in *The Enquirer*.

It was, then, probably the twin impacts of the war and Godwin which drove Shelley toward that radical humanitarianism which became the ruling passion of his life.

The "Genius of the south" (line 166) who "looked over Afric's desolated clime" from the top of Mount Atlas and "wept at slavery's everlasting moan" must have been inspired by Robert Southey's "To the Genius of Africa" (1795), which begins:

> O thou, who from the mountain's height
> Rollest thy clouds with all their weight
> Of waters to old Nile's majestic tide;
> Or o'er the dark, sepulchral plain
> Recallest Carthage in her ancient pride,
> The mistress of the Main;
> Hear, Genius, hear thy children's cry!

Southey then goes on to describe the horrors of the slave trade.

The reference to "Memnon's plainings wild/That float upon the morning ray" may also have been derived from Southey, who writes in a note to Book Ten of *Thalaba the Destroyer* on the legendary statue of Memnon:

> My design is not absolutely to deny that he might compose some head or statue of man, like that of Memnon, from which proceeded a small sound and pleasant noise, when the rising sun came, by his heat, to rarify and force out, by certain small conduits, the air which, in the cold of the night, was condensed within it.[3]

---

[3] "Shelley's favourite poet in 1809 was Southey. He had read *Thalaba* till he almost knew it by heart, and had drenched himself with its metrical beauty." (Medwin, *Shelley*, p. 44.) For some echoes of *Thalaba* in Shelley's works, see Hughes, *The Nascent Mind of Shelley*, pp. 88-9, and Shelley, *Complete Works*, I, 418 (on *Queen Mab*).

The (rather appalling) "big tear" of line 182 may come from Coleridge's sonnet to Bowles (second version), although we do not know that Shelley read Coleridge as early as 1809.

Page 144. A Translation of the Marsellois Hymn

STANZA 4 of this translation of "The Marseillaise" appeared in a letter from Shelley to his musician friend Edward Fergus Graham.[4] The letter occupies the first three pages of a double-sheet quarto; the stanza is on page 4, written in block letters. The letter is undated and bears neither postmark nor address, but its contents indicate that it was written just after a celebrated fete held by the Prince Regent on June 19, 1811, at Carlton House.

This dating is borne out by the bibliographical evidence, which also indicates where the letter was written. Examination of the manuscript in the Berg Collection of the New York Public Library shows the watermark to be "CHARLES WILMOTT/1809/." Wilmott paper was used by the Shelley family at Field Place. We find that Shelley used it at Field Place in 1810-1811 but not in London or Oxford.[5] This letter to Graham, then, was almost certainly written at Field Place. As Graham lived in London, the letter cannot have been sent by private messenger, but must have been folded inside a sheet, now lost, bearing the address and postmarks.

[4] Shelley, *Complete Works*, VIII, 109-10.
[5] *Shelley and his Circle*, II, 658. As to the specific watermark "CHARLES WILMOTT/1809/," we find it on five letters by Shelley in The Carl H. Pforzheimer Library. They have the following dates: Jan. 17, 1811 (SC 135); Jan. ?19-?21, 1811 (SC 136); May 17, 1811 (SC 160); May 21, 1811 (SC 161); and June 4, 1811 (SC 164).

In a letter of June 20, 1811, from Field Place, Shelley commented to Elizabeth Hitchener on the Prince's fete:

> What think you of the babbling *brooks* and *mossy banks* at Carlton House — the *allée[s] verts*, etc. It is said that this entertainment will cost £120,000; nor will it be the last bauble which the nation must buy to amuse this overgrown bantling of regency. How admirably this growing spirit of ludicrous magnificence, tallies with the disgusting splendors of the stage of the Roman Empire which preceded its destruction! Yet here are a people advanced in intellectual improvement, wilfully rushing to a Revolution, the natural death of all great commercial empires, which must plunge them in the barbarism from which they are slowly arising.[6]

Evidently this vulgar display aroused Shelley's republican ardor, for he proposed to Graham that he supply the words and Graham the music to an "ode" on the Royal family.[7] This ode was probably the poem which Charles Grove remembers Shelley throwing "into the carriages of persons going to Carlton House after the fete."[8]

Stanza 4, then, had been written by about June 20, 1811; and probably all the stanzas had been, for it is more likely that Shelley translated the whole poem at one time, rather than stanza 4 by itself. Perhaps he only included in the letter what he considered the most appropriately antimonarchical stanza. Nor is it likely that Shelley just happened to be working on a translation of "The Marseillaise," when he was writing to Graham. More probably

---

[6] Shelley, *Complete Works*, VIII, 108-9.

[7] The ode is referred to again in a letter to Graham of about July 13, 1811. *Ibid.*, IX, 123. (The editors date this letter July 15, but this date they have simply taken from the London postmark. As the letter was sent from Cwm Elan to London and mail between these two points took two to three days, the letter must have been written on July 12 or 13.)

[8] Charles Grove to Hellen Shelley, February 25, 1857, quoted in Hogg, *Shelley*, II, 158.

it was something he had done previously and had by him as he wrote.

As the letter was almost certainly written at Field Place, we are faced with a large span of time for the dating of the poem, for Shelley had his "younger poems" at Field Place. (In a letter to Hogg from Field Place on about June 18-19, 1811, he enclosed "Hopes that bud in youthful breasts," which is dated 1810 in the Notebook; a letter to Hogg from Field Place on January 6, 1811, contained "On an Icicle," which is dated 1809.) The radical connotations of Shelley's translation (see below) point to at least the fall of 1809.[9] "Pomp-fed Kings" of line 30 parallels "pomp-fed despots" in the final stanza of "Henry and Louisa" (late 1809). When we note also that the poem comes in a sequence of early poems, we arrive at a probable date of late 1809 to 1810.

In translating,[1] Shelley preserves some of the energy of the original, but changes the character of the poem — making it adhere more closely to his personal interest, but weakening its impact. In contrast to the concrete rallying song of the French, Shelley's translation is, characteristically, a generalized anti-tyranny poem. He changes the tone not only by his use of "you" for the original first-person plural, but also in particular instances. For example, in stanza 1, Shelley uses "slaves of power" rather than "soldiers" to translate "soldats." Again, in stanza 3, "nos guerriers," instead of "our warriors," becomes "the arm upraised for liberty." Similarly, in stanza 4, the idea that the earth itself will replace "our young heroes" with others "all ready to fight against you" is inflated to:

---

[9] See, for instance, Commentaries to "I will kneel at thine altar" and "Henry and Louisa," above, pp. 250 and 260.

[1] For this examination of the translation, I am indebted to Miss Winifred Davis.

> Our Mother Earth will give ye new
> The brilliant pathway to pursue
>   That leads to Death or Victory!

The simple "liberté chérie" (6) becomes "Thou, more dear than meaner gold . . . Liberty." "Beneath our flags" is translated as "Where conquest's crimson streamers wave." Structurally, Shelley has expanded the original eight-line form into nine lines by adding a final line rhyming with the second and fourth lines of each stanza.

Page 147. Written in very early youth

THE EARLIEST known poem by Shelley is the comical "Verses on a Cat." It exists only in a copy said to be in the hand of his sister Elizabeth, and bears the notation in another hand apparently added later: "Percy Bysshe Shelley written at 10 years of age to his Sister at School."[2] On the basis of this note the poem has been assigned to the year 1802. One might suspect, however, that it was written somewhat later. Hellen Shelley remembered only that it was "a very early effusion," and the copy bears the date 1809 in the watermark.

Next comes a four-line stanza, "Hark; the owlet," which is dated in Shelley's *Complete Works* as 1807. This date, however, is based on a statement by Medwin in *The Shelley Papers*: "I think he was then about fifteen"[3] (Shelley became fifteen in the summer of 1807); but as Medwin continues, "Shortly afterwards we wrote, in conjunction, six or seven cantos on the story of the Wandering Jew," and as *The Wandering Jew* was not begun until the winter

---

[2] Shelley, *Complete Works*, III, 314.
[3] London, 1833, p. 7.

of 1809-1810, it is apparent that Medwin was (not untypically) muddled. Furthermore, the stanza, as Medwin apparently did not know, was actually the first stanza of a horror poem in *Original Poetry* (1810) called "Ghasta, or, The Avenging Demon! ! !" This stanza, then, was probably written not in 1807 but 1809 or 1810.

"Cold are the blasts" was, as we have seen, dated by Shelley 1808 in the Notebook and July 1810 in *Original Poetry* and may be early 1809.

There is only one other attribution of a poem earlier than 1809. This again is based on Medwin, who gives in his life of Shelley two Latin poems "which he [Shelley] gave me in 1808 or 9."[4] The first of these is a translation of the Epitaph to Gray's "Elegy Written in a Country Churchyard"; the second is a poem on a young lady's watch. As this second poem is a Latin version of an English poem which appeared in *The Oxford Herald* for September 1809,[5] the dates for both poems are more likely to be 1809 than 1808.

When we examine the claims for extant poems written before 1808, then, they seem to fade away, with the exception of the verses on the cat, and the date of these verses is not certain. Certainly Shelley himself does not seem to have preserved anything earlier than 1808 or possibly 1809. Is the present poem, then, an exception? Does "very early youth" mean, say, 1806 or 1807? Possibly so, but it is apparent that Shelley himself either did not quite remember when he had written it, or, in view of

---

[4] Medwin, *Shelley*, p. 35.
[5] Denis Florence MacCarthy, *Shelley's Early Life* (London, 1872), p. 27. In Shelley's version, which is rather more juicy than *The Oxford Herald* version, the young lady's name is given as Leonora. Possibly it was Shelley who suggested "Leonora" as a title for Hogg's now-lost novel. (See above, p. 243.) The poem, of course, might have appeared in other places than *The Oxford Herald*. Shelley did not enter Oxford until the fall of 1810.

its juvenile character, wished it to appear earlier than it actually was. It is, in fact, in the same vein as the graveyard school effusions in *Original Poetry*, some of which are dated 1810. We might note also the anti-war implication of "No votarist, I, at Glory's shrine." All things considered, the most likely date seems to be 1809.

Page 148. Zeinab and Kathema

BEFORE the action of the poem opens, Zeinab has been stolen from her home in Cashmere by a band of "Christian murderers" (line 33) armed with sword and Bible, and taken to their native England. Her beloved, Kathema, following her (presumably down the Indus), is, as the poem opens, lying on a beach facing westward across the Arabian sea. He sees a ship looming up in the sunset. It is bound for England. Kathema buys passage. In England he finds himself in a corrupt society — "Famine, disease and crime even wealth's proud gates pollute" (line 102) — very different from the "natural" society in the Vale of Cashmere; but he bravely pursues his search for Zeinab. One damp December evening he comes to a "wild heath," where he collapses in exhaustion. When he wakes, the moon is up and in its dim light he perceives that he is under a gibbet on which, swinging from chains, is the naked and decayed body of Zeinab. He mounts the gibbet, winds a chain around his neck, and hurls himself out to die beside her corpse. In England, the final stanzas inform us, Zeinab had been forced into prostitution but escaped and, corrupted by a corrupt society, "waged ruthless war" against it by "its own arms of bold and bloody crime."

"Here," as Dowden commented, "is romantic ghastliness, as imagined by a boy, in extravagant profusion";

but, as Dowden also pointed out, this was not Shelley's main intent; he designed the poem "less as a piece of romantic art than as an indictment of widespread evils."[6] "Zeinab and Kathema" combines the old horror-mongering of *Zastrozzi* with social radicalism. The poem is intended primarily as an exposé of the evils of contemporary British society and an indictment of its inhuman punishments (lines 179-80):

> A universe of horror and decay,
> Gibbets, disease, and wars, and hearts as hard as they.

One might assume on the basis of the mixture of Gothic and radical elements that the poem was written when Shelley was emerging from his "votary of romance" period into that of a consciousness of "social duties," between, say, the fall of 1809 and the spring of 1810. But Shelley's penchant for romantic horror continued well beyond this time; and there are indications that the poem was later than 1809 and probably later than 1810. In the first place, Shelley himself did not date it, and, as we have seen, he usually does date his "younger poems." It seems especially unlikely that he would fail to date a poem so long as this one if it had been written in 1809 or even in 1810.

In the second place, there is the possibility of influence from Sydney Owenson's (Lady Morgan) novel *The Missionary* (1811). Dowden suggested that the use of Cashmere might have come from this novel, the locale of which is Cashmere.[6] And there is one other piece of evidence which supports this view. In October 1814, after Shelley had left Harriet, he wrote asking her to copy and send him a "poem called an Indian Tale."[7] There is no poem of this title in the Esdaile Notebook, but as Roger Ingpen has

---

[6] Dowden, *Shelley*, I, 348.
[7] October 12, Shelley, *Complete Works*, VII, 304.

suggested one (and only one) could fit it, namely "Zeinab and Kathema,"[8] a suggestion which may receive some support from the fact that the full title of *The Missionary* is *The Missionary, an Indian Tale*.

If "Zeinab and Kathema" was influenced, however slightly, by the novel, it must have been written later than early June 1811, for Shelley notes in a letter of June 11 to Elizabeth Hitchener that he has just finished reading *The Missionary*.[9] About a week later he commented to Hogg: "The only thing that has interested me, if I except your letters has been one Novel . . It is Miss Owenson's *Missionary* an Indian tale. will you read it, it is really a divine thing . . Luxima the Indian is an Angel . . What pity that we cannot incorporate these creations of Fancy, the very thought of them thrills the soul . . . Since I have read this book I have read no other . . . but I have thought strangely."[1] It is possible, then, that Shelley was working on the poem at this time or shortly thereafter (deciding to "incorporate" his strange thoughts in poetic fiction). At any rate, Shelley was fascinated by a novel about Cashmere and a Cashmere maiden in the summer of 1811, and we do not know of any other source from which he could have received an impetus for using Cashmere and Cashmere lovers for his poem. The rather idyllic pictures of Cashmere in lines 91-100, it should also be noted, are gen-

---

[8] *Ibid*. One other (rather horrible) thought, however, also occurs. Let us say that Harriet did send the "Indian Tale" to Shelley. If it was the same as "Zeinab and Kathema" she must have copied it out, but this would have been such a long job that it is difficult to imagine Harriet undertaking it. However, let us assume that the "Indian Tale" was another poem in the Esdaile Notebook and not "Zeinab and Kathema." There are two leaves torn out of the Notebook, which obviously contained a complete poem of some sixty lines. Perhaps these leaves contained the "Indian Tale," and Harriet simply tore them out and sent them to Shelley.
[9] *Ibid.*, VIII, 103.
[1] *Shelley and his Circle*, II, 810.

erally reminiscent of Miss Owenson's novel. On the other hand, the novel is definitely not a major source for the poem. It is a romantic tale of a Catholic missionary falling in love with an Indian priestess. There is nothing in it about a heroine being captured and sent to England or forced into prostitution, although in the final episodes the priestess leaps madly into the flames of an inquisitional pyre to save her lover somewhat as Kathema does on the gibbet.

It may be argued against this dating that the style of the poem seems earlier than 1811. But further reading suggests (at least to this editor) that its more ragged lines are the result of the kind of violent emotional involvement with the subject matter which Shelley in these years had not the skill to handle. We find the same phenomenon in some of the poems written at Cwm Elan in 1811 and in "a Tale of Society as it is." Moreover, some of the lines, for instance, the passionate indictment of English society, have a ring of reality which the earlier, more derivative manner did not have, and some of the images (for instance, "slow-raised surges near the strand" — line 65) seem aesthetically above anything that Shelley produced in 1809 or 1810.

The radical content points in the same direction. It is not just the general anti-kings and anti-war republicanism of "Henry and Louisa," but a deeper and more sociological radicalism. The poem, in fact, sometimes sounds rather like a creative interpretation of Godwin's remarks in *Political Justice* on unjust laws and punishments;[2] it embodies Godwin's general thesis (later taken up by Robert Owen) that social evils arise not from defects in human nature but from defects in society.

There is also one other indication of an 1811 date, slight

---

[2] Godwin, *Political Justice*, I, 12-14; II, 323.

though it is. Shelley almost certainly took the name Zeinab from Southey's *Thalaba,* in which Thalaba's mother is named Zeinab. Perhaps, then, Kathema was suggested by Kehama in Southey's *The Curse of Kehama.* Shelley, however, did not read this book until at least December 1810.[3]

In some of its general characteristics, "Zeinab and Kathema" anticipates *Laon and Cythna (The Revolt of Islam;* 1817). Laon and Cythna are also a pair of lovers; Cythna is taken off by an armed band and forced into the seraglio of "the tyrant"; Laon searches for her, finds her, and in the end the two are burned at the stake. Some of this, Shelley took from the *Ahrimanes* of his friend Peacock,[4] but there are echoes suggesting that he still had "Zeinab and Kathema" in mind. For instance, the scene in which the imprisoned and chained Laon has cannibalistic fantasies in his delirium[5] is reminiscent of the ghastly climax on the gibbet. The opening scene on the beach seems to be echoed in the opening of *Laon and Cythna,* in which Laon sees from the shore a form "like a great ship in the sun's sinking sphere."[6] In *Laon and Cythna* we also find an evil "blood-red Comet" and a good "Morning star,"[7] symbols which Shelley had not used in his poetry in the intervening years.[8] Further study would perhaps reveal other parallels.

The Missionary, as we have noted, is not a major source for "Zeinab and Kathema." Was there such a source? None comes to mind from what we know of Shelley's early read-

---

[3] Shelley, *Complete Works,* VIII, 21, 22, 99.

[4] Kenneth Neill Cameron, "Shelley and *Ahrimanes,*" *Modern Language Quarterly,* III (June 1942) 287-95.

[5] *Laon and Cythna,* I, xxv-xxvi.

[6] *Ibid.,* I, vi.

[7] *Ibid.,* I, xxvi; "Zeinab and Kathema," lines 171-4.

[8] Line 173 may have been subconsciously in Shelley's mind in the description of Claire Clairmont in *Epipsychidion* (line 368): "Thou too, O Comet beautiful and fierce."

ing.[9] It may be that, as with "Henry and Louisa," he had no such source, but combined romantic elements — the lovers violently parted, the search for the beloved — with real ones, such as those in "a Tale of Society as it is," possibly taken from some historical account of crime and punishment.

Shelley's tale is certainly fantastic, especially its conclusion, but its indictment of inhuman punishment is hardly exaggerated. Men were still hanged, drawn, and quartered in Shelley's day; and "gibbeting" was legal until 1834. Shelley, we might note, uses the word in its technical sense. A gibbet was a kind of gallows with a long wooden arm extending outward, from which the body of an executed criminal was hanged in chains (that is, was "gibbeted").[1] The bodies of highwaymen and other criminals were displayed, in particular on Hounslow Heath in Middlesex,[2] and people used to ride out from London in their carriages to observe them. When we note that Hounslow Heath was in the general vicinity of Shelley's first school, Sion House, and that a main coach road he must many times have traveled went through it, it seems probable that Shelley himself saw gibbeted bodies. Hounslow, then, is doubtless the "wild heath" of the poem (line 123). We might note also that at least two women were hanged for highway robbery (although there seems to be no record of any being gibbeted). The horror of gibbeting was still remembered in Victorian times — as witness Tennyson's "Rizpah."

---

[9] One might guess from line 48 and other lines that Shelley had recently been reading Spenser or his imitators, but this influence was probably stylistic only.

[1] For a description of a gibbet, see Patrick Pringle, *Stand and Deliver: The Story of the Highwaymen* (London, 1951), pp. 68-70.

[2] George S. Maxwell, *Highwayman's Heath: The Story in Fact and Fiction of Hounslow Heath in Middlesex* (Hounslow, 1949). Maxwell includes pictures of gibbets (pp. 177 and 192).

Page 155. *The Retrospect*

SHELLEY, as we have seen, stayed with his cousins the Groves at their Welsh estate, Cwm Elan, in July and August 1811, just prior to his elopement with Harriet Westbrook. In April of the following year, after his return from Ireland, he took a house about a mile and half from Cwm Elan and intended to settle there. He was, however, unable to secure the property, and moved, on about June 5, to Cwm Elan—with Harriet and Eliza—and stayed there until about June 20.[3]

The suggestion for the poem perhaps came from Robert Southey's "The Retrospect" (1794). Southey begins, as does Shelley, with comments on the passing of time, and then addresses the following lines to his wife:

> O thou, the mistress of my future days,
> Accept thy minstrel's retrospective lays;
> To whom the minstrel and the lyre belong,
> Accept, my EDITH, Memory's pensive song.
> Of long past days I sing, ere yet I knew
> Or thought and grief, or happiness and you;
> Ere yet my infant heart had learnt to prove
> The cares of life, the hopes and fears of love.

With these early lines, however, the comparison between the two poems ceases, for Southey goes on to describe his schooldays.

The light which "The Retrospect" throws on Shelley's first visit to Cwm Elan and his psychological state at that time, we have already discussed in commenting on the poems he actually wrote during this visit. What light does

---

[3] To Elizabeth Hitchener, June 6, 1812, June [18, 1812], Shelley, *Complete Works*, VIII, 332, 338. Harriet Shelley to Catherine Nugent, June 30, [1812], *ibid.*, IX, 3.

it throw on the period of the second visit? That second visit, one would gather, was a pleasant one. Harriet at first found Mrs. Grove rather "formal" but soon warmed up to her and to Cwm Elan: "For the present I am tied Leg and Wing by the chain of Mysticis[m] to this enchanting place."[4] Shelley's feelings toward Harriet we can gather from the poem:

> How do I feel my happiness?
> I cannot tell, but they may guess
> Whose every gloomy feeling gone,
> Friendship and passion feel alone ...
>
> Thou fair in form and pure in mind,
> Whose ardent friendship rivets fast
> The flowery band our fates that bind,
> Which incorruptible shall last ...

Professor White regarded this as a "glowing tribute to Harriet."[5] It seems to me, however, as with some of Shelley's other tributes to her, rather tame. One is reminded of his comments to Harriet on the nature of their "attachment" after his elopement with Mary Godwin: "Friendship was its basis, & on this basis it has enlarged & strengthened. It is no reproach to me that you have never filled my heart with an all-sufficing passion perhaps, you are even yourself a stranger to these impulses which one day may be awakened by some nobler & worthier than me, and may you find a lover as passionate and faithful, as I shall ever be a friend affectionate & sincere!"[6]

Certainly the emphasis in the poem is on "friendship."

---

[4] Harriet Shelley to Catherine Nugent, June 7, [1812], Shelley, *Complete Works*, VIII, 333; June 30, [1812], *ibid.*, IX, 3; to Elizabeth Hitchener, June 11, 1812, *ibid.*, VIII, 335-6.

[5] White, *Shelley*, I, 235.

[6] Shelley to Harriet Shelley, [mid-July, 1814], Shelley, *Complete Works*, VII, 294. See also above, p. 219.

"Passion," however, though placed second, is mentioned. And in the letter Shelley continued, evidently feeling that he had placed too exclusive an emphasis on friendship: "Shall I not be more than a friend? Oh, far more, Brother, Father of your child, so dear as it is to us both, for its own sake & because we love each other." What he seems to be saying is that although there was no deeply passionate love in their relationship, there was, nevertheless, love, a love similar to that of friendship but somewhat more "ardent."

"The Retrospect" is technically the best of the longer poems that Shelley had written up to this time. It has none of the awkwardness that sometimes besets "Henry and Louisa" and "Zeinab and Kathema," but is both taut and easy-flowing. Its style is in the early-nineteenth-century mode and yet is original (compared, for instance, with Southey's "Retrospect," which reads like watered-down Shenstone). We have to recognize also, however, that Shelley in these apprentice years is more adept in the couplet (as witness the first of the *Margaret Nicholson* poems) than in complex stanzaic forms.

The image in the early (unpublished) lines of time as a female monster giving birth to and then devouring her young is a striking one. It is reminiscent of Spenser's Errour (*Faerie Queene*, I, i, 15) and Milton's Sin, but its mythological origin is perhaps in the story of Saturn (Cronos) devouring his children, for Saturn (apparently through a confusion of "Cronos" with "chronos") was sometimes said by the mythologists to symbolize time.

The title of the poem, we might note, is "The Retrospect," not as Dowden and subsequent editors and biographers have given it: "The Retrospect: Cwm Elan, 1812." Shelley placed a period after "Retrospect," and put "Cwm Elan 1812" on the next line. "Cwm Elan 1812," therefore, was not intended to be part of the title but simply an indication of place of composition and date.

Page 161. *The wandering Jew's soliloquy*

THE STORY of Shelley's interest in the Wandering Jew is long and complex.[7] He perhaps first encountered him in Monk Lewis's horror novel *The Monk*. When he was still an Eton schoolboy he and his cousin Thomas Medwin began a long anti-religious narrative poem, *The Wandering Jew,* in which the Jew was presented sympathetically, and God, who had condemned him to wander forever, undying, was the villain, the "Eternal Avenger." Canto III revolved around God's refusal to allow the Jew release from his sufferings in death, and it was this theme of physical immortality that fascinated Shelley. He returned to it in *Queen Mab*, where the wandering Jew makes a brief but dramatic appearance; and he treated it in a prose fragment, which he gave to Hogg.[8]

When we turn to these various versions we find that the only one which is at all close to "The wandering Jew's soliloquy" is that in Canto III of *The Wandering Jew*. In both *Queen Mab* and the prose fragment the resemblances are merely of a general nature (the "avenger" theme). And even the parallels in *The Wandering Jew* are only with the first five lines of the "soliloquy"; for instance:

> I have cast myself from the mountain's height,
> Above was day — below was night;

---

[7] See Cameron, *The Young Shelley*, pp. 34-5, 306-13.
[8] Now in The Carl H. Pforzheimer Library, *Shelley and his Circle*, II, 649-59.

> The substantial clouds that lower'd beneath
> Bore my detested form;
> They whirl'd it above the volcanic breath,
> And the meteors of the storm;
> The torrents of electric flame
> Scorch'd to a cinder my fated frame.
> Hark to the thunder's awful crash —
> Hark to the midnight lightning's hiss!⁹

The parallels of "hell," "frame," and "lightning" — and there is a dagger at line 280 which will not quench life, as in line 5 of the "soliloquy"—show that there is some connection between the two versions, but there are also sufficient differences to show that it was not close. For instance, the casting from a mountain is not present in the "soliloquy" and the Biblical references of the second part of the "soliloquy" are not in the narrative. Furthermore, the two poems differ in verse form and in quality, the verse of the narrative having a harsh and tinny sound which makes the "soliloquy" seem relatively mature. Whatever the origin of the "soliloquy," it seems clear that it was not written as part of *The Wandering Jew*. Its level of technical skill is closer to that of *Queen Mab;* but its rhymed verse form shows that it cannot have been part of *Queen Mab* either. Apparently it was an independent poem.

When was it written? The technique indicates a date later than that of *The Wandering Jew*, which was completed by at least the summer of 1810. We can probably advance this initial date to November 1810 on the following grounds: under the heading of Chapter X of his novel *St. Irvyne,* Shelley quotes some lines from *The Wandering Jew* (on his attempts to achieve death); if he had written the "soliloquy" by that time he would presumably have preferred it to the inferior lines of *The*

---
⁹ *The Wandering Jew*, III, 171-80.

Wandering Jew; Shelley was working on *St. Irvyne* as late as November 1810. As for the latest possible date, the fact that the treatment is closer to *The Wandering Jew* than to the *Queen Mab* episode suggests that it was written before *Queen Mab* (begun in the summer of 1812).

Although, as Bennett Weaver has shown, Shelley had read widely in the Bible,[1] the Biblical references in this poem are not all exact. It may be that he was recalling commentaries on the Bible or sermons or, perhaps, antireligious works such as those of Paine and Holbach which quoted Scripture with Satanic intent, for Shelley's examples are designed to show the inhumanity and destructiveness of the Biblical God. The reference to Korah (who with his followers was destroyed for opposing Moses) is clear enough, and will be found in Numbers XVI; the fiery sword is, of course, that which expelled Adam and Eve from Eden. It is not, however, described in Genesis (or *Paradise Lost*) as "two-edged". The destruction of Sennacherib and his Assyrian army is celebrated in various places in the Old Testament (for instance, in II *Kings* XVIII-XIX), but in none of them is there a mention of a "fiery tide." Apparently Shelley meant the phrase only in a general metaphorical sense. Exactly what he had in mind in the "noonday pestilence" is not clear. Professor Weaver refers to the pestilence of I Chronicles XXI, which came upon Israel because David numbered its people.[2] But neither here nor in the retelling of the story in II Samuel XXIV is there a reference to "noonday." Perhaps this is an echo blended in from the Ninety-first Psalm: "Nor for the pestilence that walketh in darkness; nor for the destruction that wasteth at noonday."

---

[1] Bennett Weaver, *Toward the Understanding of Shelley*, University of Michigan Press, 1932.
[2] *Ibid.*, p. 134.

The word "remit" in the final line is somewhat cryptic; the Jew means that if God will take back the curse He placed upon him he can die (which is what he wishes).

Page 163. To Ianthe

SHELLEY AND HARRIET's first child Ianthe (later Mrs. Edward Jeffries Esdaile and future owner of the Esdaile Notebook — it was found in her coat pocket after her death) was born on June 23, 1813.[3] Whether she was born in London or Pimlico (where the Shelleys moved at about this time) has been a matter of controversy. And there has been some confusion on the exact form of her name.

To take the problem of the name first; some biographers give the name as Ianthe Eliza, some as Eliza Ianthe. The signature on the front endpaper of the Esdaile Notebook (presumably Ianthe's) is "Ianthe E Esdaile"; and the name on her tombstone is Ianthe Eliza Shelley Esdaile. This would appear to settle the matter. However, the baptismal record gives the name as Eliza Ianthe, and so, too, do the documents submitted by the Westbrooks and Shelley at the trial for the custody of Ianthe and Charles in 1817.[4] Possibly, Ianthe did not herself know how her name appeared on the baptismal registry and assumed that Ianthe was her first name (Shelley and Harriet and Charles in their letters call her simply Ianthe); or she may have preferred Ianthe Eliza.[5]

Shelley's cousin and biographer, Thomas Medwin, states

---

[3] Louise Schutz Boas, *Harriet Shelley* (London, New York, Toronto, 1962), pp. 129 and 176 — baptismal record and tombstone inscription. (The baptismal records are those of St. George's parish, which includes Chapel Street, where the Westbrooks lived, and — see below — Dover Street and Half Moon Street, where Shelley and Harriet lived.)

[4] Quoted in Medwin, *Shelley*, Appendix III; see pp. 463, 469, 470.

[5] Ianthe was the name of the heroine of *Queen Mab*, which must have

that Ianthe was born in a hotel in London; but he apparently based this statement simply on the fact that Shelley addressed two letters to Medwin's father from Cooke's Hotel in Dover Street, one before the birth, on June 21, one after the birth, on June 28.[6]

Hogg, contradicting Medwin, said he believed Ianthe had been born at Pimlico and not in Cooke's Hotel, for the "first time I called there [at Pimlico] was so soon after the birth of the child that it is hardly possible to suppose that she could have been removed thither from Dover Street."[7] But, as Hogg himself tells us that he was never inside the Pimlico house and obviously had no exact knowledge of the time of Ianthe's birth, his impression is not of prime importance.

There is, moreover, one piece of evidence that neither Hogg nor Medwin knew about. On June 27 Shelley sent a note by his servant from Cooke's Hotel to his Welsh friend John Williams, who was visiting London: "If you can call any time before two o'clock, I shall be at home, if afterwards, Mrs. S. will be very happy to see you . . . Dan will show you the way."[8] Harriet, then, was in London on June 27; and it is unlikely that, if she had given birth in Pimlico on June 23, she would be in London four days later. The place of birth, then, was almost certainly London. Was it, however, Cooke's Hotel?

Let us return to Hogg: "At the end of March 1813, Shelley and Harriet came from Killarney. . . . They remained a few days at a hotel in Dover Street, and then Harriet took lodgings in Half Moon Street [a few blocks

---

been published at about the time of Ianthe's birth; Eliza was presumably in honor of Harriet's sister, Elizabeth, who was always known as Eliza.

[6] Medwin, *Shelley*, p. 20. For Medwin's possession of these letters, see Ernest J. Lovell, *Captain Medwin* (University of Texas Press, [1962]), p. 311.

[7] Hogg, *Shelley*, II, 106; see also pp. 5, 68.

[8] Shelley, *Works*, IX, 72. This note was first printed in 1920.

from Dover Street], accounting the situation fashionable."[9] As no letters of Shelley bearing a Half Moon Street address have so far been published, some skepticism has been voiced on Hogg's statement. But there is a letter (unpublished) in The Carl H. Pforzheimer Library addressed by Shelley from Half Moon Street. The lodgings, then, unquestionably existed. (They appear from Hogg's descriptions to have consisted of furnished rooms, a sitting room on the ground floor and one or more bedrooms above.) It seems more likely that Ianthe was born at these "fashionable" lodgings than at Cooke's Hotel.

One question remains: if Shelley and Harriet had been living in Half Moon Street since April, why was Shelley addressing letters from Cooke's Hotel in June? Hogg tells us that he used the hotel for business meetings; and he might well have wished also to hide his true address from his pressing creditors. Shelley, then, apparently continued to retain a room at the hotel.

After a few weeks in Pimlico the Shelleys moved again, this time to the village of Bracknell (some thirty miles away). There they were visited by Thomas Love Peacock, who was impressed by Shelley's attention to the baby: "He was extremely fond of it, and would walk up and down a room with it in his arms for a long time together, singing to it a monotonous melody of his own making. . . ."[1] Harriet wrote to her Irish friend Catherine Nugent: "I wish you could see my sweet babe. She is so fair, with such blue eyes, that the more I see her the more beautiful she looks."[2] The opening of Shelley's sonnet is the poetical expression of the same feeling of happiness in the dimpled, blue-eyed baby.

---

[9] Hogg, *Shelley*, II, 68; see also pp. 5, 26.
[1] Peacock, *Memoirs*, pp. 69-70.
[2] October 11, 1813, Shelley, *Complete Works*, IX, 79.

Page 164. Evening—to Harriet

THE LINE-NUMBERED section of the Notebook ends, as we have seen (page 21), with "The wandering Jew's soliloquy." Then come the two sonnets "To Ianthe" and "Evening—to Harriet," on facing pages, "To Ianthe" on the left-hand page. They are the last poems in the book in Shelley's hand. Following them come transcriptions by Harriet.

Both poems present problems in dating of a type unusual in Shelley scholarship. As a rule, dating problems in Shelley arise because he has neglected to put down any date. For these sonnets he added too many dates.

Let us consider the sonnet "To Ianthe"—on the left-hand page—first. At the top, following the title, Shelley has written "Oct," crossed it out, and substituted "Septr. 1813." This dating is in an ink considerably darker than that used for the title and the body of the sonnet, and so was probably added later. When we look across at the right-hand page, at the sonnet to Harriet, we immediately see that the ink is somewhat darker than that of the sonnet to Ianthe, which probably means that the two sonnets were not copied into the book at the same time. Then we see that Shelley has again added a date after the title—"Sep. 1813"—and this is in the same dark ink as the other added date. As this ink is still darker than that of the sonnet to Harriet, it would seem that this date also was added after the sonnets were copied. Thus to the eye the appearance of the two pages suggests three separate times of writing: the sonnet to Ianthe, the sonnet to Harriet, the dates at the top.

If we now read through the sonnet to Harriet we find, on the line below its last line, the date "July 31st. 1813" written in ink of about the same consistency as that of the sonnet itself. The indication is that this date was added when the sonnet was copied into the Notebook. We might note also that the "from" and the crossing out of the "to" (see Textual Notes) are in ink of the same shade as the July 31 date and the sonnet as a whole. This would indicate that Shelley read the sonnet over after he had copied it, changed "to" to "from," and added the date.

Why, then, if Shelley placed the date July 31 below the sonnet shortly after composing it did he also place the date "Sep." at the top? Dowden suggested that this September dating was that "of Shelley's copying the poem into the book."[3] This is perhaps the most likely explanation, although one objection, at least, can be raised against it. If it is a date of copying, then that at the top of the sonnet to Ianthe is presumably a date of copying also; but on this date, as we have noted, Shelley hesitated, writing "Oct" first, then crossing it out and writing "Sept^r." Shelley might not always have known the date within a month, but he would normally know the month itself. Two solutions to this difficulty may be suggested: (a) Shelley might have been writing on the last day of September or the first of October, in which case he could have had some hesitation. (b) The darker ink suggests, as we have seen, that these dates were written in later. How much later, of course, the ink alone cannot tell us; perhaps a few hours, perhaps several months. If there was a long lapse of time, however, Shelley might not have remembered whether he had done the copying in September or October.

Why, one might wonder, were dates of copying added at all? As Harriet herself, as we shall see, noted a copying date, she may have regarded some of them as important

---

[3] Dowden, *Shelley*, I, 385 n.

(presumably for sentimental reasons), so that perhaps Shelley added these dates at her request. That the poems were copied in especially for Harriet is indicated by the fact that they are carefully written and fully punctuated (in contrast to the previous poems). Presumably, then, at the time they were copied the Notebook was regarded as Harriet's.

Whatever the explanation for the puzzling September dates at the top of the sonnets, however, there can be little doubt that the actual date of composition for the sonnet to Harriet was July 31, 1813.

What, then, of the sonnet to Ianthe? Here we have a certain initial date of composition, namely, that of Ianthe's birth, June 23, 1813, and the fact that this sonnet is followed by the sonnet to Harriet probably indicates that it was written at about the same time, probably earlier rather than later. That it cannot have been written long after Ianthe's birth is shown by the sonnet itself, which is clearly addressed to a very young infant (with "weak" frame and "passive eyes").

The sonnet to Harriet was apparently written (in the "evening") after a lover's quarrel. What this quarrel was about we do not know, but it more likely had to do with Eliza than Harriet directly. Peacock, who was with the Shelleys at Bracknell, tells us that Ianthe was "looked after by his wife's sister, whom he intensely disliked,"[4] and this was confirmed by Shelley himself: "It is a sight which awakens an inexpressible sensation of disgust and horror, to see her caress my poor little Ianthe."[5]

---

[4] Peacock, *Memoirs*, p. 70.
[5] To T. J. Hogg, March 16, 1814, Shelley, *Complete Works*, IX, 87.

COMMENTARIES

Page 165. To Harriett ("Thy look of love")[6]

IN THE SPRING of 1814, at least two months before Shelley became interested in Mary Godwin, his marriage with Harriet began to break up. This is apparent from a letter that he wrote to Hogg on March 16, 1814, from the village of Bracknell, where he was then living:

> I have been staying with Mrs. B[oinville] for the last month; I have escaped, in the society of all that philosophy and friendship combine, from the dismaying solitude of myself.... my heart sickens at the view of that necessity, which will quickly divide me from the delightful tranquillity of this happy home — for it has become my home.... Eliza is still with us — not here! — but will be with me when the infinite malice of destiny forces me to depart. I am now but little inclined to contest this point. I certainly hate her with all my heart and soul.[7]

The following week Shelley and Harriet were together in London; on March 24 they were remarried, as there was some doubt about the legality of their Scottish union.

The next month, on April 18, Mrs. Boinville wrote from Bracknell to Hogg:

> Shelley is again a widower; his beauteous half went to town on Thursday with Miss Westbrook, who is gone to live, I believe, at Southhampton.[8]

Also in April, Shelley wrote a poem, "Stanzas: April, 1814," in which he once more laments having to leave

---

[6] In regard to Harriet's spelling of the name, we might note Shelley's letter to Thomas Charles Medwin, October 21, 1811, asking him to draw up a marriage settlement: "I wish the sum settled on my wife in case of my death to be £700 per annum. The maiden name is Harriett Westbrook, with two T's — Harriett." (Shelley, *Complete Works*, VIII, 162.) Both Harriet and Shelley, however, usually spelled it with one "t." Apparently "Harriett" was the legal form of the name, and this Shelley wished to establish for the settlement. See also Medwin, *Shelley*, Appendix III, p. 463.

[7] Shelley, *Complete Works*, IX, 85-6.

[8] Hogg, *Shelley*, II, 145.

Mrs. Boinville's house. In the fall, looking back over these events, he wrote again to Hogg:

> In the beginning of Spring, I spent two months at Mrs. Boinville's without my wife . . . . The presence of Mrs. Boinville & her daughter afforded a strange contrast to my former friendship & deplorable condition . . . . I saw the full extent of the calamity which my rash & heartless union with Harriet: an union over whose entrance might justly be inscribed "Lasciate ogni speranza, voi ch'entrate!" had produced.[9]

Shelley, then, must have spent most of March and April at Mrs. Boinville's house, and Harriet was away. Where she was or why she was away we do not know, but she and Eliza were evidently together and there had been trouble over Eliza's presence in the household.

Shelley's stay at Mrs. Boinville's was not, as he seems to imply to Hogg in the fall, continuous. He informed Hogg on March 16 that he was returning home; this probably means that Harriet was coming back. Perhaps she did so only after the remarriage on March 24. Eliza, as we learn from Mrs. Boinville, came back with her; but by April 18 Shelley was "again a widower"; Harriet and Eliza had both left, Harriet going to London and Eliza to Southampton. Shelley then apparently went back to Mrs. Boinville's. There, it would appear from his April poem and other evidence, he began to show some romantic interest in Mrs. Boinville's daughter, Cornelia Turner. Whether Harriet later returned for a time to Bracknell from London is not known. The next we hear of her she is in Bath, early in July, and then at Bracknell.[1] In the meantime, Shelley had met Mary Godwin.

---

[9] *New Shelley Letters*, p. 76.
[1] Mrs. Godwin says that Harriet came to London from Bracknell in July. (Dowden, *Shelley*, II, 543.)

On June 8 [2] Hogg accompanied Shelley to Godwin's house:

> I stood reading the names of old English authors on the backs of the venerable volumes, when the door was partially and softly opened. A thrilling voice called "Shelley!" A thrilling voice answered "Mary!" And he darted out of the room, like an arrow from the bow of the far-shooting king. A very young female, fair and fair-haired, pale indeed, and with a piercing look, wearing a frock of tartan, an unusual dress in London at that time, had called him out of the room. He was absent a very short time — a minute or two; and then returned. "Godwin is out; there is no use in waiting." So we continued our walk along Holborn.
> "Who was that, pray?" I asked, "a daughter?"
> "Yes."
> "A daughter of William Godwin?"
> "The daughter of Godwin and Mary." [3]

Shelley and Mary, then, had obviously met before June 8. How long before, we can determine from William Godwin's Journal. In April, Godwin records no visits from Shelley (then presumably living mainly at Mrs. Boinville's in Bracknell). In May, however, the picture changes. Godwin records Shelley's presence at his house on May 5, 6, 13, 18, 20, 23, 26, 27. In June the visits become even more frequent, Shelley dining at the Godwins' on June 19, 20, 22, 24, 25, 26, 28, 29. The first declaration of love, according to Godwin, came on June 26; Shelley and Mary perhaps first actually made love on June 27. [4]

---

[2] Godwin records the date in his Journal (Abinger Manuscript, Pforzheimer microfilm).

[3] Hogg, *Shelley*, II, 148.

[4] Godwin to John Taylor, August 27, 1814, quoted in White, *Shelley*, I, 338. On August 4, 1814, Shelley wrote an entry in Mary Godwin's Journal: "Mary told me that this was my birthday; I thought it had been the 27th June." (*Mary Shelley's Journal*, p. 5.) Raymond D. Havens believed that this meant that it was on this date that "Shelley first learned of Mary's

On July 6 Harriet wrote from Bath to Shelley's friend Thomas Hookham in London: "I would not trouble you but it is now four days since I have heard from him which to me is an age."[5] On July 8 Godwin's notation "Talk with Mary" indicates his first sign of concern. By July 15 Harriet was back from Bath and called on Godwin with Shelley; Godwin was not in; but then later "call[ed] on Shelley," which indicates that Shelley and Harriet were not living together in London. Harriet was presumably at her father's house. Within two weeks Shelley and Mary had eloped — as Godwin noted with typical meticulousness in his entry for July 28 — at "Five in the morning," and Mrs. Godwin took off in pursuit by the Dover coach.

It has usually been considered that June was the month in which Shelley began to take an interest in Mary. This seems to be supported by Shelley himself. "In the month of June," he told Hogg in his letter of October 3, "I came to London to accomplish some business with Godwin that had been long depending. The circumstances of the case required an almost constant residence at his house. There I met his daughter Mary." After describing her beauties of mind and body, he concludes: "I speedily conceived an ardent passion to possess this inestimable treasure."[6]

Godwin's Journal, however, shows that it was in May and not June that Shelley's visits began. And if "speedily" means the usual Shelleyan speed, it indicates May. This too, was Mrs. Godwin's recollection. "In May," she wrote a few months later, "Mary came home from Scotland, and

---

regard for him." (*Modern Language Notes*, April 1930, p. 225.) Havens, however, does not mention Godwin's comment; and on matters of date Godwin is likely to have been accurate. On this matter, however, Shelley is likely to have been accurate also; June 27 must have had special significance — and it was the day after the declaration of love.

[5] Shelley, *Complete Works*, IX, 91.
[6] *New Shelley Letters*, pp. 77, 78.

then began all our troubles. He paid her the most devoted attentions, and my husband spoke to him on the subject. Mr. S—— declared that it was only his manner with all women. Shortly after, Harriet Shelley came up from Bracknell suddenly, and saw me and my husband alone. She was very much agitated, and wept, poor dear young lady, a great deal, because Mr. Shelley had told her yesterday at Bracknell that he was desperately in love with Mary Godwin." As Dowden points out, the chronology here is somewhat shaky.[7] Mary returned not in May but on March 30; the talk with Shelley and Harriet's visit must have occurred in July. But there is no reason to doubt the essential truth of Mrs. Godwin's story. Her memory of May as the month in which the "troubles" began is probably correct; she doubtless saw more than her husband did; and the numerous visits by Shelley in May were obviously not all motivated by an obsession with Godwin's business problems (which Shelley had successfully resisted in March and April).

Moreover, May as the starting point for Shelley's interest in Mary is indicated also, it seems to me, in this poem, "To Harriett ('Thy look of love')," written in May, and at Cooke's Hotel[8] — in Dover Street, London, where the Shelleys, as we have seen, had stayed briefly the previous spring and which Shelley used for business purposes. The poem, then, was written in London; but that Harriet was not in London in May, or in June either, is indicated by a lack of reference to her in Godwin's Journal

---

[7] Dowden, *Shelley*, II, 543.

[8] Harriet places "Cook's Hotel" (which Shelley apparently spelled "Cooke's") at the bottom of the first page, after stanza three, and the date at the end of the poem on the opposite page. Why she separated the two is not clear. Possibly she was copying from a letter (see below) and the two were separated there. Or perhaps she was in a depressed or agitated state when she was copying.

and by other evidence. She was perhaps at Bracknell; or she may have left for Bath in May. Shelley's frequent visits to Godwin indicate that he was living most of the time in London and this makes it more likely that Harriet was at Bath (108 miles from London) rather than at Bracknell (27 miles from London). In either case the probability is that the poem was mailed to Harriet in a letter and the letter was dated from Cooke's Hotel.

Dowden commented, in part, on the poem as follows:

> In this piteous appeal Shelley declares that he has now no grief but one — the grief of having known and lost his wife's love; if it is the fate of all who would live in the sunshine of her affection to endure her scorn, then let him be scorned above the rest, for he most of all has desired that sunshine; let not the world and the pride of life harden her heart; it is better that she should be kind and gentle; if she has something to endure, it is not much, and all her husband's weal hangs upon her loving endurance; for, see, how pale and wildered anguish has made him; oh! in mercy do not cure his malady by the fatal way of condemning him to exile beyond all hope or further fear; oh! trust no erring guide, no unwise counsellor, no false pride; rather learn that a nobler pride may find its satisfaction in and through love; or if love be for ever dead, at least let pity survive in its room.[9]

There is doubtless truth in this interpretation, but it seems to miss the main point. What was it that stirred Shelley to write it? Why the note of guilt:

> Then hear thy chosen own [*i.e.* admit], too late,
> His heart most worthy of thy hate.

Why the obvious suffering and moral conflict? Shelley showed no such symptoms in his letter to Hogg on March 16. The answer must be that he had begun to feel an at-

[9] Dowden, *Shelley*, I, 413.

traction to Mary and was torn between this and his duty to Harriet. The poem probably marks the beginning of that traumatic ambivalence which Peacock noted in July: "Between his old feelings towards Harriet, *from whom he was not then separated*, and his new passion for Mary, he showed in his looks, in his gestures, in his speech, the state of a mind 'suffering, like a little kingdom, the nature of an insurrection.' His eyes were bloodshot, his hair and dress disordered. He caught up a bottle of laudanum, and said: 'I never part from this.' "[1]

Seen in this light, "To Harriett" is a very different poem from what it appeared to Dowden and other commentators. Shelley, frightened by the intensity of his feeling for Mary, is trying to move back to Harriet and urges her, for this reason, finally to get rid of Eliza (the "erring guide" is obviously Eliza). Clearly Harriet still has more attraction for him than he admitted in his letter to Hogg in the fall in which he represented the charms of Mary as instantly overwhelming. At the time of writing this poem — probably late in May — he has by no means decided that his way must lie with Mary; he is, in fact, in turmoil, caught up by "the stormiest passion of my soul."

Harriet, of course, did not, when she received the poem, see all the motives behind it or the implications in it. By the time she copied it into the Notebook, however, these were doubtless apparent. When this was we do not know, but as she and not Shelley did the copying, it was probably after Shelley's elopement with Mary, and as the poem is followed by one dated 1815, probably before the end of 1815.

---

[1] Peacock, *Memoirs*, p. 91.

Page 167. Full many a mind

FOLLOWING "To Harriett ('Thy look of love')" comes a blank left-hand page, then these lines in Harriet's hand on the facing right-hand page, dated below the verses: "Stanmore. 1815." In 1815 Stanmore was a village of a few hundred inhabitants ten miles out on a main coach road — the Edgware Road — from London. It had two inns and there were several gentlemen's houses (including Lord Castlereagh's) in the vicinity. The Westbrooks do not appear to have had any connections there.[2] We had not known previously that Harriet had been there and we fail to find any reference to it in her letters or the letters and journals of Shelley and Mary. So far as the year 1815 is concerned, the few references we have to Harriet in Mary Shelley's Journal (in January and April) seem to indicate that she is in London. The Edgware Road route, however, as shown on coaching maps of the time, began at the northeast corner of Hyde Park just a few streets away from the Westbrook house on Chapel Street.

We are unable to identify the lines. The verse, however, is so poor and the sentiment in the second stanza so un-Shelleyan that they are certainly not by Shelley.

It is possible that the stanzas represent two poems and not one and that they have been copied from some book of verse. The probability, however, seems to be that they were by Harriet herself and were intended to form one poem: the irregularity of the meter and other crudities indicate an amateur poet; the fact that Harriet copied them into the Notebook must mean that they have some

---

[2] Miss A. M. Dimbleby, District Librarian, Harrow Public Library, Kenton, Middlesex, wrote in reply to an inquiry: "I have been unable to find that Harriet Westbrook or her family had any connection with Stanmore, nor have I ever seen any reference to such a connection with this district."

connection with Shelley. And if we look at them in this light they make a certain amount of sense.

The first stanza, with its "radiant genius" in "wild despair," could well—to judge his letters to her in the fall of 1814—reflect Shelley's moods in some of his interviews with Harriet. The second stanza would appear to be a pious wish that Shelley might find "peace of mind" in the legality of marriage, sanctified both by society ("Earth's laws") and by God—that is, in a return to Harriet.

The implication in the poem seems to be that Harriet was at Stanmore sometime in 1815 and that either Shelley visited her there or she there wrote down sentiments which seemed appropriate to a previous meeting in London.

Page 168. To Harriet ("Oh Harriet, love like mine")

RICHARD GARNETT, seeing this poem in Dowden's copybook, wrote to him: "I can hardly believe that the lines to Harriet dated May 1813, and in her writing, are Shelley's at all. If they are they must belong to a much earlier period." Dowden replied: "I quite agree with you about the lines in Harriet's handwriting dated May 1813."[3]

The subject matter, however, indicates that the poem is by Shelley, poor though it is. The main problem lies in the date. As Harriet dated the previous poem "1815," her May 1813 date, at the top of the poem, must be intended as a date of composition, not the date on which it was copied into the Notebook. But we also find, at the bottom, the notation "Cum Elam." Obviously either the date or the place is wrong, for neither Shelley nor Harriet was in

---

[3] *Letters about Shelley*, pp. 122, 123.

Cwm Elan in May 1813. They were, in fact, in London, and Harriet was eight months pregnant.

Shelley, as we have already seen, was at Cwm Elan (near Rhayader in Wales) on only two occasions: once, in the summer of 1811, without Harriet, and again in June 1812 with her; in May 1812 they were at Nantgwillt, but a mile and a half away from Cwm Elan, and doubtless they visited Cwm Elan. The style and sentiment of the poem, however, are not at all in accord with the poetry Shelley was writing at that time, for instance, "The Retrospect: Cwm Elan." Nor are the sentiments in general accord with Shelley's relationship with Harriet in 1812. They are, however, in accord with that relationship in the early summer of 1811 when Shelley was at Cwm Elan. (That they were to Harriet Westbrook and not Harriet Grove is shown by the reference to "my Harriet.")[4]

As for the subject matter of the poem, let us compare its sentiments with those in the letter to Hogg from Cwm Elan on August 3, 1811, in which Shelley tells of his plans for elopement: "Her father has persecuted her in a most horrible way, & endeavours to compel her to go to school. . . . I set off for London on Monday. . . . I advised her to resist . . she wrote to say that resistance was useless, but that she would fly with me, & threw herself on my protection.—. . . Gratitude & admiration all demand that I should love her *forever*."[5]

The "hour which tears thee from me" (line 29) could be the hour of Harriet's forced return to school. (There was no threat to take her away from Shelley in 1812.) "My ever dear Harriet to save" (line 18) could refer to Shelley's leaving for London to rescue her from her persecution. And the sentiment of "eternal affection" (line 17) which

---

[4] See commentary to "To November," above, p. 187.
[5] *Shelley and his Circle*, II, 856.

runs through the poem is that of the "love her *forever*" of the letter. The indications of previous suicidal tendencies in lines 25-8 are also, as we have seen, paralleled in Shelley's poems written at Cwm Elan in 1811.

If, then, the poem was composed at Cwm Elan, it was composed either late in July or in the first few days of August 1811 (Shelley left for London on August 5), and sent to Harriet by mail, either in the text of a letter (as with poems in letters to Hogg and Elizabeth Hitchener) or as a verse letter. The final line, "Adieu, my love; good night," sounds like the close of a letter; for Shelley frequently closed his early letters to Hogg with "adieu." If, then, the poem was written rapidly and spontaneously in a state of agitation and mailed off immediately to Harriet, we may have an explanation for some of its irregularities and the poor quality of the verse. Other irregularities might have arisen from Harriet's attempts to decipher a messy manuscript full of Shelley's typical first-draft cancellations and interlineations.

If, however, the poem was written in July or early August 1811, why did Harriet put the date "May 1813" at the top? We can but guess. We might note, however, that the date comes before the title. It is possible that Harriet wrote in this date and intended to follow it with some other poem and then forgot to cancel the date. Or this date may have been mistakenly placed at the top of whatever manuscript she was copying from and she copied it mechanically. Whatever the explanation, the poem was certainly not written in May 1813.

There is one other possibility we might consider. Let us assume that the notation "Cum Elam" is wrong and the date partially right. Harriet may have miscopied 1811 as 1813, and, if in an agitated state, not seen her error. In this case the poem could have been written in May 1811.

Shelley left Harriet and London on May 10 and was in Sussex for the rest of the month.[6] True, we do not know whether Shelley in May was as involved with Harriet as this poem would suggest, but we do not know that he was not. His letters to Hogg in April and May contain mysterious hints of romance, but it is difficult to decide how seriously these are to be taken.

One can only assume — on this hypothesis — that Harriet herself added "Cum Elam" and did not find it on the manuscript from which she was copying. She could — again assuming she was in an agitated state, similar perhaps to that indicated in her suicide letter — have written in "Cum Elam," thinking that that was where the poem had come from. (Shelley apparently sent her several letters from Cwm Elan.)

Whether the poem was written in May or later in the summer, it indicates that Shelley was emotionally more deeply involved with Harriet in the period before the elopement than we would gather from his letters to Hogg or Elizabeth Hitchener.

Page 170. Late was the night

THIS IS a puzzling poem. It is so poor in parts that it is hard to believe that it is by Shelley. Even in the worst of the "Victor and Cazire" *Original Poetry* we find nothing so incoherent or technically inept as, for instance, the second stanza. On the other hand, some of the lines are not bad (line 3, for example), and the subject matter — the betrayed and wandering girl — is similar to "Cold are the blasts" and a song in *Original Poetry*:

---

[6] *Shelley and his Circle*, II, 783.

COMMENTARIES

> See! o'er yon rocky height,
>   Dim mists are flying—
> See by the moon's pale light,
>   Poor Laura's dying!

One possible explanation is that this was a very early poem by Shelley, which Harriet found in a corrupt text, and that she copied it while in a state of agitation similar to that discernible in her suicide letter. Although Harriet's handwriting is usually neat, here it is almost illegible in places, and there are copying errors of a kind we do not find in the other poems. As the date indicates, the poem was copied in 1815. At some point in 1815 Harriet may have begun to realize that Shelley would never come back to her, and felt that the poem reflected her own abandoned condition, even to the dread of a "watery grave" (line 19). Perhaps she copied the poem into the book so that she might show it to Shelley when he visited her.

"Teinted" in line 2 is a variant spelling of "tainted" in its sense of "colored."

Page 171. To St Irvyne

ON APRIL 17, 1810, Harriet Grove, then visiting the Shelley's at Field Place with her family, recorded in her diary: "Still more odd, Walked to Horsham saw the Old House St Irvyne had a long conversation but more perplexed than ever walked in the evening to Strood by moonlight."[7]

Her brother Charles, some forty-seven years later, also remembered the occasion:

---

[7] *Shelley and his Circle,* II, 575. (For the "Old House," see Plate VIII.)

> I did not meet Bysshe again after that till I was fifteen, the year I left the navy, and then I went to Field Place with my father, mother, Charlotte, and Harriet. Bysshe was there, having just left Eton, and his sister, Elizabeth. Bysshe was at that time more attached to my sister Harriet than I can express, and I recollect well the moonlight walks we four had at Strode, and also at St. Irving's; that, I think, was the name of the place, then the Duke of Norfolk's, at Horsham. (St. Irving's Hills, a beautiful place, on the right-hand side as you go from Horsham to Field Place, laid out by the famous Capability Brown, and full of magnificent forest trees, waterfalls, and rustic seats).[8]

Such, then, was St. Irvyne and such the memorable walks. At first glance one might think that the poem "To St Irvyne" referred to these walks, but examination indicates that it was written earlier and must refer to another visit. Harriet, one might gather from references in her 1809 diary entries, had been at Field Place in August 1808. If we put this together with the "August Moon" (line 7) of the poem and with the fact that Shelley in a poem published in the fall of 1810 lamented that "two years of speechless bliss are gone,"[9] it seems probable that the romance began in August 1808 and that it was associated with a visit to the ruins at St. Irvyne in the moonlight. The later visits, in April 1810, with Charles and Elizabeth, perhaps had a significance for Shelley and Harriet that their companions did not know.

---

[8] Charles Grove to Hellen Shelley, February 16, 1857, Hogg, *Shelley*, II, 154-5. The parenthetical comment on St. Irving's Hills is presumably by Hellen Shelley. In this regard we might note the following in *Paterson's Roads* (1811): "*Broadbridge Heath*. On *l*, Hill Place, Lady Irwin; and on *r*, Field Place, Tim. Shelley, Esq.; and beyond it, Strood, John Commerell, Esq." The Hills estate was purchased from Lady Irvine by the Duke of Norfolk in two transactions, one in 1788, one in 1810-1811. (See William Albery, *A Parliamentary History of Horsham, 1295-1885* [Horsham, 1926], pp. 252-3.

[9] "Melody to a Scene of Former Times."

This hypothesis is also supported by what evidence we have for dating the poem. (The date of February 28, 1805, at the top cannot be the date of composition, for Shelley was only twelve in February 1805 and hardly likely to be looking back on a romance of the previous summer.) On April 22, 1810, Shelley sent his friend Edward Fergus Graham a poem which is rather like "To St Irvyne." In it a "youth with darkened brow" near St. Irvyne's "tower" is mourning his "long-lost love." Harriet Grove had arrived at Field Place on April 16 and left on April 18. Perhaps the poem was evoked by her leaving, or perhaps it was an earlier poem Shelley included in his letter, as he did with poems in letters to Hogg.

When in the fall of 1810 Shelley published his novel *St. Irvyne*, written in the main between the fall of 1809 and the spring of 1810, he included in it some of the stanzas of the poem sent on April 22 to Graham. Then in *Original Poetry* we find a song, dated April 1810, which is clearly on the same subject:

> Then ——! dearest farewell,
>   You and I love, may ne'er meet again;
> These woods and these meadows can tell
>   How soft and how sweet was the strain.

The name Harriet in the first line would fit the meter. Presumably this poem was inspired by Harriet's leaving Field Place on April 18. Its "ne'er meet again," however, seems curious in view of the fact that Shelley saw Harriet again in London on April 25. Perhaps he did not know that this would happen when he wrote the poem. Harriet gives no indication in her diary entry on leaving Field Place that she expected to see Shelley in London.[1]

Shelley, then, was writing poems of the same type as

---

[1] *Shelley and his Circle*, II, 576.

"To St Irvyne" in the spring of 1810. "To St Irvyne," however, was not written in the spring; otherwise Shelley would hardly speak of the "winter winds" (line 1) roaring around St. Irvyne's turrets. It would seem that it was written in the preceding winter.

If Shelley was writing poems in the winter of 1809-1810 and the spring of 1810 bemoaning his separation from Harriet Grove and engaging in death fantasies (both in "To St Irvyne" and in the poem sent to Graham on April 22), they must have had their orgin in the crisis of the fall of 1809. That "To St Irvyne" was part of this complex is indicated also by its tone, which is closer to that of other 1809 poems than to the deeper emotions stirred up the following year, for instance, in "Melody to a Scene of Former Times."

If the poem was written in the winter of 1809-1810, what is the meaning of the date "Feb^{ry} 28th 1805" which Harriet Shelley has placed in front of the title and which she must have found in the manuscript from which she was copying? Dowden suggested that this date might "refer to some incident of February in that year, which might be viewed as a starting-point in the course of their love."[2] The indication, however, as we have seen, is that although Shelley and Harriet had known each other previously, the romance did not begin until the summer of 1808. Could the date be that of the first meeting of Shelley and Harriet Grove? Charles Grove begins the letter to Hellen Shelley quoted above as follows:

> It is very difficult, after so long a time, to remember with accuracy events which occurred so long ago. The first time I ever saw Bysshe was when I was at Harrow. I was nine years old; my brother George, ten. We took him up to Brentford, where he was at school, at Dr. Green-

[2] Dowden, *Shelley*, I, 48.

law's; a servant of my father's taking care of us all. He accompanied us to Ferne, and spent the Easter holidays there.[3]

The "Easter holidays" normally began in the middle of February and ran for some eight weeks; according to Roger Ingpen, Charles Grove was born in 1794, but he does not give the month.[4] The "Easter holidays" referred to, then, would be either those of 1803 or 1804. But, as Grove states that he was not sure of his accuracy in surveying events of some fifty years before, it may be that this visit took place in 1805.

Material on pastedown endpapers, leaf 1, verso, and leaf 140 (final leaf), verso

THIS material is noted in the Bibliographical Description (page 329).

The front pastedown endpaper contains the name "Ianthe E Esdaile" near the top. Presumably this is Ianthe's signature (we have no other specimens of her handwriting at our disposal) and indicates that she owned the book. The uncertain letters (in an unknown hand) "GE — GY" on the verso of the first leaf are puzzling. The "E" might stand for "Esdaile."

On the final leaf Shelley made a notation on the top line — "Vol. 7. 286. Gibbon." This must refer to *The History of the Decline and Fall of the Roman Empire*, which Shelley also refers to in his Notes to *Queen Mab* (note to III, 189: "Even love is sold," a note on marriage

---

[3] Hogg, *Shelley*, II, 154.
[4] *The Journal of Harriet Grove for the Years 1809-1810*, ed. Roger Ingpen (London, 1932), p. viii.

and sex). He then added a footnote to the note: "The first Christian emperor made a law by which seduction was punished with death: if the female pleaded her own consent, she also was punished with death; if the parents endeavoured to screen the criminals, they were banished and their estates confiscated; the slaves who might be accessory were burned alive, or forced to swallow melted lead. The very offspring of an illegal love were involved in the consequences of the sentence.—*Gibbon's Decline and Fall, &c.*, vol. ii. page 210. See also, for the hatred of the primitive Christians to love and even marriage, page 269."

We have been unable to find an edition of the *Decline and Fall* in which the passage Shelley is paraphrasing appears on page 210 of Volume II. In the Dublin edition of 1788, however, we find the passage on pages 208-9; and his reference to the primitive Christians' hatred of marriage on pages 266-7. This edition, then, seems to run about two pages behind the one that Shelley was using, so that we would expect to find his reference to page 286 of Volume VII some two pages earlier. And this is what we do find. Although there seems to be nothing on page 286 that held special interest for Shelley, on page 284 we find a comment that would have interested him very much —on "Mazdak, who asserted the community of women and the equality of mankind." This sounds as though the "Vol. 7. 286" reference was made when the *Queen Mab* note on marriage and sex was being written, and indicates that Shelley had the Esdaile Notebook in his possession while he was working on the Notes to *Queen Mab*. As we have seen, Shelley wrote to Hookham on February 19, 1813: "Queen Mab is finished and transcribed. I am now preparing the Notes which shall be long and philosophical. You will recieve [*sic*] it with the other poems."

The notation "4/" on the back pastedown endpaper indicates that the Notebook cost four shillings. This seems high. Possibly they were Irish shillings. Hogg tells us that in 1813 he found Irish currency in an unstable condition.[5]

[5] Hogg, *Shelley*, I, 409-10.

Publication History

ALTHOUGH it might at first seem a simple matter to determine how many lines from the Esdaile Notebook have been previously published, it turns out to be rather complex. The problem arises from the fact that some of the poems have been published from other sources and these texts often differ from the Notebook text, so that we cannot always simply say that a certain line has or has not been published. Before we discuss this question, however, let us take up the material published from the Esdaile Notebook text itself. Here there are no particular difficulties and we can make an exact estimate.

The largest number of lines published from the Notebook are those that first appeared in Edward Dowden's *The Life of Percy Bysshe Shelley*, 1886,[1] and thereafter in editions of Shelley's poetry. Dowden, as we have noted, also copied out the whole Notebook and showed this copy

---

[1] Dowden (*Shelley*, I, viii) makes acknowledgment as follows: "My debt is great to Shelley's grandsons, Charles E. J. Esdaile, Esq., and the Rev. W. Esdaile. Mr. Charles Esdaile lent me the manuscript volume of unpublished poetry by Shelley, of which in its proper place I have given an account; and he permitted me to print for the first time all such poems or passages of poems as seemed to me of special biographical interest. The Rev. W. Esdaile enabled me to correct some errors of preceding biographers." Dowden's main comments on the Notebook will be found on pages 345-9. For an examination of the Notebook based on Dowden and other published information, see Cameron, *The Young Shelley*, pp. 233-8, 379-85.

to Richard Garnett.[2] He did not, however, attempt to publish any poems in addition to those which he was given permission to publish by Charles Edward Jeffries Esdaile, in whose possession the Notebook then was. Dowden's copy remained in the hands of his family after his death.

The year following the publication of Dowden's life of Shelley, one poem, "The wandering Jew's soliloquy," was published by Bertram Dobell in an appendix to his Shelley Society edition of Shelley's *The Wandering Jew*.[3] The fourth stanza of Shelley's translation of "The Marseillaise" was, as we have seen, published (in 1877 by H. B. Forman) from a text in a letter from Shelley to Edward Fergus Graham.[4] The whole poem, from the Esdaile Notebook text, was published in 1910 by André Koszul in an appendix to his book *La Jeunesse de Shelley*.[5]

Roger Ingpen, in editing Shelley's poems for *Complete Works* (1926-1930), republished the poems previously published by Dowden, Dobell, and Koszul, but he was not permitted to publish any others from the Esdaile Notebook. He was, however, allowed to check the texts of those already published.[6]

Nothing further was published from the Notebook until 1956 when Neville Rogers printed 73 lines in his book *Shelley at Work*.[7] And in 1962, 8 lines were published by Louise S. Boas in her biography of Harriet Shelley.[8]

---

[2] See above, pp. 32, 175-6.
[3] The Shelley Society Publications, Second Series, No. 12 (London, 1887), pp. 69-70.
[4] See above, p. 270.
[5] Pp. 401-4.
[6] Shelley, *Complete Works*, III, [v] ("Editor's Preface"), 315. To one poem, however, "A Dialogue," Ingpen added two lines from the Esdaile Notebook. Ingpen's texts for these poems are sometimes eclectic and his collations unreliable.
[7] Oxford, pp. 28, 29, 91-2, 121, 171. See also p. viii.
[8] *Harriet Shelley, Five Long Years* (London, New York, Toronto), pp. 179-80.

In addition to the poetry, the Notebook contains prose — one Advertisement and ten footnotes. Two of the footnotes have been published in full and one in part;[9] the advertisement is unpublished.

In the first of the tables below we present the poems and lines of poetry published from the Esdaile Notebook, with abbreviated titles for the works in which they appear.

Let us now consider the problem of the poems published from sources other than the Esdaile Notebook (Table II). There are four of these sources: poems in letters; manuscripts given to T. J. Hogg; manuscripts formerly owned by Sir Percy Florence Shelley (Boscombe MSS); and poems published by Shelley himself (in *Queen Mab* and *Alastor*). The poems in these manuscripts were published in the following works: Hogg's life of Shelley (1858); the Rossetti (1870) and Forman, IV (1877), editions of Shelley's poetry; Shelley, *Complete Works* (1926-1930); and *Shelley and his Circle* (1961). The poems in *Complete Works* are sometimes (as with the Hogg texts) taken from the printed text, sometimes (as with the Hitchener letters) directly from the manuscripts. All the poems in *Shelley and his Circle* are taken directly from the manuscripts. If a poem appears in a letter, *Complete Works* will include it both among the letters and among the poems. In Table II the reference is to the latter.

Although the number of lines previously published given in Table I may be taken as exact, those in Table II, as we have indicated, present more difficulty. The nature of the problem can best be shown by an example. Let us look at the first poem listed, the dedicatory poem "To Harriet ('Whose is the love')." This poem is listed as published — in the *Queen Mab* volume, where it also serves as a dedication. But actually only some of the lines are the

---

[9] Dowden, *Shelley*, I, 347; Rogers, *Shelley at Work*, pp. 28, 29.

same in both versions. For instance, stanza two runs as follows in the Esdaile Notebook:

> Whose looks gave grace to the majestic theme,
> The sacred, free and fearless theme of truth?
> Whose form did I gaze fondly on
> And love mankind the more?

In *Queen Mab* these lines run:

> Beneath whose looks did my reviving soul
> Riper in truth and virtuous daring grow?
> Whose eyes have I gazed fondly on,
> And loved mankind the more?

It would seem at first that we should record the first two lines as unpublished because they differ almost completely from the *Queen Mab* version. But, then, what is to be done about the next two lines, which differ only in a word or two? We cannot say flatly that they are either unpublished or published. This problem continues throughout. It seems impossible to construct a satisfactory yardstick. A purist in such matters might argue that if a line varied by only one word from a previous text, it was unpublished, and certainly a case can be made for such an argument. But the solution we have favored is that of recording in our tables as published in full all poems previously published and all their lines — even though there are variants in some lines — on the grounds that the poem as a whole has been published and its essential meaning is the same in both versions. We have, however, collated these poems and totaled the lines which show variants in words or phrasing. (One poem, "Cold are the blasts," has been published in two texts. Lines which these texts have in common have been counted only once.) This total (225 lines) the reader may deduct or not as he wishes from the grand total of published lines.

One special problem needs to be noted, namely, that some lines from two poems—"To Harriet ('It is not blasphemy')" and "Translation of The Marsellois Hymn" —have been published both from the Esdaile Notebook and from other sources. These lines, totaling 30, we have not counted twice, but in the Table I total only. In Table II they are placed within brackets.

In Table II we list for each set of lines the work in which it was first published and a reference to the standard edition (*Complete Works,* here abbreviated further to *Works*). For the texts first published in 1858 by T. J. Hogg in his life of Shelley ("Hogg"), we also refer to *Shelley and his Circle,* as the texts in this work were taken from the manuscripts and differ in some respects from Hogg's published transcripts.

Table III is the reverse of Tables I and II, namely, a list of the lines previously unpublished.

Some of the main conclusions indicated by the tables may be summarized as follows:

1. Of the 58 poems in the Esdaile Notebook, 9 have been published in full from the Notebook. Another 6 have been published in full from texts other than the Notebook.

2. Of the 2925 lines of poetry in the Esdaile Notebook, 511 have been published from the Notebook. Another 553 have been published from other sources; of these, 225 lines differ in wording, in one degree or another, from the corresponding lines in the Esdaile Notebook. If we count these 225 lines as previously published, we arrive at a total of 1064 lines previously published and 1861 lines previously unpublished. If we do not count these 225 lines as previously published, we get a total of 839 previously published and 2086 previously unpublished.

TABLE I: *Lines published from the Esdaile Notebook*

TITLE	PAGE	WHERE PUBLISHED	NO. OF LINES PUB.	LINE NOS.	TOTAL NO. OF LINES IN POEM
A Sabbath Walk	37	Dowden, I, 345	2	45-6	56
		Works, III, 111	2	45-6	
The Crisis	40	Dowden, I, 347	4	13-16	20
		Works, III, 111	4	13-16	
To Liberty	58	Dowden, I, 348	5	26-30	50
		Works, III, 111	5	26-30	
		Rogers, p. 171	10	41-50	
On Robert Emmet's Tomb	60	Dowden, I, 268	8	21-8	28
		Works, III, 104	8	21-8	
The Tombs	83	Dowden, I, 268	2	14-15	30
To Harriet ("It is not blasphemy")	85	Dowden, I, 286	72	1-72	72
		Works, III, 105	72	1-72	
Sonnet. To Harriet on her birth day	88	Dowden, I, 404	4	9-12	14
		Works, III, 107	4	9-12	
Sonnet. To a balloon, laden with Knowledge	89	Dowden, I, 294	14	1-14	14
		Works, III, 108	14	1-14	
Sonnet. On launching some bottles	90	Dowden, I, 294	14	1-14	14
		Works, III, 108	14	1-14	
A Retrospect of Times of Old	95	Rogers, p. 28	17	1-4, 71-83	83

(318)

TITLE	PAGE	WHERE PUBLISHED	NO. OF LINES PUB.	LINE NOS.	TOTAL NO. OF LINES IN POEM
THE VOYAGE	98	Rogers, pp. 91-2	42	40-62	298
		p. 121		60-2	
		p. 29		102-11	
				120-8	
A TRANSLATION OF THE MARSELLOIS HYMN	144	A. Koszul, *La Jeunesse de Shelley*, pp. 402-4	58	1-58	58
		Works, IV, 341-2	58	1-58	
ZEINAB AND KATHEMA	148	Dowden, I, 347	6	79-84	180
		Works, III, 97	6	79-84	
THE RETROSPECT	155	Dowden, I, 270-4	154	15-168	168
		Works, III, 99-103	154	15-168	
THE WANDERING JEW'S SOLILOQUY	161	Dobell, pp. 69-70	29	1-29	29
		Works, III, 77-8	29	1-29	
TO IANTHE	163	Dowden, I, 376	14	1-14	14
		Works, III, 111	14	1-14	
EVENING—TO HARRIET	164	Dowden, I, 385	14	1-14	14
		Works, III, 112	14	1-14	
TO HARRIETT ("THY LOOK OF LOVE")	165	Dowden, I, 413	30	1-30	30
	167	*Works*, III, 115	30	1-30	
FULL MANY A MIND		Boas, p. 179	8	1-8	8
TO ST IRVYNE	171	Rogers, p. 38	4	17-20	24

TABLE II: *Lines published from other sources*

TITLE	PAGE	WHERE PUBLISHED	NO. OF LINES PUB.	LINE NOS.	TOTAL NO. OF LINES IN POEM
TO HARRIET ("WHOSE IS THE LOVE")	37	*Queen Mab*, 1st ed., 1813, p. [iii] *Works*, I, 65	16	1-16	16
FALSHOOD AND VICE	44	Notes to *Queen Mab*, 1st ed., pp. 30-5 *Works*, I, 136-8	108 108	1-16 1-86 89-110 1-86 89-110	110
A TALE OF SOCIETY AS IT IS	62	Shelley, Rossetti ed., 1870, II, 526 ("Mother & Son"), from letter to Elizabeth Hitchener, Jan. 17, 1812 *Works*, III, 95-7	79	1-79 1-79	120
THE SOLITARY	67	Shelley, Rossetti ed., 1870, II, 507-8, from copy by Richard Garnett of	18	1-18	18

TITLE	PAGE	WHERE PUBLISHED	NO. OF LINES PUB.	LINE NOS.	TOTAL NO. OF LINES IN POEM
TO THE REPUBLICANS OF NORTH AMERICA	71	Boscombe MS *Works*, III, 72-3 Shelley, Rossetti ed., 1870, II, 528 ("The Mexican Revolution"), from letter to Elizabeth Hitchener, Feb. 14, 1812 *Works*, III, 98	18 40 40	1-18 1-30 41-50 1-30 41-50	50
TO DEATH	74	Hogg, I, 198-9, from MS given to Hogg by Shelley *Works*, III, 73-4 *Shelley and his Circle*, II, 641-3	48 48 48	1-48 1-48 1-48	68
THE PALE, THE COLD AND THE MOONY SMILE	79	*Alastor*, 1st ed., 1816, pp. 61-3	30	1-30	30

II—Lines published from other sources (CONTINUED)

TITLE	PAGE	WHERE PUBLISHED	NO. OF LINES PUB.	LINE NOS.	TOTAL NO. OF LINES IN POEM
TO HARRIET ("IT IS NOT BLASPHEMY")	85	Works, I, 204	30	1-30	30
		Notes to Queen Mab, 1st ed., 1813, p. 210	[12]	58-69	72
		Works, I, 157	[12]	58-69	
		Shelley, Forman ed., 1877, IV, 359, from copy by Richard Garnett of Boscombe MS	[9]	5-13	
A DIALOGUE	108	Works, III, 105	[9]	5-13	44
		Hogg, I, 197-8, from MS given to Hogg by Shelley	40	1-10 13-30 33-44	
		Works, III, 70-1	42	1-30 33-44	
HOW ELOQUENT ARE EYES!	110	Hogg, I, 398, from letter to Hogg [June 18-19, 1811]	7	33-9	40

TITLE	PAGE	WHERE PUBLISHED	NO. OF LINES PUB.	LINE NOS.	TOTAL NO. OF LINES IN POEM
		Shelley, Rosetti ed., 1870, II, 530, from copy by Richard Garnett of Boscombe MS	13	1-13	
		p. 525 (last stanza of "Love's Rose")	7	33-9	
		Works, III, 75-6	13	1-13	
		p. 75 (last stanza of "Love's Rose")	7	33-9	
		Shelley and his Circle, II, 811	7	33-9	
Hopes that bud in youthful breasts	112	Hogg, I, 397-8, from letter to Hogg [June 18-19, 1811]	14	1-14	21
		Works, III, 75 ("Love's Rose")	14	1-14	
		Shelley and his Circle, II, 811	14	1-14	

II—*Lines published from other sources* (CONTINUED)

TITLE	PAGE	WHERE PUBLISHED	NO. OF LINES PUB.	LINE NOS.	TOTAL NO. OF LINES IN POEM
TO THE MOONBEAM	113	Hogg, I, 377-8, from letter to Hogg, May 17, 1811 ("To the Moonbeam")	28	1-28	28
		Works, III, 71	28	1-28	
		Shelley and his Circle, II, 790	28	1-28	
DARES THE LAMA	123	Hogg, I, 351-2, from letter to Hogg, April 28, 1811	36	1-36	36
		Works, III, 89-90 ("Bigotry's Victim")	36	1-36	
FRAGMENT . . . BOMBARDMENT OF COPENHAGEN	127	Hogg, I, 165, from letter to Hogg, Jan. 11, 1811	14	1-14	21
		Works, III, 316-17	14	1-14	
		Shelley and his Circle, II, 702	14	1-14	

(324)

TITLE	PAGE	WHERE PUBLISHED	NO. OF LINES PUB.	LINE NOS.	TOTAL NO. OF LINES IN POEM
On an Icicle	128	Hogg, I, 103-4, from letter to Hogg, Jan. 6, 1811	21	1-21	21
		Works, III, 88-9	21	1-21	
		Shelley and his Circle, II, 688-9	21	1-21	
Cold are the blasts	129	Hogg, I, 125-6, from MS given to Hogg by Shelley	39	1-22 24-40	40
		Original Poetry, Victor and Cazire, 1810	39	1-22 24-40	
		Works, I, 9-10	39	1-22 24-40	
A Translation of The Marsellois Hymn	144	Shelley, Forman ed., 1877, IV, 353, from letter to Edward Fergus Graham [undated]	[9]	32-40	58
		Works, III, 91-2	[9]	32-40	

TABLE III: *Lines not published*

TITLE	PAGE	NO. OF LINES NOT PUB.	LINE NOS.	TOTAL NO. OF LINES IN POEM
A Sabbath Walk	38	54	1-44, 47-56	56
The Crisis	40	16	1-12, 17-20	20
Passion	41	50	1-50	50
To Harriet ("Never, O never")	43	20	1-20	20
Falshood and Vice	44	2	87-8	110
To the Emperors of Russia and Austria	48	50	1-50	50
To November	50	30	1-30	30
Written on a beautiful day in Spring	52	18	1-18	18
On leaving London for Wales	53	72	1-72	72
A winter's day	56	34	1-34	34
To Liberty	58	35	1-25, 31-40	50
On Robert Emmet's Tomb	60	20	1-20	28
A Tale of Society as it is	62	41	80-120	120
The Monarch's funeral	68	76	1-76	76
To the Republicans of North America	71	10	31-40	50

(326)

TITLE	PAGE	NO. OF LINES NOT PUB.	LINE NOS.	TOTAL NO. OF LINES IN POEM
Written at Cwm Ellan	73	16	1-16	16
To Death	74	20	49-68	68
Dark Spirit of the desart rude	77	46	1-46	46
Death-spurning rocks!	81	30	1-30	30
The Tombs	83	28	1-13, 16-30	30
Sonnet. To Harriet on her birth day	88	10	1-8, 13-14	14
Sonnet. On waiting for a wind	91	14	1-14	14
To Harriet ("Harriet! thy kiss to my soul is dear")	92	32	1-32	32
Mary to the Sea-Wind	94	16	1-16	16
A retrospect of Times of Old	95	66	5-70	83
The Voyage	98	256	1-39, 63-101, 112-19, 129-298	298
A Dialogue	108	2	31-2	44
How eloquent are eyes!	110	20	14-32, 40	40

(327)

III—*Lines not published* (CONTINUED)

TITLE	PAGE	NO. OF LINES NOT PUB.	LINE NOS.	TOTAL NO. OF LINES IN POEM
Hopes that bud in youthful breasts	112	7	15-21	21
To Mary I	116	28	1-28	28
To Mary II	118	21	1-21	21
To Mary III	119	37	1-37	37
To the Lover of Mary	121	33	1-33	33
I will kneel at thine altar	125	36	1-36	36
Fragment ... Bombardment of Copenhagen	127	7	15-21	21
Cold are the blasts	129	1	23	40
Henry and Louisa	131	315	1-315	315
Written in very early youth	147	23	1-23	23
Zeinab and Kathema	148	174	1-78, 85-180	180
To Harriet ("Oh Harriet, love like mine")	168	37	1-37	37
Late was the night	170	24	1-24	24
To St Irvyne	171	20	1-16, 21-4	24

Bibliographical Description

THE ESDAILE NOTEBOOK

Holograph manuscript, 183 pages, in notebook of 140 leaves (7.1 × 4.4 in.)—including stubs of two torn-out leaves—unnumbered, ruled (22 rules to page), half-bound in original red roan and marbled boards (7.3 × 4.8 in.).

Wove paper.

Contents: pastedown endpaper: "Ianthe E Esdaile"; leaf 1, recto, blank, verso: "[?]GE — [?]GY"; leaves 2 and 3 blank; leaf 4, recto, writing in Shelley's and Harriet Shelley's hand, verso, blank; leaf 5, recto, to leaf 92, recto, writing in Shelley's hand (leaves 78 and 79 torn out, stubs remaining, with traces of writing); leaf 92, verso, to leaf 97, recto, writing in Harriet Shelley's hand (leaf 93, verso, blank); leaf 97, verso, to leaf 140, recto, blank; leaf 140, verso: "Vol. 7. 286. Gibbon" (in Shelley's hand); pastedown endpaper: "4/" (in pencil).[1]

---

[1] The following page numbers appear in ink in Shelley's hand: "104" (leaf 56, verso); "127" (leaf 68, recto); "134" (leaf 73, verso); "158" (leaf 84, verso); "167" (leaf 90, recto). The following page numbers appear in pencil in an unknown hand: "48" (leaf 28, recto); "50" (leaf 29, recto); "70" (leaf 39, recto); "90" (leaf 49, recto); "100" (leaf 54, recto); "150" (leaf 81, verso).

Textual Notes

As I have noted in the Introduction, the text presented, although (hopefully) exact, is not literal. I shall now indicate in what ways we have departed from the manuscript, first in regard to words, and then in regard to punctuation.

TEXTUAL CHANGES INVOLVING WORDS

1. Titles. When Shelley has put a title on a poem we have used it, unless it is simply a date. Otherwise we have used the first line or the first phrase as a title, with two exceptions (see page 354 below). All dates given below titles are Shelley's.

2. Abbreviations and ampersands. Abbreviations, such as "cd" for "could," have been written out and ampersands given as "and" without indication in the notes.

3. Misspellings and slips of the pen are recorded in the notes and corrected in the text.

4. Apostrophes and hyphens have been supplied as needed in the text and are recorded in the notes only if meaning is involved (e.g., if an apostrophe could indicate either a singular or a plural possessive). If Shelley's apostrophes or hyphens have been deleted, this is recorded.

5. Capital letters are supplied as needed and recorded

in the notes. (Shelley had a habit of using a period and then beginning his next sentence with a small letter.)

6. Canceled words are not given in the text but are recorded in the notes. If a whole line is canceled, however, it is given in the text within brackets. Sometimes Shelley canceled a word by strokes of the pen, sometimes by smudging it out with his finger. We note smudged-out words because they may indicate haste in copying or composition.

7. Interlineations are given on line level in the text but recorded as interlineations in the notes.

8. Illegible words or letters are shown by brackets, the spacing of which roughly indicates the number of illegible letters.

It should, therefore, be possible from these notes to reconstruct Shelley's text in regard to the actual wording, with the exception of abbreviations, ampersands, aspostrophes, and hyphens.

CHANGES INVOLVING PUNCTUATION

1. Commas, periods, and semicolons have been added as needed and not recorded in the notes unless the addition could affect the sense. (See, for instance, "To Mary I," line 2.) If, however, Shelley's own commas, periods, or semicolons have been deleted or changed, this fact is recorded.

2. Colons, question marks, exclamation marks, dashes, quotation marks, and two or more dots. If these have been supplied, the addition is recorded in the notes by indicating Shelley's own punctuation or lack of it. If Shelley's colons, etc., have been deleted or changed, this fact is recorded. Thus any colons, etc., which are in the text and not recorded in the notes may be taken to be Shelley's. Shelley's underlinings in the text are shown by italics.

It should, therefore, be possible to reconstruct from the

notes the more significant elements of Shelley's original punctuation. Commas, periods, and semicolons, as we have seen, he apparently regarded either as routine and not worth including systematically, or, in a manuscript intended for publication, as details to be left up to an editor. If most of these commas, etc., were deleted in the present text, the result would not be very different from the original. If Shelley's punctuation were thus reconstructed, it might at first seem to be merely eccentric, but it represents a combination of punctuation practices current in Shelley's day and Shelley's own special use of punctuation to convey mood and sense rather than grammatical logic. For instance, Shelley will sometimes put an exclamation point where the logic of the sentence demands a question mark, if the general content and mood call for an exclamation point. In passages in which the syntax is complex he will put in colons or dashes as general guide lines to his thought. Shelley, in fact, seems to have been getting at a point which has never been properly solved, namely, that conventional punctuation, although adequate for the needs of expository prose, often fails to serve the more subtle patterns of poetry. We have retained Shelley's punctuation as much as possible, and indicated any major deviations from it, but our main criterion has been that of intelligibility. (The above rules apply also to the poems in Harriet Shelley's hand.)

The text which has resulted from these editorial methods will not, of course, prove satisfying to the textual scholar. Hope, however, is on the horizon. When these poems and their notes are reprinted in *Shelley and his Circle,* the text will, in accordance with the principles laid down in that work, give a "close approximation of the manuscript, retaining the spelling, punctuation, and so on of the original."

One matter which falls under neither word change nor punctuation change is that of indicators for footnotes. Shelley usually put an *X* or a cross in the text and a similar mark below, but sometimes he failed to do so. We have used asterisks uniformly.

Indentions follow Shelley's intent insofar as it can be determined. Sometimes he indented in the early stanzas of a poem and not in the later. In such cases we have indented throughout, following the pattern he has set.

References to Dowden's readings are to his copybook (now in The Carl H. Pforzheimer Library). Shelley's own line counts have been indicated within brackets.

A few bibliographical details have been commented on if they seemed helpful — for instance, on ink shading as indicating revision — but no attempt has been made in this edition to present systematic bibliographical descriptions.

PAGE 37. TO HARRIET ("Whose is the Love")

Title. "To Harriet" is in Harriet Shelley's hand. (See Plate III.)
l. 3. *praise:* There is a small curved stroke between *a.* and *i.*
l. 9. *thine.* —

PAGE 38. A SABBATH WALK

Heading. There is a short rule below *Poems.*
l. 5. *labyrinth: labyrith*
l. 6. *truth*
l. 20. *shrine: shine.* For a similar type of error in transcription, see line 46.
l. 29. *Its:* Shelley began to write *This* or *The* and then

TEXTUAL NOTES

wrote *It* through *Th* and changed the following half-formed *e* or *i* into *s*.

l. 40. prejudice: j written through g
l. 46. living: lving
l. 49. hireling: hirelng
l. 51. melody. The: melody. the
l. 52. pervadeth,
l. 53. its: it's; apostrophe so used in Shelley's day

PAGE 40. THE CRISIS

l. 2. Falshood: an early spelling, recorded in the NED
its: it's
l. 3. Tyranny: Tyrranny
l. 9. Monarchs: Monachs
l. 19. day star

PAGE 41. PASSION

Subtitle. The parenthesis of the subtitle is not completed. The space between *the* and the period measures 1.2 inches.
l. 3. conceal: originally written *concel* and corrected in darker ink by changing the final *l* into an *a* and adding *l*
l. 6. lawyer: written over ?*curat,* and blotted
l. 8. no. the
l. 16. wretch: wreth
l. 18. willed: The *ed* is in a much darker ink and slightly apart from the final *l* of *will*. See line 30 below. Shelley must at some time have checked over this poem after having copied it.
l. 23. the is written through some smudged-out letters, possibly *sp*.

(335)

l. 25. courage!
l. 30. weird: wierd; originally written *grey,* which was canceled, and *wierd* written above it; *wierd* is in the same dark ink as *ed* of *willed* in line 18.
l. 37. Falshood's: see note on "The Crisis," line 2.

PAGE 43. TO HARRIET ("Never, O never")

l. 1. O: o
l. 10. The parallel line above (line 4) was left unpunctuated by Shelley. We have punctuated it conventionally in the thought that Shelley wished special emphasis only in the last line of the stanza. A short rule appears below this line, separating the two stanzas.
l. 12. lovebeaming

PAGE 44. FALSHOOD AND VICE

Title. Falshood: See "The Crisis," line 2. There is a short rule below the title.
l. 1. their: thier. Shelley often had trouble with *ei* and *ie.* Sometimes it is difficult to tell which he intended. Here the *ie* is clear.
l. 4. their: thier
  veins: Shelley wrote *viens,* then put a dot over the *e.*
l. 6. frenzied: frienzied
l. 7. with: text in Notes to *Queen Mab* reads "wields"
l. 14. toil'd: The *l* and the ascender of the *d* are in a very dark ink. See "Passion," line 18; Shelley apparently corrected the text of a number of these poems at one time. See also line 84.
l. 30. more. this
l. 56. o'er: written through ?*of*

TEXTUAL NOTES

l. 67. sated: sat crossed through with three short diagonal strokes but no other letters or word substituted
l. 75. extacies: obsolete form
ll. 81-82. These lines are canceled in the Notebook.
l. 84. in: originally *with*; canceled and corrected in very dark ink
l. 87. all. without
l. 91. well.—the
l. 99. frenzied: frienzied
l. 107. boots.—thy
[Below line 110, Shelley's line count: 256]

PAGE 48. TO THE EMPERORS OF RUSSIA AND AUSTRIA

Title. Austerlitz: austrelitz. Shelley apparently had trouble with the spelling of the word. He first wrote *austrr,* then hesitated, and made a stroke between *rr.* There is a short rule below the title.
l. 7. deep
l. 10. rest.
l. 16. whistling: whilstling
l. 19. secure.—on
l. 30. form
l. 33. where: possibly *when.* It is not always possible to distinguish Shelley's *when* from *where.*
l. 38. beneath:
l. 42. thou
l. 43. fears. be
[Below line 50, Shelley's line count: 306]

PAGE 50. TO NOVEMBER

Title. There is a cross following the title which perhaps indicates that Shelley intended to add a footnote.

l. 15. thy rage: the rage. Shelley's eye perhaps jumped ahead to *the* of *the Heaven.*
l. 19. may. the
l. 22. manymingling
l. 27. Month!
l. 28. of written through *at*
l. 29. nothings
l. 30. won.
[Below line 30, Shelley's line count: *336*]

Page 52. WRITTEN ON A BEAUTIFUL DAY IN SPRING

Title. There is a short rule below the title.
l. 2. is written through *in*
l. 3. woe worn
l. 8. its: it
l. 9. recurs
[Below line 18, Shelley's line count: *354* (slightly smudged)]

Page 53. ON LEAVING LONDON FOR WALES

l. 10. full: Dowden first transcribed "*full*" then interlineated "*free(?).*" On the opposite page he comments: "I incline to *free,*" and below the comment is a penciled notation: "And I., R. G.," i.e., Richard Garnett. There is one stroke too many for *free* but the word could be *full* if Shelley made his *l*'s short, something which he occasionally did. *Full* also makes better sense, especially in view of *burdened* in the next line.
l. 22. tightening: tightning
    steel
l. 27. In a much darker ink and thinner penpoint. So, too, perhaps, in line 19, the *l* of *Hail* and the dot over the *i* of *wind,* and a few other letters in other lines. Pre-

TEXTUAL NOTES

sumably line 27 was added later and Shelley might have touched up the rest of the stanza at the same time. Dowden comments: "This line in fresher ink and a handwriting of a different date—evidently filling up a line that had been left blank."

l. 36. lowers: Dowden comments: "lowers might be towers (but t not crossed)." *Towers* is possible but *lowers* seems more likely. Shelley's initial *t*'s and *l*'s are sometimes rather similar.

      all
l. 39. spirit breathing
l. 43. Reason: R written through *r*
l. 44. unfurled
l. 48. pert: Dowden comments: "pert=?past or pert or great." The word, however, seems quite clearly to be *pert*.
l. 58. with: The *t* and *h* are jammed together into one composite letter and the word runs on into *the*.
l. 66. light:
l. 68. fear,
l. 69. Their: Thier
[Below line 72, Shelley's line count: 427 (last number blotted)]

PAGE 56. A WINTER'S DAY

l. 2. reviving: reving with *vi* interlineated
      year
l. 8. O: o
l. 11. whirlwinds.
l. 14. endure
l. 15. bloom written through *prim*. Shelley's eye must have caught *prime* on the next line as he copied.
l. 20. doom

(339)

l. 27. alone
l. 32. pulses
[Below line 34, Shelley's line count: *461*]

PAGE 58. TO LIBERTY

l. 11. Say.
l. 14. not
l. 18. Sees Paradise written through *Yet bravely*; see line 20
l. 20. true
l. 25. shall: sha written through *wi*
    Revenge!: Rev written at margin, *enge!* written above.
l. 31. employer: first written *employers*, then *s* canceled
l. 37. planned. which
l. 42. ye
[Below line 50, Shelley's line count: *511*]

PAGE 60. ON ROBERT EMMET'S TOMB

Title. There is a short rule below the title.
l. 4. shrine: shine
l. 14. heart:
l. 16. depart
l. 18. There is a large X in the right-hand margin following the line. Perhaps Shelley intended to add a footnote.
l. 20. Like the tears: Li corrected from initial *Th*
l. 21. Lines 21 and 22 and parts of line 23 are in much darker ink, of about the same shade as line 27 of "On leaving London for Wales." Perhaps all these lines and other corrections in black ink were added at the same time.

(340)

l. 23. caresst: carest
l. 25. daybeam: second *a* written over *e*
[Below line 28, Shelley's line count: *540*]

Page 62. A TALE OF SOCIETY AS IT IS

Subtitle. 1811 is in a darker ink and was presumably added later.
l. 3. decay: decary
l. 7. energy
l. 11. Poverty the   stain
l. 20. will.
l. 23. The *A* of *And* has left a clear blot on the opposite page, whereas other equally dark letters in lines below have not. Shelley perhaps went back and touched up the *A* before he turned the page.
l. 28. might'st: mighst
l. 32. ghastly: an additional stroke between *t* and *l*
    eye:
l. 34. run
l. 35. was,
l. 39. grieve
l. 47. round
l. 56. wing
l. 58. sway.
l. 59. they
l. 77. spirit sinking
l. 84. borne: born
l. 92. from originally written *by,* and canceled; then *from* written above *by*
l. 95. flowers: flowr's
    thus. thou
l. 96. them. the

l. 107. to door
l. 110. dead.
[Below line 120, Shelley's line count: *661*]

PAGE 67. THE SOLITARY

Date. 1810: The *o* has apparently been formed from *1*.
l. 11. remove
l. 15. others.
[Below line 18, Shelley's line count: *679*]

PAGE 68. THE MONARCH'S FUNERAL

l. 11. crimson: c written through *g*. Apparently Shelley started to write *glow*.
l. 15. As written through *?If* and blotted
l. 22. fell: The first *l* has a very short ascender, giving it the appearance of *e*.
l. 24. pile
l. 29. the: t written through *?w*
l. 30. Gather: A final *s* has been canceled.
l. 35. insatiate: first *t* written through *s*
l. 38. dine
l. 46. fleeting: Shelley apparently first wrote *flelting* and then drew a curved line to cut the second *l* at *e* level.
l. 72. tear.
l. 73. no. 'tis
l. 75. People,
[Below line 76, Shelley's line count: *755*]

PAGE 71. TO THE REPUBLICANS OF NORTH AMERICA

Title. outh Am is written through *New Spain,* which, except for the *N*, has been lightly erased and smudged out.

l. 9. catch: the *tc* of *catch* has been corrected from a final *tt*, and the *h* then added.

l. 13. Start: ar written through ?ra

l. 14. groan!.

l. 25. O!: o!

l. 33. bloodless: written through *quivering,* which has been partly erased

l. 37. Let: written through ?*That*

[Below line 50, Shelley's line count: *805*]

PAGE 73. WRITTEN AT CWM ELLAN

l. 14. glen: rocks canceled, and *glen* written above

l. 15. tongued: Dowden reads *tangled,* but this is not a possible reading of the letters. The word appears to be written *tungued.*

[Below line 16, Shelley's line count: *821*]

PAGE 74. TO DEATH

l. 8. this

l. 9. When in: first written immediately under *Death* (line 8) then partly erased, and repeated under *Thou* (line 8)

l. 13. sacrifice: sacrifize

l. 17. mine

l. 23. sway

l. 45. land

l. 48. There is a penciled line below *strand*. Dowden has a note to this line: "Here the printed fragment ends —." Possibly Dowden added the penciled line.

l. 49. '*Twere:* written through some partly erased and rubbed-out letters

    well: The *w* seems to have been formed from some other letters, perhaps *th*. Dowden suggests *Hell* as an alternate reading.

l. 52. receives: recieves

l. 57. gaze

l. 64. Not: originally *Can*; *Can* crossed out, and *Not* written above

l. 65. Can liberate: written through some partly erased and rubbed-out words, possibly *My Triumph th* from the next line

l. 66. shame

l. 67. thee

[Below line 68, Shelley's line count: *889*]

Page 77. DARK SPIRIT OF THE DESART RUDE

Title. No title in manuscript

l. 1. desart: in use in Shelley's day

l. 3. wood.

l. 6. jetty   musical. The space was left by Shelley as though a word were to follow *jetty*.

l. 16. day's: d written through partly erased ?*t*[ ]

l. 19. By: written through partly erased *on*

l. 22. eyeballs

l. 26. O: o, written through *a*

l. 31. their: there

l. 33. Earth's sweet: written through *Natures* [ ]

l. 35. Oak written through ?*rock*

l. 37. Whose written through [ ]

TEXTUAL NOTES

l. 44. And: and; *and* was first written above *That* and partly erased and smudged; then another clearly written *and* was interlineated.
[Below line 46, Shelley's line count: *935*]

PAGE 79. THE PALE, THE COLD AND THE MOONY SMILE

Title. No title in manuscript
l. 14. perceive: percieve
l. 16. steel
l. 26. veil: viel
    come
[Below line 30, Shelley's line count: *965*]

PAGE 81. DEATH-SPURNING ROCKS!

Title. No title in manuscript
l. 3. palsied: written through ?*dread*
l. 9. away
l. 11. A: written through *The*
l. 12. wonders. on
l. 14. snares: originally *pangs*, then canceled, and *snares* written above *pangs*. *snares* is written more neatly and in a darker ink. It was probably added later.
    lay
l. 16. tear
l. 18. of: written through *&*
l. 20. veins: viens
l. 22. shew: written through [ ]
l. 25. back. the
l. 29. Chance
    misery
l. 30. die

(345)

PAGE 83. THE TOMBS

l. 3. thy: the
l. 6. tombs. am
l. 7. skulls: sculls
l. 10. life!
l. 13. love. Shelley, both in these poems and in his early letters, often uses a period as a general indication of pause. Sometimes, if writing hastily, he will use two dots in the same way. He often omits punctuation at the end of a line, taking the end itself as a pause. Here, for instance, he puts a period after *love* in the middle of the line but no punctuation mark after *thought* at the end.
l. 19. every: originally written *all the,* then canceled, and *every* written above, in a lighter ink and more neatly. Evidently it was added later.
    shape: original final *s* crossed out
l. 25. 1020 is written at end of this line, in faint ink, and small numerals.
[Below line 30, Shelley's line count: *1025*]

PAGE 85. TO HARRIET ("It is not blasphemy")

l. 17. fibres.
l. 19. existence,
l. 26. chill: c corrected from original *f*
l. 28. souls,
l. 31. its: it's
l. 36. supersede: supercede
l. 38. me.
l. 55. fears: fear's
l. 65. being. if

TEXTUAL NOTES

[At end of line 69, Shelley's line count: *1096*]

l. 70. *Fortitude:* written through a blurred

$$\begin{array}{r} 1025 \\ 71 \\ \hline 1096 \end{array}$$

l. 71. *Purity*

[Below line 72, Shelley's line count: *1100*]

PAGE 88. SONNET: TO HARRIET ON HER BIRTH DAY

Title and subtitle. Sonnet To Harriet
                On her birthday August 1. 1812

l. 1. *smile*

l. 2. *indexing*

l. 5. *as on:* originally *as on* followed the first *thus;* then *as on* was canceled, and a second *thus* written and followed by a new *as on*

l. 7. *dyes:* changed from *dies*

PAGE 89. SONNET: TO A BALLOON, LADEN WITH KNOWLEDGE

Subtitle. laden: n written through a second e, Knowledge underlined

l. 5. *shall:* possibly *shalt*

l. 11. *tyrants*

PAGE 90. SONNET: ON LAUNCHING SOME BOTTLES

Subtitle. Knowledge underlined

l. 3. *ye:* y written through w
    stern: Dowden reads *stem* but the word is clearly *stern* (used as a verb meaning "to steer through").

l. 5. *deigned: deighned*

l. 8. blow,
l. 11. on: Dowden reads *in,* but the *o* is probably compressed; *on* is the more likely reading.
l. 12. Its: It's

PAGE 91. SONNET: ON WAITING FOR A WIND

Title. the Bristol channel: originally written *the channel,* and *Bristol* interlineated
    Wales.
l. 2. Spirit: possibly *spirit,* the *s* is about halfway in size between a capital and small letter. Shelley occasionally forms such initial letters when he seems hesitant on how much emphasis to give to a word.
l. 9. sigh. ye
l. 12. sails
l. 13. receive. The final *e* is followed by a slight curl which might be a half-formed *s.*
[Below line 14, Shelley's line count: *1156*]

PAGE 92. TO HARRIET ("Harriet! thy kiss to my soul is dear")

l. 4. a look: a loo smudged; followed by *look*
l. 26. its: it's
[Below line 32, Shelley's line count: *1188*]

PAGE 94. MARY TO THE SEA-WIND

l. 1. thee I: second *e* written through *?n* or *?re*
l. 6. heath: heatth
l. 7. yet: written through *but*
l. 9. inhale
l. 10. kind

TEXTUAL NOTES

l. 11. And written through *That*
[Below line 16, Shelley's line count: *1204*]

PAGE 95. A RETROSPECT OF TIMES OF OLD

l. 11. worship. oh
l. 13. Kings
l. 17. Death,
l. 18. the: *e* written through *is*
    world: originally *word*; then *l* inserted
l. 20. Death! — .yet
l. 21. thou'lt: originally written *thou wilt, wi* canceled and apostrophe added. (Opening and closing quotation marks have been supplied.)
l. 22. Dream of fame!: written through *?brilliant piles!* (see line 29)
l. 29. lay
l. 30. fled.
l. 33. features
l. 34. day
l. 36. steel: stell; stell . . . the
l. 37. blade
l. 44. torrent. the
    stormy: probable reading
l. 45. its: it
l. 47. moment! and he dies hark
l. 50. veil: viel
    hid
l. 51. flown written through smudged *?glow*
Footnote. *that* written after *record* and then canceled
    parallel: parallell
    former
l. 52. roll: first written *rolls,* and *s* canceled
    tide

THE ESDAILE NOTEBOOK

l. 54. not: originally *nor, r* canceled and *t* inserted
l. 55. slept!: Shelley first wrote *slept*, and then added the exclamation mark above the comma.
    gone
l. 56. bone
l. 61. gorgeous: gorg written over *blood*
l. 66. drowned: A *d* appears to have been inserted before *n*.
    each: ea written through *?to*
    moan
l. 67. away
l. 70. Heroes,
l. 71. come
    Shelley began to form the *X* for his footnote after *come*, then smudged it out.
Footnote. There appears to be an extra pen stroke after the first *a* of *Buonaparte*.
l. 72. gloom
l. 73. die
l. 83. better: Dowden reads *latter*, which is possible.
[Below line 83, Shelley's line count: *1287*]

Page 98. THE VOYAGE

Title. Shelley apparently first began to write *The ?J* at left-hand margin, then smudged and crossed it out, then wrote *The ?Journey*, centered, crossed and scratched it out, and wrote *The Voyage* above it. (See Plate IV.)
Subtitle. *Fragment: Fragment. .*
l. 2. Each: E written through *?I*
    puissant: puisant; ant written through smudged-out letters
l. 17. sorrow!
l. 19. loveliness

(350)

TEXTUAL NOTES

l. 27. clash: probable reading; Dowden reads *dash*, which is possible.
l. 37. mind
l. 39. pain
l. 40. now: written through smudged-out ?*here*
l. 50. heads;
l. 65. atmosphere
l. 67. long
l. 78. Of is perhaps a transcription error for *As.*
l. 85. Their: Thier with the dot over the *e*
l. 98. hazard. smil'd
l. 104. it
l. 107. power
l. 108. work
l. 109. paths
Footnote. There is no asterisk in the text but the reference is clearly to lines 108-9.
    peculiarly: peculiarely
    engaging,
    possess: posess
l. 125. cradled
l. 134. pure: there is an extra stroke to the *u.*
l. 141. body,
l. 167. barren: written through smudged ?*fruitless*
l. 173. He was first written on the (blank) line above and smudged out. "He struggled" perhaps did not begin a new stanza in the manuscript from which Shelley was copying.
l. 174. But: Shelley apparently began to write a *T* and changed it to *B.*
l. 188. forth. the
l. 208. withered: ed written through a fainter and smaller *ed* ?*li*
l. 215. sight

l. 219. them: then
l. 221. Town
l. 225. town written through ?*den*
l. 227. spot. should
l. 236. their robberies: there robberies
l. 237. sailor: sailors
l. 246. him. to
l. 257. handkerchief: handcherchief
l. 277. selfishness. — the
l. 278. vallies; early spelling recorded in the NED; so, in Blake
l. 281. footstep. the
l. 283. Nature's: Nature fair Earth; possibly intended for *Nature, fair Earth.*
l. 289. the vale: h written through a ?*v*
ll. 292-8. The quotation marks are supplied.
l. 293. with: written through ?*f*[ ]
l. 295. thee. — get
[Below line 298, Shelley's line count: *1588*]

PAGE 108. A DIALOGUE

l. 1. brave: brav. The *v* comes at the right edge; there is no *e*. If Shelley has one or two more letters to get into a word, he will, as a rule, bend the word downward at the margin sufficiently to fit them in. But in this case he has not done so, nor has the page (or any other page) been trimmed.
l. 2. grave: gra; written partly below the line and crowded into the margin
l. 8. steeps: The *t* is not crossed, giving it the appearance of *l*.
l. 14. me
l. 21. Death: D changed from *d; e* is a capital. Apparently

TEXTUAL NOTES

Shelley began to write a small *d*, realized he wanted a capital, inadvertently wrote a capital *E*, then went back and capitalized the *d*.

l. 22. shore
l. 23. mortal
l. 26. above
Footnote. another
    Contains
    transgress: trangress
l. 32. its: it's; written above canceled *thy*
l. 36. day
l. 38. Death
l. 43. shrine: shine; crowded into the margin
l. 44. destroyer: written *destroyers* with *s* canceled
[Below line 44, Shelley's line count: *1632*]

PAGE 110. HOW ELOQUENT ARE EYES!

Title. No title in manuscript
Date. There is a short rule under the date.
l. 2. frenzied: frienzied
l. 28. desire
l. 38. shrine: shine
l. 40. joy
[Below line 40, Shelley's line count: *1672*]

PAGE 112. HOPES THAT BUD IN YOUTHFUL BREASTS

Title. No title in manuscript
l. 1. bud written through *live*, which has been lightly smudged out.
l. 2. time: Shelley has a colon after *time;* in his day a colon

would sometimes be used where today we would use a semicolon.

l. 6. mine: m written through ?w

l. 11. planted: planten. Shelley's eye, in copying, was perhaps caught by the *n* of *Heaven* or *riven*.

l. 17. sin

[Below line 21, Shelley's line count: *1693*]

PAGE 113. TO THE MOONBEAM

Title. No title in manuscript, but so titled by Shelley in letter to T. J. Hogg. See above, p. 240.

l. 5. grow

    grow: There is a space between the *g* and *r;* the *r* is long and irregularly shaped; Shelley's eye perhaps strayed from the page as he was copying.

l. 10. shadow: ad written through *?rou*

l. 12. Yet written through *And*

l. 15. mine: i written through *y*

[Below line 28, Shelley's count: *1723*]

PAGE 115. POEMS TO MARY (General title supplied by editor.)

Advertisement: There is a short rule under the word *Advertisement*.

    are: a written through *we*

    discriminating: Either the first loop of the first *n* rises high and gives the letter the appearance of *ti,* or Shelley, in copying, has inadvertently written *ti* twice (*discrimitiating*).

    me, will

    that time

    before inserted above a canceled *after*

PAGE 116. TO MARY I

Date. The date appears one line below the last line of the *Advertisement* and one line above the title *To Mary I.* (Rule supplied.)

Title. Mary—I

l. 2. so

l. 11. forgiven.

Footnote. This footnote was apparently written before the copying of the poem was completed. It begins on leaf 56, verso, continues on the last three lines of leaf 57, recto, then on the last four lines of 57, verso, and ends on the last four lines of 58, verso, with the footnote to "To Mary II" above it. But "To Mary I" ends on 57, recto, about halfway down the page; after it there come seven blank lines. So that Shelley could have ended the note on this page, and presumably would have done so had he realized that the space would be available. The indication seems to be that the note was not in the manuscript from which he was copying. The final sentence has been heavily canceled.

blasphemy.—

alone.—

I instead: I ever instead with *ever* canceled

side.—

[Below line 28, Shelley's line count: *1751*]

PAGE 118. TO MARY II

Title. II is in heavier ink and blotted on opposite page. It was probably added later.

l. 3. art?

l. 4. me

l. 17. There is not: written in very black ink through erased and smeared ?*Indeed, tis*

Page 119. TO MARY III

l. 3. stone
l. 4. Pours none written through smudged *Where mur* (see following line)
l. 6. fell
l. 8. decree.
l. 16. love
l. 17. I wretch! weep
l. 20. tie
ll. 24-5. Shelley copied these lines in the reverse order, and then attempted to correct it. Opposite line 24 (his line 25) he put a *1* in the left margin, opposite line 25 a *2*.
l. 30. eternal: written above a canceled *heavenly*
l. 37. feeds
[Below line 37, Shelley's line count: *1809*]

Page 121. TO THE LOVER OF MARY

l. 6. tenantless
l. 7. thy warm: thy originally *thine;* the *y* was written through *in;* the *w* of *warm* was partly formed from the *e* of *thine.*
  caress
l. 19. veil: probably *viel; iel* written through *?ale*
l. 21. when: possibly *where*
[Below line 22, Shelley's line count: *1831,* canceled]
ll. 23-33. This stanza is written in a different ink and with a different penpoint. These facts plus the canceled line-count number below line 22 indicate that the stanza was added later. The next line count (*1867*)—at the end of the next poem ("Dares the Lama")—does not allow for this stanza. Nor does the final count

TEXTUAL NOTES

(2822). Hence, the stanza was added after the next poem had been copied, and, presumably, after Shelley had completed the line count for the Notebook. The indication from the ink and other evidence is that Shelley counted lines as he went along.

l. 32. eternal: Shelley completed only one stroke of an X above *eternal* to indicate the footnote (paralleling *eternal love* with *virtue*).

l. 33. holier: holeir

Footnote. synonimous: This spelling is recorded in the NED as used by Samuel Johnson.

PAGE 123. DARES THE LAMA

Title. No title in manuscript
Date. Underlined twice
l. 8. death: d written through *y*
l. 11. brood: The word looks rather like *blood*, but apparently Shelley's pen slipped upward on the *r* (he was writing near the gutter of the book) and gave it the appearance of an *l*.
l. 13. blood
l. 23. frightful: frighful
l. 24. And: A written through *?W*
l. 26. withered: it written through *hi*
l. 34. its: it's
l. 35. me. it
    fly
l. 36. remains: slightly blotted and smudged
    die
[Below line 36, Shelley's line count: *1867*]

Page 125. I WILL KNEEL AT THINE ALTAR

Title. No title in manuscript
Date. Underlined with two dark heavy lines converging at each end
l. 16. adore
l. 17. live.—
l. 23. to written through *the*
l. 29. destroyed
l. 30. Gold
l. 31. alloyed
l. 34. *its: it's*; *i* written through smudged-out *t*
l. 35. nations.—it
[Below line 36, Shelley's line count: *1903*]

Page 127. FRAGMENT ... BOMBARDMENT OF COPENHAGEN

Title. Immediately below the last line of the title, there is a row of *X*'s across the page.
l. 3. perceives: percieves, with the dot over the *e*
l. 6. clots: written through smudged-out *?tinges*
with: inserted above the line
l. 17. orient: Shelley apparently first wrote *oriet*, or *orient* with the *n* and *t* too close; then the *t* or *nt* was blotted, and he added another *t* but left the top of the first one sticking out from the blot.
l. 19. shrieks: shieks; see *shine* for *shrine*, "A sabbath Walk," line 20. These are not misspellings but miswritings. Apparently, forming the bottom loop of an *h* if an *r* was to follow, gave Shelley the impression that he had written the *r*. It is an error similar to writing *n* for *m*.
l. 20. pride: The descender of the *p* is short—something

we find from time to time in Shelley's writing—giving the word the appearance of *bride*.
[Below line 21, Shelley's line count: *1924*]

PAGE 128. ON AN ICICLE

Date. Date appears above title.
l. 11. racking pain: racking is written into the margin, *pain* written above.
l. 12. insult . to
l. 14. there
[Below line 21, Shelley's line count: *1945*]

PAGE 129. COLD ARE THE BLASTS

Title. No title in manuscript
l. 11. Till a
    sorrow
l. 12. babes
ll. 21-4. quotation marks supplied
l. 22. tempest: es formed from *?le*
l. 23. blame: b written through *p*
l. 25. flowers: flowrs
l. 27. drops. then. Such dots as these Shelley does not intend as periods. They seem to be a kind of nondescript, generalized form of punctuation. Usually they just indicate a pause, but sometimes they are found where a dash or even a question mark is required.
ll. 29-32. quotation marks supplied
l. 30. on: n written through *f*
l. 33. Louisa. — &
[Below line 40, Shelley's line count: *1985*]

Page 131. HENRY AND LOUISA

Footnote. Spencer: "Spenser" was spelled "Spencer" in the first edition of *Colin Clouts Come home againe* (1595) and occasionally in later references.

portraiture: Shelley apparently started to write *pour* and corrected it to *por*.

pronounced: prounounced

Date. Date appears above title. (See Plate V.)

l. 3. canopy: y written through *ies*

l. 8. ay: following *ay* is a small cross apparently intended for a footnote that was not written

l. 9. blood-boltered: archaic; see the NED under "blood"

l. 10 misery;

l. 21 Heaven

Stanzas III, IV, and part of V missing. Shelley has left the page blank except for the stanza numbers: *III* (then 9 blank lines), *IV* (9 blank lines), and *V* (1 blank line). The line of dots does not appear in the Notebook.

l. 22. Space for 5 lines has been left blank at the top of the page (before line 22). Lines 22-4 close the incomplete stanza V, and are written in darker ink than stanzas VI and VII.

l. 31. felt

l. 44. returned.

l. 51. Here. in this breast. thou

l. 52. empire be. b written through *m*.

heart: Shelley seems to have first written *healt*, then put an *r* beside the top of the *l*.

throne." (quotation marks supplied)

l. 53. fair: fairs, s canceled

l. 58. away: followed by a smudged question mark
l. 61. ray
l. 68. its: it's
l. 71. shalt
  God
  recieve: possibly *recieve;* written partly below the line
l. 89. fears is the last word on the line; *entwine* is crowded in below the line; the quotation marks are above the line over *fears.*
l. 99. spoke. the
l. 120. memory;. The long sentence beginning at line 104 ends here; the semicolons at lines 107 and 116 are Shelley's.
l. 126. soulreviving
l. 128. spring-flowers: Shelley's hyphen
l. 138. tale
l. 140. Tho': o written through ?*at*
l. 142. sacrificed: sacrifized
l. 152. succeed —
  never, never
l. 155. weep
l. 156. die. The *e* has an extra upstroke at the end, as though for emphasis, and there appears to be a dot under it.
[Below line 156, Shelley's line count: ?*2167;* 21 is clear, 67 is blurred.]
l. 169. Deep wept: wept written through ?*En*[ ]?*t.*
  moan and *groan* (line 170) are both followed by a stroke giving an appearance of *s.*
l. 176. this changed from *there*
  sand
l. 177. woe.
l. 184. fixed. dim

(361)

l. 187. victory's shame: originally written *victory stern;* *stern* crossed out and *shame* written above it; *'s* added to *victory* (in lighter ink)

l. 190. timid: probable reading

l. 194. There is a stroke before the second *is* as though Shelley began to repeat *H.*

dead: question mark and quotation marks supplied

l. 195. Half: initial letter originally *F,* then changed to *H*

l. 196. is my: is my is written through *is ?he;* Shelley perhaps intended to make a change but abandoned it.

dead

l. 197. Henry.

l. 199. whelmed: written above crossed-out *dried*

l. 202. fling.: period and quotation marks supplied

l. 216. her: he written through *th*

l. 224. break

l. 225. unformed —

l. 230. bend

l. 252. pale. deaths

l. 253. the chain: large *e* written through *ose*

l. 254. binds: bind; Shelley originally intended *those chains* in line 253.

soul,

l. 256. thine

l. 257. shine: period and quotation marks supplied

l. 258. voice. the

l. 267. crumbling: cru written through *?ru*

l. 272. bed;

l. 277. death;

l. 278. hate

l. 279. breast: re written through *os.*

l. 281. Why?: original *!* changed to *?* by Shelley

l. 300. When: possibly *Where*

TEXTUAL NOTES

l. 311. steady: written above a crossed-out *bronzed*
[Below line 315, Shelley's line count: *2326*]

PAGE 144. A TRANSLATION OF THE MARSELLOIS HYMN

Title. There is a short rule below the title.
l. 1. Band
l. 2. thee
l. 8. joy
l. 9 family
l. 13. soil
l. 18. you. on
l. 22. free: followed by a short line which is perhaps the beginning of an exclamation mark
l. 24. tyranny
l. 25. hope: hopes, s crossed out
l. 28. Koszul (*Jeunesse*, p. 403) silently adds *in* before *despots* and is followed by Ingpen (Shelley, *Complete Works*, IV, 342), but the phrase could be in apposition to *despots.*
l. 29. head
l. 30. quake: qu written through *sh*
  dread
l. 32. Man
l. 33. country
l. 40. Victory
l. 49. cruelty
l. 58. Victory
[Below line 58, Shelley's line count: *2384*. Shelley's next line count indicates 60 lines of text missing on torn-out pages immediately following (leaves 78 and 79); see Bibliographical Description, above p. 329.]

(363)

Page 147. WRITTEN IN VERY EARLY YOUTH

Title. Short rule under title
  very: verry
l. 14. traitorous: traiterous
l. 16. tired: The word looks more like *tried* than *tired* but Shelley's *ir*'s and *ri*'s are not always distinguishable. Shelley uses "tired frame" in "To the Moonbeam," line 11.
l. 18. shrine: shine; as before
[Below line 23, Shelley's line count: *2467; 2* written through *1*]

Page 148. ZEINAB AND KATHEMA

Title. Short rule under title
  Kathema: An *h* has been smudged out following the final *a*. Shelley apparently thought of spelling the name Kathemah. Possibly it was so spelled in the manuscript he was copying.
l. 18. sun written above the line, punctuation (as given here) follows *setting*
l. 19. A faint *He thought*, smudged-out, appears on the top line of the page. Shelley, after writing *He thought* on the top line decided to begin one line down. His object was doubtless to make it clear that the words began a new stanza. His previous stanza had finished on the last line of the preceding page because it had been forced down on the page by the presence of the title. Normally, for this poem, the final stanza on a page ends two lines up from the bottom.
l. 24. care
l. 26. gave;

TEXTUAL NOTES

l. 35. Zeinab: Zeniab
l. 36. invaders
   brand: written below the line
l. 39. peace,
l. 54. mother's gore: written below the line. Usually Shelley has no apostrophes; this time he has two — one under the *r* of *dear* on the line above and one in the space between the two words. The shade of the ink indicates that the one under the *r* was placed at the time of the writing. The second perhaps indicates a rereading in which Shelley failed to see the first apostrophe which is close to the *r* of *dear*.
l. 68. heap the
   God!" : exclamation point and quotation marks supplied
l. 73. now
l. 78. endeared
l. 80. unvarying: v written through *w*
l. 86. sown
l. 93. There: corrected from *Their*
l. 95. Whilst: lst written through *ch*
   zone
l. 100. veil: viel
l. 108. frames
l. 109. Art: A written through *a*
l. 111. Heaven: Heavn, crowded downward into the margin
l. 116. wide altered
l. 120. Safe,
l. 123. came to a written through smudged out *th*[ ]*a ?city ?of.* If this is *thro' a city of,* it may mean that Shelley inadvertently began to copy from a stanza which he did not include in the Notebook version.
l. 128. deathy: apparently first written *deth*; the ascenders

of this *t* and *h* were then joined to make a large *a*, and *thy* was added.
l. 133. its: first written *her, er* crossed out, *i* added before the *h*, the *h* crossed to make *t*, and *s* inserted
l. 140. filled. he
l. 142. avail'd: written above the line
l. 149. creak: There is an ascender written in over the *r*; Shelley perhaps thought of changing the word to *clank.*
l. 150. weight,
l. 152. Calmly.—in
l. 156. guest": quotation marks supplied
l. 157. He: H formed from *Th*
[At end of line 160, Shelley's line count: *2628*, faint]
l. 166. was: w written through [ ] (See Plate VI.)
l. 170. With: written through smudged-out *An crime*
l. 172. rays written above crossed-out *beams*
   grace written (in browner ink) above crossed-out *mark*
l. 173. Changed to written (in browner ink) above crossed-out *Even like*
l. 177. hope written above crossed-out *heart*
l. 178. plan
[Below line 180, Shelley's line count: *2648;* below it, another number, very faint: *2600*]

Page 155. THE RETROSPECT

Date. 1812: 2 written through *o*
l. 12. steel,: steel; Shelley's semicolon replaces four smudged-out dots.
l. 48. mien: mein
l. 56. Heaven: followed by a blotted period or comma
l. 70. misery,

TEXTUAL NOTES

l. 74. its: it's
l. 81. my: m formed from *an*
l. 84. sought. it
l. 90. perish,
l. 92. could: co is written through *w*
l. 96. ray
l. 115. vale
l. 118. its: it's
l. 129. mien: mein
l. 131. brain
l. 134. sadness
l. 146. feeling: written through crossed-out *passion*
l. 148. see: se written through *?p* or *?fr*
l. 164. crown: written above crossed-out *coronets*
    bleeding: above the line with caret below. *Crowns, bleeding* and the caret are in darker ink and were presumably added later.
[Below line 168, Shelley's line count: 2767]

PAGE 161. THE WANDERING JEW'S SOLILOQUY

l. 1. Triune: above the line and indicated by a caret
l. 5. swells
l. 9. Light: Liight
l. 15. contempt
l. 18. that: at written through *en*
l. 22. crew
l. 24. their: thier, dot over *e*
l. 25. their: thier
l. 26. foreknown
l. 27. omniscient: There is a line through *omn;* perhaps Shelley intended to cross out the word and then changed his mind.

l. 29. remit
    then: n appears to have been formed from s
[Below line 29, Shelley's line count: 2796
$$\frac{16}{2822}]$$

PAGE 163. TO IANTHE

Date. Septr originally written *Oct; Oct* canceled
l. 1. sake:
l. 12 O: o; over the *o* is a mark that looks like a circumflex accent.
    fair: air written through *rail*

PAGE 164. EVENING — TO HARRIET

l. 8. dream,
Below line 14. *31st: 1* written through *o*

PAGE 165. TO HARRIETT ("Thy look of love")

[From this point on all writing (including all dates) is in Harriet Shelley's hand until we come to Shelley's notation on leaf 140, verso; see Bibliographical Description, above, p. 329.]
l. 9. give (See Plate VII.)
l. 11. own too late
l. 13. from: originally written *to*, canceled, and *from* written above
l. 14. state
l. 16. hate
l. 25. guide
l. 30. love
    Cook's Hotel appears below line 18, and is on the last

(368)

TEXTUAL NOTES

line of the page on which the poem begins. *May 1814*
is written below line 30.

PAGE 167. FULL MANY A MIND

Title. No title in manuscript
l. 4. despair

PAGE 168. TO HARRIET ("Oh Harriet, love like mine")

Title. Following "To Harriet" there is a series of nine
   dots.
l. 2. destroy
l. 3. woes,
l. 4. grief
l. 24. unvarying: unvayrying
l. 28. misery's: miseries
       pain
l. 36. For: preceded by smudged-out *fo*
On line 37: *Cum Elam* [sic]

PAGE 170. LATE WAS THE NIGHT

Title. No title in manuscript
l. 2. walls: wals
l. 4. mountain: possibly *mountains*
ll. 5-8. These lines are obviously corrupt, but there seems
   no easy way of amending them. Perhaps Harriet, in
   copying, reversed the order for the rhyme words at
   the end of lines 6 and 7. This would be easy to do
   if the manuscript from which she was copying had
   these words in the margin crowded above or below
   the line — a common practice with Shelley. Even so,
   however, the lines still would not make much sense.

l. 6. murderer's: murderes; an extra stroke has been added to the first *r*.

l. 8. murderer: murderes

l. 17. he can save: possible reading if some of the letters (almost illegible) are highly compressed; perhaps simply *can save*. Possibly the original read "See that fair form heav'n can save." We find "Rest awhile, hapless victim, and heaven will save" in "Bereavement," one of the poems in *St. Irvyne,* and in his early poems on similar subjects Shelley often repeated phrases. Harriet could conceivably have misread "that" for "Heav'n" in Shelley's script.

l. 18. bare

l. 20. around her: her interlineated

ll. 20-21. A stanza space has been supplied here; in the original there is no break.

l. 21. mile

l. 22. victim: victims

l. 24. cold-stricken: cold-striken; written above crossed-out *wide,* which comes just before *wild*

Page 171. TO ST IRVYNE

l. 3. more
l. 4. past
l. 7. night
l. 8. by
l. 9. sigh
l. 10. confess
l. 24. on me

Reference Sources
Abridged Title List

ABINGER MANUSCRIPTS. The manuscripts and letters of William Godwin, Mary Wollstonecraft, and others in the possession of Lord Abinger (Pforzheimer Microfilm).

CAMERON, *The Young Shelley*. Kenneth Neill Cameron: *The Young Shelley, Genesis of a Radical*. New York, 1950.

DOWDEN, *Shelley*. Edward Dowden: *The Life of Percy Bysshe Shelley*. London, 1886.

GODWIN, *Political Justice*. William Godwin: *Enquiry Concerning Political Justice and Its Influence on Morals and Happiness*, ed. F. E. L. Priestley. Toronto, 1946.

GRABO, *A Newton among Poets*. Carl Grabo: *A Newton among Poets*. Chapel Hill, N. C., 1930.

HOGG, *Shelley*. Thomas Jefferson Hogg: *The Life of Percy Bysshe Shelley*, in *The Life of Percy Bysshe Shelley...*, ed. Humbert Wolfe. London, 1933. (Vols. I-II.)

HUGHES, *The Nascent Mind of Shelley*. A. M. D. Hughes: *The Nascent Mind of Shelley*. Oxford, 1947.

INGPEN, *Shelley in England*. Roger Ingpen: *Shelley in England: New Facts and Letters from the Shelley-Whitton Papers*. London, 1917.

KING-HELE, *Shelley.* Desmond King-Hele: *Shelley, the Man and the Poet.* New York, 1960.

KOSZUL, *Jeunesse.* André Koszul: *La Jeunesse de Shelley.* Paris, 1910.

Letters about Shelley. Letters about Shelley Interchanged by Three Friends—Edward Dowden, Richard Garnett and Wm. Michael Rossetti, ed. R. S. Garnett. London, 1917.

Mary Shelley's Journal. Mary Shelley's Journal, ed. Frederick L. Jones. Norman, Okla., 1947.

MEDWIN, *Shelley.* Thomas Medwin: *The Life of Percy Bysshe Shelley,* ed. H. Buxton Forman. Oxford, 1913.

NED. *New English Dictionary on Historical Principles.* Oxford, 1949.

New Shelley Letters. New Shelley Letters, ed. W. S. Scott. New Haven, Conn., 1949.

Paterson's Roads. [Daniel] Paterson: *A New and Accurate Description of All the Direct and Principal Cross Roads in England and Wales and Part of Scotland.* London, [various dates].

PAUL, *Godwin.* C. Kegan Paul: *William Godwin, His Friends and Contemporaries.* London, 1876.

PEACOCK, *Memoirs.* "Memoirs of Percy Bysshe Shelley," *The Works of Thomas Love Peacock,* ed. H. F. B. Brett-Smith and C. E. Jones (Halliford Edition). London, 1934, Vol. VIII.

PECK, *Shelley.* Walter Edwin Peck: *Shelley, His Life and Work.* Boston and New York, 1927.

Shelley and his Circle. Shelley and his Circle, 1773-1822, ed. Kenneth Neill Cameron. Cambridge, Mass., 1961.

SHELLEY, *Complete Works. The Complete Works of Percy Bysshe Shelley,* ed. Roger Ingpen and Walter E. Peck (Julian Edition). London and New York, 1926-1930.

SHELLEY, FORMAN ED., 1877. *The Poetical Works of Percy*

Bysshe Shelley, ed. Harry Buxton Forman, Vol. IV. London, 1877. (Vols. I-II, 1876, III-IV, 1877.)

SHELLEY, ROSSETTI ED., 1870. *The Poetical Works of Percy Bysshe Shelley*, ed. William Michael Rossetti. London, 1870.

TRELAWNY, *Recollections*. Edward John Trelawny: *Recollections of Shelley & Byron* in *The Life of Percy Bysshe Shelley* . . . , ed. Humbert Wolfe. London, 1933. (Vol. II.)

WHEATLEY, *London*. Henry B. Wheatley: *London Past and Present, Its History, Association, and Traditions*. London, 1891.

WHITE, *Shelley*. Newman I. White: *Shelley*. New York, 1940.

Index of Titles

A Dialogue *108*
A retrospect of Times of Old *95*
A sabbath Walk *38*
a Tale of Society as it is *62*
A Translation of The Marsellois Hymn *144*
A winter's day *56*
Cold are the blasts *129*
Dares the Lama *123*
Dark Spirit of the desert rude *77*
Death-spurning rocks! *81*
Evening—to Harriet *164*
Falshood and Vice *44*
Fragment   bombardment of Copenhagen *127*
Full many a mind *167*
Henry and Louisa *131*
Hopes that bud in youthful breasts *112*
How eloquent are eyes! *110*
I will kneel at thine altar *125*
Late was the night *170*
Mary to the Sea-Wind *94*
On an Icicle *128*
On leaving London for Wales *53*
On Robert Emmet's tomb *60*
Passion *41*
Sonnet. On launching some bottles *90*
Sonnet. On waiting for a wind *91*

Sonnet. To a balloon, laden with Knowledge *89*
Sonnet. To Harriet on her birth day *88*
The Crisis *40*
The Monarch's funeral *68*
The pale, the cold and the moony smile *79*
The Retrospect *155*
The solitary *67*
The Tombs *83*
The Voyage *98*
The wandering Jew's soliloquy *161*
To Death *74*
To Harriet ("Harriet! thy kiss to my soul is dear") *92*
To Harriet ("It is not blasphemy") *85*
To Harriet ("Never, O never") *43*
To Harriet ("Oh Harriet, love like mine") *168*
To Harriet ("Whose is the love") *37*
To Harriett ("Thy look of love") *165*
To Ianthe *163*
To Liberty *58*
To Mary I *116*
To Mary II *118*
To Mary III *119*
To November *50*
To St Irvyne *171*
To the Emperors of Russia and Austria *48*
To the Lover of Mary *121*
To the Moonbeam *113*
To the Republicans of North America *71*
Written at Cwm Ellan *73*
Written in very early youth *147*
Written on a beautiful day in Spring *52*
Zeinab and Kathema *148*

Index of First Lines

Bright ball of flame that thro' the gloom of even *89*
Brothers! between you and me *71*
Cold are the Blasts when December is howling *129*
Coward Chiefs! who, while the fight *48*
Dares the Lama, most fleet of the Sons of the Wind *123*
Darest thou amid this varied multitude *67*
Dark Spirit of the desart rude *77*
Dear girl! thou art wildered by madness *116*
Death-spurning rocks! here have ye towered since Time *81*
Death, where is thy victory! *74*
Drink the exhaustless moonbeam where its glare *121*
Fair are thy berries to the dazzled sight *41*
Fair one! calm that bursting heart *118*
Full many a mind with radiant genius fraught *167*
Harriet! thy kiss to my soul is dear *92*
Haste to battle, Patriot Band! *144*
Hopes that bud in youthful breasts *112*
How eloquent are eyes! *110*
I implore thee, I implore thee, softly swelling Breeze *94*
I love thee, Baby! for thine own sweet sake *163*
I will kneel at thine altar, will crown thee with bays *125*
I'll lay me down by the church yard tree *147*
In that strange mental wandering when to live *52*
Is it the Eternal Triune, is it He *161*
It is not blasphemy to hope that Heaven *85*
Late was the night, the moon shone bright *170*

THE ESDAILE NOTEBOOK

Mary, Mary! art thou gone *119*
May the tempests of Winter that sweep o'er thy tomb *60*
Moonbeam! leave the shadowy dale *113*
Never, O never, shall yonder Sun *43*
O let not Liberty *58*
O month of gloom, whose sullen brow *50*
O take the pure gem to where Southernly Breezes *128*
O thou bright Sun! beneath the dark blue line *164*
O thou, whose radiant eyes and beamy smile *88*
O! wintry day! that mockest spring *56*
O'er thy turrets, St Irvyne, the winter winds roar *171*
Oh! for the South's benign and balmy breeze *91*
Oh Harriet, love like mine that glows *168*
Quenched is old Ocean's rage *98*
She was an Aged Woman, and the years *62*
Sweet are the stilly forest glades *38*
The glowing gloom of eventide *68*
The ice mountains echo, the Baltic, the Ocean *127*
The mansions of the Kings are tenantless *95*
The pale, the cold and the moony smile *79*
These are the tombs. O cold and silent Death *83*
Thou miserable city! where the gloom *53*
Thy look of love has power to calm *165*
To trace Duration's lone career *155*
Upon the lonely beach Kathema lay *148*
Vessels of Heavenly medicine! may the breeze *90*
When the peasant hies him home, and the day planet
    reposes *73*
When we see Despots prosper in their weakness *40*
Where are the Heroes? sunk in death they lie *131*
Whilst Monarchs laughed upon their thrones *44*
Whose is the love that gleaming thro' the world *37*
Yes! my dagger is drenched with the blood of the brave *108*

A NOTE ON THE TYPE

THE TEXT of this book was set on the Linotype in *Baskerville*. Linotype Baskerville is a facsimile cutting from type cast from the original matrices of a face designed by JOHN BASKERVILLE. The original face was the forerunner of the "modern" group of type faces.

John Baskerville (1706-75), of Birmingham, England, a writing-master with a special renown for cutting inscriptions in stone, began experimenting about 1750 with punch-cutting and making typographical material. It was not until 1757 that he published his first work. His types, at first criticized, were in time recognized as distinct and elegant, and both they and his printing were universally admired.

Composed, printed, and bound by
The Haddon Craftsmen, Scranton, Pa.
Typography and binding design by

WARREN 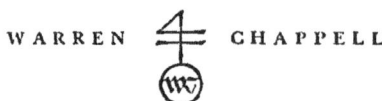 CHAPPELL

Deacidified using the Bookkeeper process.
Neutralizing agent: Magnesium Oxide
Treatment Date: May 2009

PreservationTechnologies
A WORLD LEADER IN COLLECTIONS PRESERVATION
111 Thomson Park Drive
Cranberry Township, PA 16066